The Christian God

The Christian God

Richard Swinburne

CLARENDON PRESS · OXFORD

Oxford University Press, Great Clarendon Street, Oxford OX2 6DP
Oxford New York
Athens Auckland Bangkok Bogota Buenos Aires Calcutta
Cape Town Chennai Dar es Salaam Delhi Florence Hong Kong Istanbul
Karachi Kuala Lumpur Madrid Melbourne Mexico City Mumbai
Nairobi Paris São Paolo Singapore Taipei Tokyo Toronto Warsaw
and associated companies in
Berlin Ibadan

Oxford is a registered trade mark of Oxford University Press

Published in the United States by
Oxford University Press Inc., New York

First published in hardback and paperback 1994
Reprinted in paperback 1995, 1996, 1998

British Library Cataloguing in Publication Data
Data available

Library of Congress Cataloging in Publication Data
Swinburne, Richard.
The Christian God / Richard Swinburne.
Includes bibliographical references and index.
1. God.   2. Trinity.   3. Incarnation.   I. Title.
BT102.S947   1994   231'.044—dc20   94-4969
ISBN 0-19-823513-5
ISBN 0- 19-823512-7 (pbk.)

1 3 5 7 9 10 8 6 4 2

Printed in Great Britain
on acid-free paper by
Biddles Ltd., Guildford and King's Lynn

Acknowledgements

I have delivered previous versions of most of the material of this book as lectures and seminar papers in graduate classes at Oxford and as a visiting lecturer in other universities; and I appreciate the many comments and criticisms received on these occasions from students and colleagues, which I have been able to take into account in writing the final version. I am most grateful to those who read previous versions of parts of the book and provided helpful comments—Sarah Coakley, Norman Kretzmann, and Michael Redhead. Some of the material of Chapters 4, 8, and 9 has received prior publication in the following papers, 'God and Time', in Eleonore Stump (ed.), *Reasoned Faith* (Cornell University Press, 1993); 'Could there be More than One God?', *Faith and Philosophy* (1988), 18: 287–312; and 'Could God Become Man?' in G. N. A. Vesey (ed.), *The Philosophy in Christianity* (Cambridge University Press, 1990). I thank the editors and publishers concerned for permission to reuse the material. And finally I am most grateful to Mrs Alicia Loreto-Gardner for her patient typing and retyping of many versions of this book.

R. G. S.

Contents

Introduction

My book *The Coherence of Theism* was published in 1977. In it I sought to distil from the tradition of Western religious thought a coherent account of what it is for there to be a God. The present work also has this as part of its aim; and the account which it develops is not (except in one respect) significantly different from that of the earlier work. However, half this book is devoted to fundamental metaphysical prolegomena—the nature of substance, cause, time, and necessity—which received very inadequate treatment in the earlier work. By contrast, the issue of religious language, also of considerable importance for a correct view of this matter, gets little treatment here in view of my discussion of it there. I do however take for granted here the results of *The Coherence of Theism* with respect to the need for some analogical use of words (in the way described there) in our talk about God. In *The Christian God*, I move quite quickly over the central issue of the *Coherence of Theism*, discussing it only in Chapters 6 and 7. I move thus quickly because I seek to develop here my account of the divine nature so as to expound the two claims, peculiar to Christianity, about that divine nature—that God is 'three persons' (Father, Son, and Holy Spirit) 'in one substance', and that one of those persons (the Son) became incarnate at a particular moment of time as a human being, Jesus Christ.

I am concerned with giving a coherent account of the meaning of these further claims; and examining what grounds we could have, given that there is a God, for supposing them to be true. There are, I believe, arguments of pure reason in favour of the necessary truth of the doctrine of the Trinity. There could not be such arguments in favour of the doctrine of the Incarnation; since that doctrine says that God voluntarily chose to become incarnate, it could not be shown that he had thus to become incarnate. But there could be arguments of pure reason showing that God had good reason to become incarnate and so was quite likely to do so. But such

arguments would need to be backed up by arguments from history
and revelation, showing that he had indeed become incarnate (and
anyway arguments of pure reason could hardly show when and
where he would become incarnate). Yet before arguments from
history and revelation can be produced, we need to investigate
what sort of arguments of this kind would show that God had
become incarnate; what would the historian need to show in order
to show that a certain human was God incarnate? And to answer
that question is a philosophical task. In the case of both doctrines,
the Trinity and the Incarnation, there are arguments from
revelation—that they are part of revealed truth. In a previous book,
Revelation, published in 1992, I analysed the grounds for believing
some religious doctrine to be revealed truth; and the results of that
book have application to these doctrines. But there are independent
arguments that Jesus Christ was God incarnate from historical
evidence about what Jesus did and what happened to him, as well
as from revelation, and their status will need separate examination
herein. So, in summary, my concern in this book is with the Christian doctrine of God, and with the arguments of pure reason and
the nature of other arguments which would show to be true the
Christian additions to the core Western doctrine of God.

The respect in which *The Christian God* differs significantly in
its account of the divine nature from that of *The Coherence of Theism*
concerns the possibility of there being more than one divine individual. In the original edition of *The Coherence of Theism* (1977),
using the terminology not of 'divine individual', but of 'personal
ground of being', I denied the possibility of there being more than
one such individual. I realized subsequently that the argument
given on p. 225 of that work, against the possibility of more than
one such individual, was unsound; and in the revised edition (1993),
I wrote that the original argument was unsound; and said that the
work was to be regarded as an account of the nature of the personal
ground of being, on the assumption that there is only one such.
Crucial for opening up this issue is the distinction made in Chapter
5 of the present work between 'metaphysical' and 'ontological'
necessity; *The Coherence of Theism* had only one kind of necessity
corresponding to these two—'necessity of kind [D]'. I shall be
arguing that a divine individual is properly thought of as having
metaphysical but not ontological necessity, and that there is reason
to suppose that there are three such mutually dependent individuals;

but that the three together form a whole (the Trinity) which is ontologically necessary. *The Christian God* thus constitutes a more sophisticated account of the divine nature than does *The Coherence of Theism*. But the latter remains an approximately true account of the nature of each divine individual, many aspects of which it develops much more fully than does the present work.

The Christian God is the third volume of a tetralogy, examining the meaning and justification of central Christian doctrines. The first volume, *Responsibility and Atonement*, was concerned with the doctrines of the nature and destiny of humans—such as sin, original sin, the Atonement, sanctification, Heaven, and Hell. The second volume, *Revelation*, analysed the grounds for believing some doctrine to be a revealed truth; which is what Christianity has traditionally claimed for its central doctrines. I plan a final volume of the tetralogy, on *Providence*, concerned with God's providential care of humans on this earth, and why He allows evil to occur as part of that care—seeking to shed light on this issue in part with the help of such Christian doctrines as that the Incarnate God shared our suffering, that there is life after death, and that the world will come to an end.

In each of the two previous volumes of the tetralogy, as indeed in all my writings on the philosophy of religion, I have found it necessary to develop at length views on straight philosophical questions, which could then be applied subsequently to the philosophy of religion. In *Responsibility and Atonement* I developed an account of the nature and application of central concepts of moral philosophy before discussing religious doctrines which utilized them. In *Revelation* I developed an account of meaning—literal, analogical, and metaphorical—before I went on to discuss the meaning of documents purporting to contain revealed truth. Since religious issues are more contested even than general secular philosophical issues, we are more likely to reach clear and justified conclusions about the former if we start with a firm base in the latter. My strategy in *The Christian God* is the same. Part I is concerned with general metaphysical issues—with the nature of substance, causality, time, and necessity. Part II then expounds the account of the divine nature given by Western religion, with the aid of these concepts, and shows how it can naturally be extended to embrace the doctrines of the Trinity and the Incarnation.

PART I

Metaphysics

1

Substances

Terminology

The world consists of substances. Examples of substances, in the sense which I shall shortly begin to elucidate, are such individual things as this table and that chair, the tree over there, you and I. Substances have properties. Properties include both monadic properties, properties that things possess independently of their relations to things, such as being square or red, or having such-and-such a mass or electric charge; and relations (alias relational or polyadic properties), such as being taller than, being to the left of, or lying between, that relate two or more things. (Properties may be possessed by 'things' of various kinds, including other properties and events; but I shall be concerned almost entirely with properties possessed by substances.) Events, as I shall understand the word, are the instantiations of properties in substances (or other events) at times, (or the comings-into-existence, existing or ceasings-to-exist of substances at times). Events thus include both unchanging states, such as this tie being now green or Oxford being situated between London and Birmingham in 1991, and changes of state such as my car moving from London to Oxford yesterday, as well as things being made and destroyed.

Substances are individual, concrete (i.e. real, non-abstract) things. Properties by contrast are universals, in that they can be instantiated in many different things. Being brown or being a table have many instances. But this table before me now is an individual; there can be only one instance of it. The number 5 is also an individual; there can be only one number five. But it is an abstract individual, created by an arbitrary act of language users. Abstract individuals are fictional individuals; they do not really exist at all. There is a property of being five-membered which belongs to groups of things under some description; the group of things on my shelf described as 'bottles on my shelf' has the property of being five-membered.

We then describe the situation as there existing a number, five, which is the number of bottles on my shelf; and go on to say that this number exists, whether or not any group of things under any description has five members. It is, however, an arbitrary fiction, though in view of what we can do with mathematics a convenient fiction, to say so.[1] The table by contrast is no fiction; it really does exist, whether or not recognized and described as a table. And hence it counts as a concrete thing. There are other individual, concrete things which are real enough, but talk about which is really talk about the other individual concrete things of kinds that I have already given as paradigms of substances. Smells and sounds, holograms and magnetic fields are real enough, but talk about them is reducible to talk about how things smell or sound or look to animals and humans, or how bits of metal behave. Talk about places too, and the space which they form, is, I suggest, just talk about how those substances that are material objects are or could be related to each other. To say that there is a place between this book and that book is to say that you can put another material object between the two books. Talk of times and the time that they form is, I believe, also reducible to talk about substances—but as this is a more contentious issue, and one more important for my purposes, I shall postpone discussion of it until a later stage.

Properties are only manifested in the concrete way in which substances exist when they are instantiated in substances. The property of redness is only manifested when there are red things. One could say that the property of redness exists, whether or not there are red things; it exists waiting to be instantiated in things. But to talk in this way, as Plato did, is to create by linguistic fiat a fictional existence like that of the number 5; a misleading way of talking which I shall not endorse. Properties occur or are manifested, and may then be said to exist, when and only when they are instantiated in substances. Redness only exists when there are red things. Events occur at times, and may be said to exist then and only then. So properties can only exist as instantiated in substances, and events can only exist when substances exist. But that does not establish any priority in the scheme of things for substances, for substances can only exist in so far as they have properties, and some of those properties are essential to the substance being the particular substance

<hr />

[1] See Additional Note 1.

it is. To be this desk, a substance has to be a desk, that is, to be similar in shape and construction to objects used by humans for writing at and to be used or designed for that purpose. And to be this tree (i.e. the oak tree outside my window), a substance has to be an oak tree, that is, similar in shape, and appearance, and growth patterns, and genetic constitution to standard oak trees. Not all the properties of a substance, of course, are essential to it—being brown is not essential to the substance that is my desk being that particular substance.

Substances (and, I think we should say, properties also) exist all at once. My desk exists in its totality at a moment; so too does the property of being brown, whenever something is brown. Events however do not exist in their totality all at once. My going from London to Oxford yesterday lasted for an hour, and what happened during the first half an hour was only a part of the event. Events thus have temporal parts. Substances exist all at once, but they persist through time from when they begin to exist to when they cease to exist. Substances can causally influence other substances—they can bring them into being or destroy them, or cause them to gain or lose properties. The carpenter creates the desk, the painter makes it brown, and so on. I shall consider in Chapter 3 the alternative view, that it is events rather than substances that cause, and I shall reject that view.

Those substances whose essential properties are such that they must occupy space (i.e. be spatially extended) I shall call material objects. The substance that is my desk could not be a desk unless it occupied space. Not all such substances are very naturally called 'material objects'—for example, the fundamental particles of physics of which the solid objects around us are composed, such as protons and electrons, do not seem very 'material' in the natural usage of that term, but they count as material objects on my definition.[2] If there is a substance which does occupy space but need not, it does not count as a material object on my definition.

Substances may have parts (not temporal parts, but coexisting parts). My desk has drawers and a top. Those parts are then also

[2] According to some theories of physics, 'fields' of force and even chunks of 'space' are causally efficacious components of macroscopic material objects. In that case they too will count as material objects—contrary to what I claimed earlier, on the supposition that talk of fields and places was reducible to talk about other things.

themselves substances. Any substance which occupies space, as all material objects must, will have parts, because it will have spatial parts (even if of physical necessity we cannot separate those parts). Being spatially extended it will have parts that occupy different regions of the space, of which the whole substance occupies the whole. Substances, including material objects, that are composed of other substances I shall call impure substances. There are pure substances that do not occupy space and do not have parts, spatial or non-spatial. A material object that does not have any non-spatial parts I will call a mere material object. My claims that some substances do not have others as parts, and that there are substances which do not occupy space are both highly contentious, and I will give arguments for them shortly.

Anything designatable by a predicate that can characterize different things, and in particular substances and groups thereof, is, as I shall understand the notion, a property. Some philosophers have wished to restrict the notion 'property' so that not all predicates designate properties. On this restrictive view only those characteristics picked out in scientific laws as making a difference to the way things behave are properties. Thus being exactly 2.351 miles away from the Eiffel Tower makes no difference to the way something behaves and so is not a property, whereas being 4,000 miles from the centre of gravity of the Earth does make a difference and so is a property. And on this view predicates that pick out characteristics that make the same difference really pick out the same property, though it may take a scientific discovery to show that—a gas having a certain temperature is the gas having the same property as it having molecules with a certain mean kinetic energy. One could talk this way, but if one did, one would need—in order fully to describe the world—another word than 'property' to designate what is picked out as belonging to things by non-synonymous predicates. I suggest that it makes for a neater description of the world if we so understand 'property' that (with a small exception to which I will come in Chapter 2) every predicate designates a property, and every non-synonymous predicate designates a distinct property— even if some properties make no difference to the way things behave and others, such as a gas having a certain temperature and having its molecules with a certain mean kinetic energy, always go together.

Our knowledge of the world by observation is basically recognition of which properties are instantiated when. For we pick out substances as the substances they are almost entirely by the unique combination of properties which they manifest. We pick out a certain desk largely by its monadic properties (being red, and of such-and-such a shape) and its location—in a certain room (picked out by its properties—the one at the top of the staircase marked '8'). An indexical element does, however, also finally enter in—we may need to distinguish between particular substances with otherwise identical properties by their relations to me (e.g. 'on my left'), me not being distinguishable from other substances solely by my properties. (On this, see further Chapter 2.)

With substances, unlike properties, however, there is a lot more to them than appears on the surface—they have parts and an inner nature of which initially we may be unaware.

Material objects are 'composed' of form and matter—not in the sense that they have these as parts, but in the sense that they are chunks of matter possessing certain properties, some of which are essential to an object being an object of its particular kind. A substance continues to exist while (more or less) the same chunk of matter continues to exist and continues to possess those essential properties. The essential properties are the substance's essential form. My desk is composed of certain matter (wood) on which is imposed a certain form (that of a desk), and while (more or less) the same wood is organized into forming a desk, the substance continues. The coming into existence of a material object consists in the imposition on matter of the object's essential form; its ceasing to exist consists in that matter no longer being organized so as to possess that form. In the case of substances of some kinds, for example, plants such as trees, the matter does not need to remain even more or less the same; it suffices that the new matter be obtained by gradual replacement of the old.

It is a somewhat arbitrary matter how one cuts the matter of the world up into chunks, and under which forms one traces the continuity of matter (i.e. which properties of a chunk of matter one regards as the essential ones). Some chunks of matter have more of a natural unity to them, in the sense of their remaining chunks for a longer time and there being many more and more influential causal interactions between the different bits of the chunk than causal relations between the chunk and the outside world, than do other chunks. And if we trace the chunks under certain forms rather than others, they will continue to exist for longer and make more evident differences to the world. Regarding the chunk of wood which forms my desk as a relevant chunk, rather than the chunk which forms the left half of my desk and the floor beneath it, picks out a chunk which continues as a whole because it sustains itself in being through causal interactions between its parts. And regarding the chunk as (essentially) a desk rather than as (essentially) a-desk-used-for-writing-philosophy allows us to trace a more useful form of continuity, for example, because it makes similar differences to the carpet beneath it and to the way it is valued by antique dealers whatever its use. But what should be apparent is that there are innumerable different ways of cutting up the world into chunks and tracing continuities, and that the differences between them concern matters of degree—degree of internal causal unity, persistence, influence on things—so that it is unjustified to say that there is one 'correct' way of describing the world.

Some philosophers have wanted to say that there is one correct way of describing the world, which we get by recognizing as substances only things whose essential properties are those of a 'natural kind'. Those properties which are fundamental in determining the behaviour of matter in accord with natural laws come together in bundles and are instantiated in things which behave in fundamentally different ways from other things. Thus each kind of chemical element—iron, copper, or hydrogen, for example—forms a natural kind, because the properties which make an atom of one kind rather than another (e.g. the number of protons in the nucleus of the atom) are fundamental in determining the behaviour of those atoms. Those bundles of properties then constitute a natural kind, and an object is a substance only if its essential properties are those of a natural kind. So an atom of iron is a substance, whereas a heap of unconnected atoms is not. But groups of atoms of different elements, joined together in ways that form objects picked out as distinct from other objects by essential properties fundamental in determining characteristic behaviour, are also substances, because they too belong to natural kinds. Thus each species of plant (elm tree, or oak tree, say) forms a natural kind, because picking out chunks of matter as plants belonging to a species involves picking them out by properties (namely, those of the genotype underlying the characteristic colour and shape of the plant) fundamental in determining the behaviour of those chunks in accord with natural laws. But useful though these particular ways of classifying are, they provide neither an exclusive nor an exhaustive system of cutting up the world into substances. Each oak tree has various chemical element atoms as parts of it. And many things which have a natural unity to them, such as sticks and stones and human artefacts, do not belong to any natural kind. Rather, there are different systems of describing the history of the world, some of them more useful than others. Hence it seems proper to regard as a substance anything (including the thing currently formed of the left half of my desk and the floor beneath it) traceable through time under a form (that is, a system of essential properties which it has to preserve in order to be that substance). One can regard the thing currently formed of the left half of my desk and the floor beneath it as having an essential shape and appearance, and as continuing to exist while roughly the same matter preserves that shape and appearance. That thing which we have now formed the concepts to recognize is a substance, and would be one even if we never picked it out as such. The world is full of innumerable, unrecognized, and unevident substances.

To tell the full history of the world, or any spatio-temporal segment of it, however small, we have at least to describe fully the continuities of matter and the properties exhibited by chunks thereof; and some of the many ways of doing this will entail others. A description of what happened to all the atoms will entail what happened to all the larger objects composed of them. But it is characteristic of any impure substance that we can tell the full history of the world without needing to mention it or anything which has it as an essential part—we need tell only what happened to its parts, or to other substances whose essential parts include its parts. I tell you what happened to my desk if I tell you what happened to a substance consisting essentially of the left half of the desk and something else, and also to a substance consisting essentially of the right half of the desk and something else. Many of our ordinary language terms for picking out substances leave somewhat vague the conditions for their correct application—it is often unclear how much original matter has to remain, and also whether it can be disassembled and reassembled, for the same substance to persist. But language can always be improved so that its terms have even more precise conditions for their correct application.

There is a philosophical distinction between phase-sortals and substance-sortals. A sortal is simply a word which applies to a substance in virtue of some property or properties which belong to it, for example, 'boy', 'desk', or 'red object'. A substance-sortal is a word which applies to a substance while it has its essential form, that is, while it exists at all. A phase-sortal is a word which applies to a substance while and only while it has certain of its non-essential properties, while, that is, it goes through a phase of its existence. Thus, it is said, 'oak tree' is a substance-sortal, because while the substances which are oak trees exist, they cannot but be oak trees; whereas 'sapling' is a phase-sortal, because the substance which is a sapling may continue to exist when it is no longer a sapling, but becomes a full-grown tree. Nevertheless if *a* and *b* are the same substance at one time, they will be the same substance at all times— for a thing cannot cease to be identical with itself; this principle is known as 'the necessity of identity'. The sapling is the same substance as the full-grown oak, even though we will not describe it as a sapling when it is full-grown.

Among substance-sortals, are narrowest substance-sortals which pick out substances in virtue of the largest conjunction of properties that must belong to a substance while it has its essential form. Thus, if 'oak tree' is a substance-sortal so is 'tree'; but 'oak tree' is a narrower substance-sortal than 'tree'. A given substance which is an oak tree then has to remain an oak tree in order to continue to exist, merely remaining a tree will not suffice. If a given oak tree can lose or gain any properties so long as it remains an oak tree, then 'oak tree' is a narrowest substance sortal, it picks out the minimum essential form or kind to which particular oak trees belong.

Our understanding of some referring expression as picking out a substance involves an understanding of what it is, what must be the case for some expression on another occasion to pick out that same substance, and so an understanding of the minimum essential kind under which we trace its continuity. It follows that if '*a* is the same as *b*' is true, '*a* is the same ϕ as *b*' is also true, where ϕ is any substance sortal which applies to *a*, including the narrowest substance-sortal, and conversely. And the same holds if ϕ is any sortal at all, not just a substance-sortal. For given that a sortal must apply to a substance—even if technically it is not a substance-sortal, 'being the same ϕ as' entails 'being the same substance which is ϕ as' which entails 'being the same substance as'. ϕ simply picks out a property that is preserved along with sameness of substance. If *a* is the same red object as *b*, there is something which *a* and *b* both are, and that can only be if there are criteria of identity associated with that thing. So if a is the same ϕ as b, it is the same substance as b, and so there can be no ψ such that a is ψ but not the same ψ as b.

The suggestion that it is possible for a substance a which is ϕ and ψ to be the same ϕ as b but not the same ψ as b, is the suggestion of the possibility of 'relative identity', an identity that is not absolute, but only relative to a sortal. Various examples have been put forward in recent years of possible cases of relative identity.[3] Suppose a statue of Napoleon made of brass, a, gradually to have its old brass replaced by new brass, so that a new brass statue is formed, b. Is it not the case, asks the champion of relative identity, that a is the same statue (ϕ) as b, but not the same lump of brass (ψ) as b? But the question must be asked, does 'a' pick out a statue made of brass, or a lump of brass formed into statue shape? Is a essentially a statue, or essentially a lump of brass? If the former, then a is not as such a lump of brass, although it is made of brass. If the latter, a is not as such a statue, although it may be formed into the shape of a statue. Neither 'being made of' nor 'being formed into' is the same as 'being the same as'. It may be said that we are often unclear in using an expression designed to pick out a substance, just what kind of thing we are picking out—that is, what is the minimum essential kind to which it belongs. No doubt, but to that extent there is no clear meaning to 'a is the same ϕ as b'. It cannot be the case where a and b have clear criteria of use, and ϕ and ψ are sortals, that a is ϕ and ψ, the same ϕ as b, but not the same ψ as b.

However, as I have pointed out, there are many different ways of cutting the world up into substances. The same phenomena can be described by the same words with a slight change in the meaning of these words. A word previously used as a phase-sortal may be used as a substance-sortal, or conversely. We could think of what happens when the sapling ceases to be a sapling, as one substance ceasing to exist and a different one coming to be formed from the molecules of the sapling. We could describe this by saying 'the

---

[3] The best-known champion of relative identity is Peter Geach. See his *Reference and Generality* (Cornell University Press, 1962); and 'Identity', *Review of Metaphysics*, 21 (1967–8), 3–12. For full-length qualified defence of relative identity see Nicholas Griffin, *Relative Identity* (Clarendon Press, 1977). For arguments against relative identity, which I endorse, see David Wiggins, *Sameness and Substance* (Blackwell, 1980), esp. ch. 1; and John Perry, 'The Same F', *Philosophical Review*, 79 (1970), 181–200.

sapling ceased to exist, and the oak tree began to exist' and in that case we would have turned 'sapling' into a substance-sortal, and restricted the range of plants which count as 'oak trees'. This would be a less useful but possible way of talking. But it remains the case that for any given way of cutting up the world relative identity is not possible.

There are substances, however, other than material objects, that, I shall argue, are pure substances—ones which do not have other substances as parts. We human persons have two parts—a body, which is a mere material object, and an immaterial part, a soul, which is a pure substance. As I have argued for this view at some length elsewhere,[4] my arguments here will be fairly brief.[5]

Humans: Body and Soul

It will be useful to begin by distinguishing, among properties, between physical and mental properties. I understand by a 'physical property' one such that no one individual has necessarily a means of discovering that it is instantiated that is not available to any other individual. Physical properties are public; there is no privileged access to them. Thus, having a mass of 10 pounds, being 8 feet tall, and being square are all physical properties. So too are the typical properties of neurones in the brain—being in such-and-such an electrical state or releasing a transmitter chemical. Anyone who chooses can find out by the same means as can anyone else whether something is 8 feet tall, or in a certain electrical state. 'Physical events' are those that involve the instantiation of physical properties. 'Mental properties', as I shall understand the term, are ones to which one individual has privileged access, that is, he has a means for

---

[4] See my *The Evolution of the Soul* (Clarendon Press, 1986), pt. 2.

[5] In 'Substance: Prolegomena to a Realist Theory of Identity', *Journal of Philosophy*, 88 (1991), 69–90, Michael Ayers lists six characteristics that philosophers have traditionally ascribed to substances—(1) They are the ultimate subjects of predication, and hence logically independent of other things, (2) they have a natural unity, (3) they are composed of matter and form, (4) they exist all at once and persist through time, (5) they have causal properties, and (6) they belong to natural kinds. I have adopted a concept of substance based on (1), (4), and (5), suggesting that (2) and (6) would be unnecessary and arbitrary restrictions on the concept. I shall in effect argue in the next chapter that (3) does not apply to all things picked out by (1), (4), and (5); and so to all substances in my sense.

discovering whether they are instantiated that is not available to anyone else. Such properties as being in pain or having a red after-image, are mental, for any individual in whom they are instantiated does seem necessarily to have a way of knowing about them not available to anyone else. For whatever ways you have of finding out whether I have a red after-image (e.g. by inspecting my brain-state or studying my behaviour) I can share; yet I have an additional way of finding this out—by my own awareness of my own experience. 'Mental events' are events which involve the instantiation of mental properties (e.g. John being in pain at midday yesterday).

Some mental properties have physical properties as components. Some property has another as a component if the instantiation of the former entails the instantiation of the latter. 'Raising an arm intentionally' entails 'having an arm rise'. The former is a mental property for the person in whom it is instantiated has a means of knowing that it is instantiated not available to others; I know in a way others cannot do whether any arm rising was intended by me, because I alone can form my intentions. But 'having an arm rise' is a physical property—anyone can observe as well as anyone else whether someone's arm rises. I shall call a property a pure mental property if it has no physical components. Impure mental properties have both pure mental and physical components. Analagously pure mental events are ones which do not have physical events as components (i.e. entail their occurrence); impure ones do have physical components.

There are, I suggest, five kinds of pure mental event that characterize humans, which I shall call sensations, thoughts, purposings, desires, and beliefs.[6] By sensations I mean experiences of the kind normally brought about by the senses or ones similar thereto in experiential content, such as my experiencing the patterns of colour in my visual field, sensations of taste or smell, mild aches and pains, sensations of hot or cold in parts of my body; together with their pale imitations in my recalling memory images or my imagining imagined images. By thoughts I mean those datable conscious occurrences of particular thoughts that can be expressed in the form of a proposition. Often these are thoughts that occur to a person, flit through his mind, or strike him without him in any

---

[6] For more detailed analysis of these five kinds of mental event, see *Evolution of the Soul*, pt. 1.

way actively conjuring them up. It may occur to me that today is Tuesday, or that this is a receptive audience, or that the weather is cold. By a person's purposings I mean his endeavourings to bring about some event, meaning so to do. Every intentional action, everything that a person does meaning to do it, consists of the person bringing about some effect or trying but failing to do so. Yet when the person brings about some effect, their active contribution may be just the same as when, unexpectedly, they try but fail to bring about the effect. When I move my hand, I bring about the motion of my hand. Normally this action involves no effort and is entirely within my control. But on some occasion, I may find myself unexpectedly paralysed. My active contribution is the same as when I move my hand successfully. For this intentional contribution, for an agent's setting himself to bring about some effect (even when effort or failure is not involved) I will use the word 'purposing'.

A person's beliefs are his view of how the world is, his 'picture' of how things are. A person's desires are his natural inclinations to do things, experience things or have things happen—what he feels naturally inclined to do or let happen, if he has the opportunity— but for contrary desire, or some strong effort of will, that is, purposing, to do otherwise. Beliefs and desires are continuing mental states, states that are mental because the subject can make himself aware of them if he chooses, but that may exist for a long period of time while he is unaware of them, asleep or doing other things. Sensations, thoughts, and purposings, by contrast, are conscious episodes—if we have these, we must to some extent be aware at the time of having them.

In order to tell the full history of the world I need to say not merely which physical properties have been instantiated, but which mental ones too. I need to say not merely what has been going on in your brain in terms of which electrical circuits have been set up by the transmission of which chemicals, but also which sensations and thoughts you had. But if we supposed that human beings were mere material objects and that mental properties (having this or that sensation or thought) were properties of those material objects, something all-important would have been left out. For full information about which physical and mental properties were instantiated in which mere material objects would still leave one ignorant of whether some person continued to live a conscious life or not.

Knowledge of what happens to bodies and their parts will not show you for certain what happens to persons. This point is illustrated very clearly by the example of brain transplants. The brain consists of two hemispheres and a brain stem. There is good evidence that humans can survive and behave as conscious beings if much of one hemisphere is destroyed. Now suppose my brain (hemisphere plus brain stem) divided into two, and each half-brain taken out of my skull and transplanted into the empty skull of a body from which a brain has just been removed; and there to be added to each a half-brain from some other brain (e.g. the brain of my identical twin) whatever other parts (e.g. more brain stem) are necessary in order for the transplant to take and for there to be two living persons with lives of conscious experiences. Which would be me? Probably both would to some extent behave like me and make my memory claims; for behaviour and speech depends, at any rate in very large part, on brain-states, and there is a very considerable overlap between the 'information' carried by the two hemispheres that gives rise to behaviour and speech. But both persons would not in a strict sense be me. For if they were both identical with me they would be the same person as each other (if *a* is the same as *b*, and *b* is the same as *c*, then *a* is the same as *c*) and they are not. They now have different experiences and lead different lives. I shall consider a little later whether in some attenuated sense, both could be me, that is, my 'successor persons', but there are three other clear possible outcomes of the transplant—that the person with my right half-brain is me, or that the person with my left half-brain is me, or that neither is me. But we cannot be certain which holds. It follows that mere knowledge of what happens to bodies does not tell you what happens to persons.

It is tempting to say that it is a matter of arbitrary definition which of the four possibilities is correct (or three possibilities, if we rule out both persons being in some sense me as self-contradictory). But this temptation must be resisted. There is a crucial factual issue here—which can be shown if we consider the situation of someone knowing that his brain is about to be split, knowing that the person to be formed from his left half-brain is to have a life of great enjoyment and the person to be formed from his right half-brain is to be subjected to a life of great pain. Whether I shall have an enjoyable future life is a clearly factual question (only someone under the grip of some very strong philosophical dogma would deny that), and yet, as I await the transplant and know exactly what will happen to my brain, I am in no position to know the answer to what will happen to me. Maybe neither future person will be me—it may be that cutting the brain stem destroys a person's connection with that brain once and for all, and repairing the severed stem creates a new human person, so that the whole process creates two new conscious human persons, neither of whom is me. Perhaps I will be the left half-brain person, or maybe it will be the right-brain person who will be me. Even if one subsequent human resembles the earlier me more in character and memory claims than does the other, that one may not be me. Maybe I have survived the operation but am changed in character and have lost much of my memory as a result of it, in consequence of which the other, subsequent person resembles the earlier me more in his public behaviour than I do. And even if there is the possibility that both later humans are to some extent me, neither science nor philosophy could show conclusively that that, rather than one of the other three possibilities, was the actual outcome, for all the evidence which could ever be obtained would be compatible with the other possibilities as well.

Reflection on this thought experiment shows that however much we know about what has happened to my brain (and other parts of my body), we are not necessarily in a position to know what has happened to me. From that it follows that there must be more to me than my brain, a further immaterial part whose continuing in existence is necessary if the brain (and so body) to which it is linked is to be my brain (and body), and to this something I give the traditional name of 'soul'. (I thus use the word 'soul' as the name of a kind of substance, as did Descartes; and not as the name of a kind of form, a way of living and behaving, as did Aristotle.) I am my soul plus the brain (and body) it is connected to. Normally my soul goes where my whole brain goes, but in unusual circumstances (such as when my brain is split) it is uncertain where it goes.

Take a slightly different example. I die of a brain haemorrhage which today's doctors cannot cure, but my relatives take my corpse and put it straight into a deep freeze in California. Shortly thereafter there is an earthquake as a result of which my frozen brain is split into many parts, a few of which get lost. However, fifty years later, when medical technology has improved, my descendants take the bits of my broken corpse, warm it up and mend it, replacing the missing parts from elsewhere. The body becomes the body of a living person which behaves somewhat like me and seems to remember quite a lot of my past life. Have I come to life again, or not? Maybe, maybe not. Again there is a truth here, about whether I have survived the haemorrhage as I wanted to, and yet a truth of which we cannot be sure however much we know about the story of my brain, and however much we know about the mental lives of the earlier me and the later revived person. Hence, my survival consists in the continuing of something else, which I call my soul, linked to my previous body; and I survive in this reconstituted body only if that soul is connected with it.

These two thought experiments show that something else than my body has to continue if I am to continue, and that something else I have called my soul; but they do not show that the continuing of that alone is all that is necessary for my survival. Maybe, as far as these thought experiments show, some of my brain has also to continue to exist if I am to continue; and in that case I would be a material object, though not a mere material object. Other thought experiments can be adduced to rule out that suggestion, but to show that no part of the body need continue to exist if I am to continue, I prefer at this stage to adduce a straight philosophical argument to be found in embryo in Descartes.

In this argument I use the notion of the logical possibility; and I had better state briefly what I understand by this notion, and the associated notions of logical necessity, contingency, and impossibility. A more thorough treatment of these notions will be provided in Chapter 5. The logically necessary is what could not but be for reasons of logic; to deny it is ultimately to contradict yourself. It is logically necessary that any red object is coloured, that all squares have four sides, and that $5 + 7 = 12$. The logically impossible is what cannot be for reasons of logic—such as there being a red object which is not coloured. The logically contingent is that which is neither logically necessary nor logically impossible—such as there being six chairs in my room, or there being seven chairs in my room. The logically possible is whatever is either logically contingent or logically necessary. The logically contingent is the world being this way rather than that, when both ways are logically possible.

My straight philosophical argument begins by claiming that it is logically possible that I who am now conscious might continue to exist if all my body were suddenly destroyed. I could have just mental properties—have thoughts, and sensations, and purposes—without having a body. And surely it must be that any religious believer who claims that he will live after the destruction of this body and without acquiring a new body does not contradict himself; anyone can understand the claim that he is making because it is a coherent one. The argument then goes on to claim that if anything is to continue to exist over time, (either the whole or) some part of it must continue to exist—and that is surely true of anything. My desk cannot continue to exist, if every part of it is destroyed—and so on. So, the argument concludes, if it is to be logically possible that I survive when all my body is destroyed, there must now already exist another part of me (an immaterial part) whose survival guarantees my survival—and that I have called the soul.[7] My mere existence as a conscious person at some time entails that I have an immaterial part, which I call the soul, at that time; and if I do survive, the argument shows that it is sufficient that that part survives—for my survival is compatible with all else being destroyed. Hence I am not a material object, since I can exist without occupying space.

The pure mental properties which are instantiated in human beings belong to them in virtue of belonging to their souls. For pure mental properties could not be instantiated in mere material objects such as bodies or brains, since the instantiation of a pure mental property—some individual being in pain, for example—leaves open the possibility that some earlier individual was the individual who would later have that experience and so would have reason in advance to fear it (or hope for it). But since knowledge of what has happened to mere material objects is not sufficient to show whether some earlier individual was so positioned, whereas knowledge of what has happened to souls is sufficient, but would be sufficient only if the pure mental property was instantiated in a soul, the pure mental property must have been instantiated in a soul. Pure mental properties characterize souls, not bodies. Impure properties characterize (soul plus body).

So I have argued that there are immaterial as well as material substances. Human souls are such immaterial substances, and so

---

[7] This argument has often been wrongly accused of various formal fallacies. For a watertight formal presentation of it, in the apparatus of modal logic, see ibid. 314 f., add. n. 2.

too are any other immaterial subjects of mental properties whom I also call souls. I believe that the higher animals are animate beings, that is, are subjects of mental properties, and hence by my previous argument they too have souls. If those individuals who are animals can also exist in a disembodied state—as I believe, but have not argued—then they are essentially souls, as are humans. But if a dog, Fido, say, has to have a body in order to exist, then it would be a material object; but, because it has a soul as an essential part, it is not a mere material object. Humans and animals on this earth both have bodies as well as souls—although the bodies are non-essential parts of, at any rate, humans.

Are souls pure substances? Alternatively, do they have parts, that is non-spatial parts? I think not. They are pure substances. If a substance has parts, then there are properties which characterize only a part but not the whole (or characterize the whole in virtue of characterizing a part, or characterize the whole in virtue of different properties characterizing different parts). Each of the seven drawers of my desk weighs 8 lb., the top weighs 5 lb., and hence the desk weighs 61 lb. The whole desk is brown because all its external surfaces are brown, even though not all the external surfaces of the drawers are brown. And so on. Similar points apply to the relations between a human being and its parts, body and soul. The human weighs 100 lb. because its body weighs 100 lb. The human walks, because its soul purposes to walk, its body's legs make walking movements and the former causes the latter. But there are no analogies here for the soul. Each pure mental property that characterizes the soul, the subject of experience, is fully present to that subject. There is no part of the subject that experiences some property which contributes to the whole experiencing a different property. It is the same I who have a blue after-image, hear your voice, think about breakfast, decide to go for a walk; and no part of me has the one experience and not the other (although the parts of the brain that cause me to have the different experiences are different).

It is difficult to see how fission or fusion of humans and thus of their essential parts, their souls, could take place unless souls had parts. For fission involves the splitting of something previously joined together; and 'fusion' the joining together of things previously separate. And if souls do not have parts, that explains why fission and fusion of souls and so of humans are not possible. And there are independent arguments to show that fission and fusion are not possible.

Some writers, notably Derek Parfit,[8] have supposed that what happens (and not merely could happen, but would happen) in the split-brain experiment, is that although both later humans would not, strictly speaking, be me, they would be my successor persons, partly me, my 'later selves'. Just as two later cars each formed from some parts of one earlier car and other parts as well, would be both in part the same car as, in part a different car from the earlier car, it would be the same, Parfit claims, with humans. This would be fission. But there is a powerful objection to the coherence of supposing that animate beings, unlike inanimate things, can split. If I became partly both the later humans, I would presumably in part have both their experiences; yet how on earth can this be, since there would be no one person who has simultaneously the experiences that each of the subsequent persons has at a given time?

There are similar logical difficulties in the way of fusion. The soul, and so the human being, is a subject of mental properties. It only exists in so far as it is capable of a mental life. It follows that it must be logically possible that a person (and so his soul) have experiences of his continuing existence at each moment of that existence. Now no human could have the experience of himself as being formed from the fusion of two humans. For suppose P_2 to be formed from the fusion of P_1 and P_1^*. If P_2 was so formed and having experiences while being so formed, it would seem that he must have two incompatible experiences at the same time. He would have to experience himself as experiencing P_1's experiences in a continuing stream as they occur and coming suddenly to acquire awareness of P_1^*'s experiences subsequent to their occurrence; and also as experiencing P_1^*'s experiences in a continuing stream as they occur and coming suddenly to acquire awareness of P_1's experiences subsequent to their occurrence. The experience of fusion cannot be described coherently; which suggests that no subsequent human can in any real sense to any degree be both of two earlier humans, for if he could, he ought to have been able to some extent to have experienced both their experiences.

Continuity of experience—one individual being the same individual as had or will have some experience—is a very important

---

[8] See D. Parfit, *Reasons and Persons* (Clarendon Press, 1984), pt. 3.

feature of the world. And the full history of the world must describe (as well as the continuities of matter) what continuities of experience there are. Given that souls do not have parts, the continuities of experience cannot be described in ways more fundamental than that of the continuities of souls; whereas the continuity of any material object with a later one can be described in terms of the continuity of its parts, or terms that entail the latter. It follows that any full history of the world must treat souls as continuing substances and describe the properties instantiated in them, even though no mention needs to be made of many impure substances such as material objects of many kinds.

The Nature of Humans

What makes an animate being (i.e. one characterized by some mental properties, and so having a soul) a human being (*homo*, man, in the sense in which both females and males are men) as opposed to, say a mere animal, a Martian, an angel, or God?

I argued earlier that the human soul is characterized by the continued or intermittent possession of mental events of five kinds. It may, however, well be that not all the higher animals who have mental events have mental events of all these kinds—maybe some of them, for example, do not have occurrent thoughts. But the principal difference between the mental life of human souls and the mental life of animal souls lies, I suggest, in the normal human soul, in contrast to animal souls, having further properties characterizing its mental life. The human soul is capable of logical thought (of drawing out mentally in a sequence of thoughts the consequences of earlier thoughts), and of moral awareness (having beliefs about actions being obligatory or, more generally, good); it has free will (its purposings, i.e. initiations of actions, not being fully caused by earlier events), and it has to it a structure (beliefs and desires are kept in place by other beliefs and desires; we have and see ourselves as having various beliefs and desires because we have other beliefs and desires which give them support). That the first two and (possibly) the fourth of these further properties characterize humans and not animals is fairly obvious. Whether humans have free will of this kind, that is, 'libertarian free will' is highly disputable; I have argued elsewhere[9] that they do. Not much turns on this for present purposes, but I shall need in a much later chapter to assume that humans do have libertarian free will.

All of this suggests a theory of a human being as constituted by a human soul, one having the above characteristics, connected to a human body, defined as one largely similar in its anatomy, physiology, and capacities for action (e.g. running, talking, etc.) that can be realized through it, to the paradigm examples of human bodies (those of our friends and neighbours) by which we are surrounded. The 'connection' involves the subject being able to operate on the world through that body (his purposings to move the limbs of that body are efficacious and make a difference to the world), acquiring beliefs about the world through that body (stimuli impinging on the eyes and ears of that body give him beliefs about how the world is), feeling things in and desiring to act through that body.

However, this theory of human nature may be challenged on various grounds as not sufficient, or as not necessary. I consider first the challenges to its sufficiency. The first objection (which is related to a similar challenge to its necessity) is the objection that 'man', unlike, say 'desk', is a natural-kind word. Natural kinds are, we saw earlier, kinds picked out in virtue of essential properties that are fundamental in determining the behaviour of things in a world with natural laws. But although we may reasonably conjecture (because of their characteristic appearance and patterns of behaviour) that most objects with certain observable properties belong to the same natural kind, that is have in common essential properties fundamental in determining behaviour, we may not know what those essential properties, which determine the exact boundaries of that kind, are—scientists may not yet have found that out.

What makes something a desk is a matter of observable features (e.g. shape and solidity). But what makes something water is not its taste, its transparency, its density, etc., but its chemical composition (H_2O), which underlies and is causally responsible for the observable properties. Something with the same observable properties but a different chemical composition would not be water. If we did not know the essence of water (as we did not before the nineteenth century), we could go badly wrong in our judgements about which samples of liquid are samples of water—even if we were the best

---

[9] See *Evolution of the Soul*, pt. 3.

experts available and took much trouble. Conversely, something with the chemical composition of water but which, because of external factors (change in our taste buds, odd lighting and atmospheric conditions, etc.), tasted or looked differently would still be water. Its observable features are normal but not completely reliable indicators that a substance before us is water.[10] So, the argument goes,[11] 'human' is like this. The features which I have listed, by which in general we rightly judge something to be a human, are largely experienceable or observable, but what makes something to be a human is the 'essence' which underlies the observable features of (most) paradigm examples of humans and is causally responsible for those observable features. The latter features which, following Putnam, I shall call the human stereotype, are only features of a human if the underlying essence that gives rise to them is the same as in standard examples of humans; and sometimes the essence might be present without the stereotype. What sort of essence are we talking about? As regards bodily features, genetic constitution is the obvious analogue to chemical constitution. Whether genetic constitution is causally sufficient to produce a human soul may be doubted,[12] and what else has to be added to it to produce a sufficient cause for the human soul is totally unclear. However, whatever the underlying cause of the stereotypic features, the issue remains whether 'human' is a natural-kind term like 'water' or instead a term like 'desk'. Why should not someone with the stereotypic features that I have listed be a human, even if those features were brought about by a quite different cause from the one that operates in normal humans? It seems to me that our criteria for the use of the word 'human' are simply unclear here. Some speakers might

[10] For this doctrine, see Hilary Putnam, 'The Meaning of "Meaning" ' in his *Mind, Language and Reality: Philosophical Papers*, ii (Cambridge University Press, 1975).

[11] This is the claim apparently made in Thomas V. Morris, *Understanding Identity Statements* (Aberdeen University Press, 1984), ch. 9; and developed in his *The Logic of God Incarnate* (Cornell University Press, 1986), esp. chs. 2 and 3. Morris, however, in fact argues (ibid. ch. 2) that, although humanity is a natural kind and so has an underlying 'essence', it does not follow that every individual which is human is so essentially; an individual who is human may belong simultaneously to another natural kind, and then lose its humanity while continuing to exist as a member of that other kind. Morris thus understands 'essence' in a looser sense than I have understood 'essence', 'essential form' or 'nature'. All that follows on Morris's understanding of 'essence' from an individual being human, is that its underlying human essence is what explains the human properties that it possesses.

[12] See *Evolution of the Soul*, ch. 10 and App., for reason for doubting that.

use the word one way and some might use the word another way. There is no right answer to my question.

A similar response, in my view, must be given to the other two objections that I shall consider to the sufficiency of my suggested list of essential features for humanity. The next is what I shall call the limitation objection. It is the objection that the powers and knowledge of an individual must be limited to some extent if he is to be a human. An individual's powers over the world outside himself must be confined almost entirely to ones that he exercises through his human body; his knowledge about the world must be confined almost entirely to that obtainable through its effects on his body (namely, through his sense-organs). An individual's powers to move the furniture about must be confined almost entirely to the power of moving it with his arms or legs, and his knowledge of where it is must be confined almost entirely to what he sees or feels or someone tells him. A *small* amount of telekinesis and telepathy might perhaps be compatible with humanity, but too much means that we no longer have a human. A human who becomes able to move mountains on distant continents just by willing, or knows what is going on in distant galaxies without using a telescope or listening to what others tell him ceases to be a human. Such is the claim of the objector. But whether his claim is correct seems to be quite unclear, because some of us might use the word 'human' in such a way that someone with such superhuman powers could not be a human, whereas others might use the word 'human' in such a way that someone with superhuman powers would be a human so long as he had normal human powers as well. Our criteria for use of the word 'human' are just not precise enough for there to be a right answer as to whether the possession of powers far beyond those of normal humans would rule out someone from being a human.

The final objection to the sufficiency of the listed features is what I shall call the historical objection. Even if my listed features are caused by the genetic or other essence, a being cannot be a human, the objection goes, unless his ancestry is right—unless the physical causes, namely, the genes, come from human parents or are otherwise obtained from the gene pool of the human race.[13] If we make an ovum in a laboratory, synthesize its genes from inorganic

---

[13] 'Even if creatures *exactly* like men arose from dragons' teeth, they would not be men, because not children of Adam,' Michael Dummett, *Frege, Philosophy of Language* (Duckworth, 1973), 144. Other writers make the point that having a common

material and fertilize it with a similar synthesized sperm cell, implant it in a tissue culture and grow the embryo in an artificial environment, the resulting being would not be human—even if the genes involved are qualitatively similar in chemical make-up to human genes. To be human you have to belong to the human race. Once again, whether our criteria of humanity involve a historical criterion seems to me unclear. If they do, the further question arises how thoroughly that criterion has to be satisfied—if for example, an individual's genes come only from his mother (parthenogenesis), can that individual still be a human? I would have thought that the use of the word 'human' by most of us is such as to yield the answer 'Yes' to the latter question.

I come now to objections to the necessity of my conditions for humanity, that to be a human an individual must have a human soul with the listed features, connected with a human body, defined as such by its physiology, anatomy, and capacities for action. First it may be objected that an infant who has only potentially some of the listed features ought to count as human. That seems right, whether or not we insist that the right causal essence ought to lie behind the infant's potentiality to develop the listed features. So long as normal growth will lead to the infant possessing the listed features, that infant is human. Secondly, why should we insist on all the listed mental features? Could there not be a human who did not have sensations, but could acquire beliefs about his environment through bodily processes without their being mediated via sensations?[14] Or—a question of especial relevance to a later chapter—could there not be a human who was not subject to desire, or at any rate to desire to do any action which he believed morally wrong? Again, our criteria for humanity yield no clear answer.

The final difficulty with the suggestion that the conditions stated earlier are necessary is—is the human body necessary? Is not a

---

evolutionary history is an important criterion used by biologists for distinguishing between species. (See e.g. Graeme Forbes, *The Metaphysics of Modality* (Clarendon Press, 1985), 201 n. 9.) One can understand the emphasis on that criterion by biologists who are concerned mainly with bodily differences formed gradually by a long process of evolution by natural selection. But it does not follow that that criterion ought to have similar importance when we are concerned with species valued primarily for their special mental features, the process of formation of which remains very mysterious (see my *Evolution of the Soul*, 183–99).

[14] On the separability of sensation and belief-acquisition as component parts of perception, see *Evolution of the Soul*, ch. 2.

disembodied human possible; and, if so, could there be a human who was never embodied (but was human in virtue of the type of mental life he had, including sensations of a kind caused in other humans by bodily processes, and desires of a kind manifested in other humans through bodily movements)?

Now I did earlier assume that I who am human could become disembodied, but my question here is not quite the same and the answer is not quite as obvious. If someone who is human cannot but be human, then since I can become disembodied, it would follow that having a body is not necessary for being human (and if, as earlier discussed, some kind of genetic constitution was involved in being human, the involvement could only be that any body a human has would have to be caused by a certain constitution, even if he could be human without having a body and so having that genetic constitution). But if I who am human can become disembodied, and yet being embodied is necessary for being human, what follows is that being human is not an essential property of those individuals who are human—one could cease to be human and become a being of some other kind, while remaining the same individual; just as a child can cease to be a child and become adult, while remaining the same individual. In the technical terminology introduced earlier, 'human' would be a phase-sortal rather than a substance-sortal.

It should be clear that with our rough present usage of 'human' there are different ways of making that usage precise. Someone clearly is human on any understanding if he satisfies all my original conditions, together with an 'underlying essence' condition, the limitation condition, and a historical condition (to meet each of the three objections to the sufficiency of the original conditions). But you get wider and wider understandings of humanity as you drop more and more conditions. There comes a point obviously where it is unreasonable to call a being 'human'—where hardly any of the conditions apply. But there is plenty of scope for different explications of what it is to be human. Yet on any plausible explication of our normal usage, 'human' cannot be a substance-sortal and so being human cannot be an essential form. For the body of some human, call him John, could gradually be turned into an animal body, into a body to all appearances like that, say, of a gorilla; and even if we insist on conditions of genotype or origin for a body being that of a gorilla, whatever else the body was it would not be that of a human. And John's human soul could gradually become a soul capable only of a gorilla-like mental life. The resulting body-and-soul would not be a human being, whatever else it was. Yet John would still exist. For suppose John knew in advance what was going to happen, and knew too that the gorilla would suffer much pain, he would rightly fear that pain for the same reason as he would fear any future pain of his. The same subject of mental properties could persist through the change. That shows that we name individuals who are humans in such a way that what is essential to their continuing to exist, namely their souls continuing to exist, is not those souls continuing with peculiarly human properties, let alone connection to a human body.

So there is no need to reform usage in order to turn 'human' into a phase-sortal; it is one already. But what is unclear in our present usage is just what are the boundaries of being human. How much by way of powers an individual has to gain or lose in order to cease to be human is unclear. But it follows from my earlier arguments that I (and any other human) who gain or lose powers or body am essentially a soul, a subject of mental properties, someone with a capacity for feeling, thought, or intentional action.

Souls are immaterial substances. There may also be pure imma-terial substances other than souls, but souls are those substances capable of having mental properties. Among souls are souls of dif-ferent kinds, differing in the kinds of mental life they are capable of and the kinds of body they are connected with. A normal use for the word 'person', which I shall adopt, is to call someone a person if he has a mental life of at least the kind of richness and complexity which humans have (or is capable of such a life, i.e. would have it as a result of normal processes of growth). Then, given that use, as well as humans, angels as traditionally depicted, and many fictional inhabitants of other planets as described in works of science fiction whom we may call 'Martians', would also, if they existed, be persons. (I shall not use the word 'person' in a very precise way, and so there is no need for me to define 'kind of richness and complexity', which would be needed if I were to try to give a precise sense to 'person'.) 'Person' must also, however, in this normal use, be a phase-sortal, since an individual could cease to have a mental life of that complexity; and yet in continuing to have sensations, continue to exist.

A crucial question about souls is whether they too, like material objects, are composed of form and some sort of stuff analogous to physical matter. I shall come to that question towards the end of the next chapter. Souls of some kinds may be able to become souls of other kinds—it is logically possible. I have argued that it is logically possible that a human soul could become the soul of a non-human animal, and I suggest also that a human soul could become a very powerful disembodied spirit. But there may be logical limits to such change. There may be souls which, given that they are of one kind, could not possibly become souls of various different kinds. I shall raise this issue again when we come to discuss the divine nature in Chapter 7.

2

Thisness

We saw in the last chapter that there are different possible systems of describing the history of the world, different ways of cutting the world into substances and tracing the continuities thereof. But if we are to tell the full history, we must trace at least the instantiations of properties in all pure substances and so their continuity over time. Although there are different ways of doing this, any system will involve thinking of each substance as belonging to a minimum essential kind. There will then be some properties which make it a substance of a particular kind, and something else which makes it the individual substance. There are certain properties which make an object a desk and something else which makes it the individual desk it is. We can, I suggest, give no content to the notion of a substance which does not belong to some minimum essential kind; for such a substance could lose all its properties and acquire quite different ones and yet remain the same substance. But, if that were possible, something which was a material object could cease to be one—my desk could become disembodied; or something which was not a material object could become one—a ghost could become my desk. Yet these are suppositions to which we can give no sense— there is nothing which would constitute something lacking spatial extension becoming my desk. Rather, as we saw in Chapter 1, in order to have some grip on (to understand and communicate) which substance we are referring to by some expression, we need to have some understanding of when some other expression on another occasion would pick out that substance, and we can only do that if we can say which properties the substance would need to continue to possess, that is, to which minimum essential kind it belongs. I can only have a concept of a substance Hesperus, I can only have a grip on what 'Hesperus' refers to, if I can say that (for example) it is essentially a planet. Thereby I set a limit on what Hesperus can become—it cannot for example become me.

What Thisness Is

For any minimum essential kind, the question arises as to what makes a substance of that kind the particular individual that it is, and there are two possibilities—that further properties suffice to individuate substances, or alternatively that although further properties might play a part in individuating they do not suffice to do so. In the latter case I shall say that a substance has *heacceitas*, or thisness. An individual (whether substance or other thing) has thisness in the sense at which I am aiming if a very weak form of the principle of the identity of indiscernibles does not apply to it. The principle states that an individual is the same as any individual which has all the same properties, but takes different forms according to what is allowed to constitute a property.

In the previous chapter I distinguished between monadic and relational properties by defining monadic properties as ones that things possess independently of their relations to things, and relational properties as ones that relate two or more things. I need now to be a little more precise. I understand by a relational property one that a thing has in virtue of how it is related to some actual thing (past, present, or future). Thus being-the-son-of-a-blacksmith is a relational property that belongs to an individual in virtue of the way he was conceived in the past. Whereas the property of being-square is one which something has independently of its relation to anything. But there are properties which things have intrinsically that concern how they could or would interact with other things under certain circumstances. In particular, causal powers are like this. The power to lift a 100 lb. weight, although it in some sense concerns a relation which I might have to some other thing, is on my definition a monadic property, because it does not concern a relation to any actual thing—my having this causal power is to be distinguished from my exercising it. (I could have it without there ever being any 100 lb. weights or anything else.)

In addition to distinguishing between monadic and relational properties, I distinguish among the latter between general ones which do not involve a relation to particular individuals, from particular ones which do. Thus being square or yellow are monadic properties; being 10 feet away from a round steel ball or living in a big city are general relational properties; and living in London or standing to the left of John are particular relational properties. 'General properties' covers both monadic and general relational properties. Properties, monadic and relational, may be hard or soft. A hard property is one that belongs to an individual at a certain time solely in virtue of how things are at that time. A soft property is one that belongs to an individual at a time solely or partly in virtue of how things are at other times. A soft future-directed property is one that belongs to an individual at t in virtue of how things will be at times later than t. A soft past-directed property is one that belongs to an individual at t in virtue of how things were at times earlier than t. Thus being-the-next-century's-greatest-pianist is a soft future-directed property, because it belongs to an individual now in virtue of how things will be in the next century. Being-sixty-years-old is a soft past-directed property, because it belongs to an individual now in virtue of what happened sixty years ago (that he was born then). Whereas being-today's-greatest-pianist is a hard property, because it belongs to an individual in virtue of how things are now. These distinctions among kinds of property give rise to many different forms of the principle of the identity of indiscernibles.

In my descriptions and subsequent discussion of these forms all properties of the above sorts will count as properties, except the properties of being identical with named individuals—e.g. being-identical-with-John[1]—I ignore these latter 'properties' because the whole point of a principle of the identity of indiscernibles is to analyse the identity or distinctness of individuals in terms of other properties which they possess. If being-identical-with-John counted as a property for present purposes, then it would be trivially and unilluminatingly true that if anyone had all the properties which John had including that property, he would be John. It is a consequence of this restriction that I shall count something as a property if and only if it is a universal, that is, can (at any rate in a different possible world, i.e. under different logically possible circumstances) be possessed by different individuals (or is a conjunction of universals—for example 'red and round'). Maybe only one individual can be the eldest son of John in this world; but since a different individual could be the eldest son of John in another world, being

[1] Or properties which entail these—such as the property of not-being-identical-with-James-in-a-universe-where-there-are-only-two-individuals, John and James. 'Named individuals' should be understood, more technically, as 'individuals picked out by rigid designators' (as this term is explained in Ch. 5).

the eldest son of John is a universal. But the 'property' of being identical with John is not a universal, because only one individual could have it (nor is it a conjunction of universals). I now distinguish six forms of the principle useful for my purposes. They concern the identity of two individuals at a time. I assume—by the necessity of identity (see Ch. 1)—that if two individuals are the same at one time, they are the same at all times.

[A] Any two individuals who have all the same properties are the same individual.

[B] Any two individuals who have all the same hard and past-directed soft properties are the same individual.

[C] Any two individuals who have all the same hard properties are the same individual.

[D] Any two individuals who have all the same general hard and past-directed soft properties are the same individual.

[E] Any two individuals who have all the same general hard properties are the same individual.

[F] Any two individuals who have all the same general hard monadic properties are the same individual.

These forms of the principle are clearly not the only ones possible, but they are the only ones to have been seriously entertained; and they are listed in order of increasing strength (except that, while [C] and [D] are both stronger than [B] and weaker than [E], they are not comparable with each other with respect to strength).

There may well be kinds of individual to whose individuation the strongest form, [F], applies. Aquinas seems to claim that [F] is true of God; and indeed that only the properties essential to divinity are needed to individuate God. Any individual who had the essential divine properties of omnipotence, omniscience, etc. would be the same individual; in other words, there could not be a possible universe in which different individuals were God.[2] I shall return to this issue in Chapter 7. But clearly this principle does not apply to individuals which have spatial relations to other distinguishable individuals. Two qualitatively identical iron balls would not be the same if they differed in their spatial relations to other distinguishable individuals.

---

[2] 'God himself is his own nature . . . It is therefore in virtue of one and the same fact that he is God and this God' (*Secundum idem est deus et hic deus*), Thomas Aquinas *Summa theologiae*, 1a. 11. 3.

[D] differs from [E], and [B] from [C], by weakening the latter form to require sameness of properties which belong to individuals in virtue of how things have been in the past. [E], and its weaker form [D], claim that mere general properties (monadic and relational) suffice to individuate. [E] is plausible for abstract objects, for example, numbers. Two integers, each of which was > 7 and < 9 (7 and 9 also being distinguished by their general properties) would be the same integer. It also applies, surely, to laws of nature, in the sense of principles determining the behaviour of objects (rather than the sentences which state them). Two laws which had the same general properties—of causing any (actual or possible) objects of such-and-such kinds to do so-and-so in circumstances of such-and-such kinds would be the same law. If Heisenberg's laws of Quantum Theory are equivalent to Schrodinger's in the sense that they have the same consequences for material objects, they are the same laws.

Symmetrical universes do, however, seem to present an obstacle to the suggestion that [E] applies to material objects, and the obstacle applies to [D] as well. 'Isn't it logically possible that the universe should have contained nothing but two exactly similar spheres?' asked Max Black.[3] Each would be of the same size, shape, 'made of chemically pure iron', at a distance of 2 miles from a sphere of that kind, and—we may add—with a qualitatively similar history, for example, each is spatio-temporally continuous with a sphere with the same hard properties for infinite past time; and yet the two spheres would be different.

This consideration moves us, for material objects, in the direction of the weaker forms [C] and [B] as the strongest which can be asserted. Each individual in a symmetrical universe would, by principle [C], be a different individual in virtue of being differently related spatially to a different individual. Thus iron sphere *a* would have the property of being 2 miles away from iron sphere *b*; whereas iron sphere *b* would not have that property, but would have instead the property of being 2 miles away from iron sphere *a*. Hence they would seem to be different.

Yet although [C] is a different principle from [E], its consequences for material objects in a world containing only material

---

[3] Max Black, 'The Identity of Indiscernibles', *Mind*, 61 (1952), 153–64, see 156.

objects, and so the objections to it, are exactly the same.[4] For since on [C] it suffices to make *a* the particular iron sphere it is for it to have the same general monadic properties as *b* and also be 2 miles away from *b*, it follows that any sphere with the same general monadic properties in its place would be the same iron sphere. By a similar argument any similar iron sphere in *b*'s place would be the same iron sphere as *b*. Hence [C] individuates in this example in exactly the same way as [E], and so [B] individuates in exactly the same way as [D], and so the objections to them remain. If two iron spheres 2 miles away from each other came out the same on [E] or [D], they will come out the same on [C] or [B]. But [A] differs from [B] only in allowing that future-directed soft properties might make all the difference. Yet that is not plausible. Two individuals can only have a different future history (e.g. one cease to exist at *t*, and the other continue to exist after *t*) if there are already two individuals distinct in virtue of other considerations, who might subsequently have different histories.[5] If we accept that the two qualitatively identical iron spheres 2 miles away from each other in an otherwise empty universe are different, we are forced to deny that even [A] has application to them. To say that individuals have thisness in the sense in which philosophers who have used the notion were doing is, I suggest, just to say that form [A] does not apply to them. There can be distinct individuals which have all the same properties. I shall consider shortly whether it is possible to say anything further about how thisness arises. But, as I am using the term, to say that individuals have thisness is simply to say that they are not individuated solely by any properties (in the sense which I have distinguished) which they have. Its thisness is distinct and intrinsic to each individual which has it.

[4] Black's example assumes that the world contains no individuals of any other kind than material objects, which have thisness (as defined below). If the world contained souls which have thisness, then material objects might be distinguished from each other by their different relations to them—e.g. this sphere is the one of which I have an image (i.e. which causes me to have an image), and that is the one of which you have an image; you and I might have all the same properties and so the spheres come out as the same by [E] but not by [C]. Alternatively, if places had thisness, then material objects could be distinguished by the places they occupy, and then again [E] and [C]—as also [D] and [B]—would individuate differently. I argue below that souls do, but places do not, have thisness.

[5] For this argument, see R. M. Adams, 'Primitive Thisness and Primitive Identity', *Journal of Philosophy*, 76 (1979), 5–26, 18 f. My whole discussion of thisness takes off from the distinctions and arguments of Adams's paper.

Do Material Objects and Human Souls Have Thisness?

It is not, however, clear that material objects do have thisness despite the initial plausibility of the example of the two iron spheres. For modern physics gives some reason for supposing that the small-scale components of material objects, the fundamental particles of which all matter is made, are really just fields of force. Just as there could not be a different magnetic field of a certain shape and strength occupying a given location from the one actually occupying it (its shape, strength, and location make it the field it is), so maybe there could not be a different photon travelling from A to B from the one which is travelling thither.[6] On this account fundamental particles are just fields of force, giving rise to observable properties, but with nothing underlying those properties to individuate them. If fundamental particles do have thisness, the large-scale material objects which they compose will, of course, also have thisness. But if fundamental particles do not have thisness, then the large-scale material which they compose cannot have it either. And in that case symmetrical universes, such as the two iron spheres' universe, though apparently logically possible, are not really so. How in that case has it come about that we have been deceived about the logical possibility? The most plausible answer must be that, although it is logically possible that iron spheres, or perhaps we should say objects qualitatively indistinguishable from iron spheres, have thisness, and so there can be a symmetrical universe; as a matter of fact, in our universe, iron spheres do not have thisness and so this universe and any universe like ours in having fundamental particles lacking thisness, could not be symmetrical. That does, of course, rule out certain apparently possible arrangements of the matter of this universe as really impossible, given what that matter is, for logical reasons. That could be right. There could still be, made of the matter of our universe, nothing but an iron sphere 2 miles away from an iron sphere—but, unless iron spheres have thisness, it would be two miles away from itself, space being curved.[7]

There is, however, to my mind a far stronger case for supposing that human souls (and souls of many other animate beings) have

[6] See Additional Note 2.

[7] This possible interpretation of the datum of there being an iron sphere 2 miles away from an iron sphere was drawn to our attention by Ian Hacking, 'The Identity of Indiscernibles', *Journal of Philosophy*, 72 (1975), 249–56.

thisness. The world could have been such that a human who had all the same general properties and relations as myself—the same bodily constitution and history (however these are individuated) and the same conscious mental life—described in general terms, for example, a pain followed by a thought that people were hostile, followed by a blue image, etc. That human could also have had all the same particular relational properties, for example, being born of particular individuals X and Y at time *t* (however these are individuated). And yet that person could have been quite other than myself. Hence what makes me is not solely the properties that I have, but also their underlying thisness. The example of the split-brain transplant discussed in the last chapter reinforces this conclusion. It is logically possible that the left-brain person be (the same person as) the earlier me, and logically possible that it be not me; and yet the difference between it being me and not being me does not turn on its hard properties; nor does it turn on its past-directed soft properties, for example, 'continuity of experience with (the earlier) me', unless 'continuity of experience with' is analysable so as to entail 'being the same subject of experience as' and so entails 'being identical with'. And a 'property' which entails the 'property' of 'being identical with me' cannot count as a property. Innumerable other thought experiments bring out that being me is not solely a matter of having certain properties.

In these cases, surely it is a factual matter whether I survive some brain operation, yet not one entailed by what happens to the brain matter and what experiences the subsequent person has. Yet if all else could be the same, and yet either I survive or I do not, it must be something other than my properties which makes an individual me—namely, my thisness. Here the intuition of logical possibility is immensely stronger than in the two iron spheres' case, because surviving is something of which we have experience from moment to moment. The instantiation of every mental property (e.g. being-in-pain, having-a-red-image) is its instantiation over a period of time, and therefore involves its instantiation over the first half of the period and over the second half of the period being its instantiation in the same subject of experience. My experience of every mental property which is instantiated in me is thus an awareness of it as instantiated in a continuing subject—me. Again, my awareness of myself as having simultaneously two different sensations—hearing a noise and having a visual image—is an

awareness of the two properties as coinstantiated in the same individual—me.[8] One's grasp of the concept of oneself is involved in
one's grasp of the mental life, the succession of events to which the
subject has privileged access and upon which all his other knowledge of the world is dependent. The understanding each of us
grasps of themself (and so of any other human person there may
be) is an understanding of a continuing subject of experience whose
existence does not entail, although it may normally accompany, the
existence of certain brain matter.

In view of the intimacy and all-pervasiveness of our awareness of
ourselves, if we do not know what we are conceiving in conceiving
events happening to ourselves, we do not know what we are conceiving about anything. If we cannot make judgements of logical
possibility here, we cannot make such judgements anywhere; and
if we cannot do that, we cannot do philosophy (or pursue any
other discipline—e.g. science—where we argue that some proposition p follows deductively from some other proposition q. For
to claim that is to claim that it is not logically possible that p-and-
not-q.) The judgements of logical possibility that this intimate
and pervasive awareness of ourselves licenses are judgements of
the logical possibility of a different human person having the same
succession of properties as myself, and of me surviving having this
half-brain, or alternatively that half-brain, or no brain or body at
all. Such awareness also licenses judgements of some animate being
currently not human, but say a monkey, having the same succession of properties as myself, or of me surviving with the mental life
and body of a higher animal.

Yet of the iron spheres we have only an external and more fallible
awareness, not an awareness of them as inhering in a continuing
subject which experiences them intimately. Because our awareness
is external and more fallible, we could more readily be mistaken in
supposing there to be some things in which the properties of the

---

[8] This despite Hume's famous remark: 'When I enter most intimately into what
I call myself, I always stumble on some particular perception or other, of heat or
cold, light or shade, love or hatred, pain or pleasure. I never catch myself at any
time without a perception' (*Treatise of Human Nature*, 1. 4. 6). It may well be that
Hume never catches himself without 'a perception' (i.e. a conscious episode) but his
bare datum is not just 'perceptions'; he does not just observe perceptions at a
distance and wonder whose they are. Rather his datum is successions of overlapping
perceptions, experienced by a common subject, he who is also aware of them. He is
aware of them as bound together by occurring to a common subject.

iron spheres inhere and which is distinct from them. Hence souls
(of human beings and of many other animate beings) are far stronger
candidates for having thisness than are material objects. And I
have the ability to pick out the soul that is me in a way which does
not involve picking it out solely in virtue of properties in the sense
so far distinguished. I can distinguish you from me even if you are
the subject of the same mental properties as I am, and our bodies
are qualitatively the same and are located in a symmetrical universe.

Times and places by contrast cannot have thisness. A given time
(whether period or instant) or place (whether volume or point) are
what they are in virtue of their relations to other things. Times
could not but have the temporal relations to other times that they
do, and surely any time which has the same temporal relations as
1990 would be 1990. There could not be a different year which
occurred after 1989 and before 1991, and in which there occurred
events otherwise the same as in our 1990. So [A] must be true of
times and times cannot have thisness. The same applies to places;
there could not be a universe which differed from our universe
only in there being in it a different place from the place now occupied
by the sun, a place which was itself occupied by the sun and surrounded by the same other places and material objects. Places too
cannot have thisness.[9] It remains the case that the most plausible
candidates for having thisness are substances, and of those, human
souls are a far better candidate than material objects.

We saw in Chapter 1 that material objects are 'composed' of
matter and form. They are what they are in virtue of the matter of
which they are made and the form imposed upon it. Forms are
conjunctions of properties. If material objects do not have thisness,
then properties alone suffice to individuate them (i.e. to make them
the particular individuals of their kind which they are), and so being
composed of the same matter will be reducible to some sameness or continuity of properties. We saw in Chapter 1 that one can
trace continuity of substances under very different and sometimes

---

[9] I claim this without pronouncing on any of the many philosophico-scientific
issues of the absoluteness of space and time. These include the issues of whether
there are absolute standards of simultaneity, of temporal interval, or spatial interval,
or spatio-temporal interval; and whether in some sense there are distinctions to be
made between absolute rest, absolute velocity, and absolute acceleration. The latter
issues involve the issues of whether times and places are what they are only in
relation to other times and places, or whether they are individuated also or ultimately
by their relations to other things such as the material objects which occupy them.

arbitrarily chosen bundles of essential properties. But clearly spatio-temporal continuity with an object with similar essential properties and other hard monadic properties is a normal crucial convention for the sameness over time of the matter of which material objects are made, and, if there is no thisness, what makes the matter the same. A normal crucial criterion for this desk being the same desk as that here last week is spatio-temporal continuity with the earlier desk (which makes the matter the same), as well as having the same shape, mass, etc., as it (which makes the form the same).

Modern physics sometimes claims that the fundamental particles, such as electrons, 'jump' from one place to another without passing through the intermediate space. Saying that involves dropping spatio-temporal continuity as a criterion for their identity over time and so either abandoning all talk of identity of particles over time (not regarding the particle at the end of the 'jump' as the same particle as that at the beginning of the 'jump' and so treating 'jumping' as having a highly analogical sense), or allowing such identity to be determined in another way. But for larger objects clearly spatio-temporal continuity is a crucial criterion. In sum, given the irrelevance of future-directed properties—if material objects lack thisness, what makes a particular object the object it is, is just some set of its hard and past-directed soft properties. The strongest principle of identity for material objects would then seem to be [B], if—as I have urged—the world contains individuals of other kinds with thisness—namely souls—by their relations to which material objects can be individuated (see n. 4), or [D] if there are none of the latter.

If, however, material objects do have thisness, then, since forms are simply conjunctions of properties, as we shall see more fully shortly, it will arise from the matter of which they are made. Chunks of matter would differ intrinsically from each other in their thisness. In that case, I suggest, we would naturally regard our use of spatio-temporal continuity as a 'criterion' of identity over time as our use, not of a logically necessary condition of such identity, but merely as inductive evidence of it. A watch having the same hard monadic properties (shape, organization, etc.) and made of the same matter as an earlier watch would be the same watch, even if it were not spatio-temporally continuous with it. We normally suppose that if there is no spatio-temporal continuity, the material object is not the same, but only because we suppose that in that case the matter is not the same. But there seems no logical reason why, if matter has thisness, it has to preserve spatio-temporal continuity. I have just noted that modern physics sometimes claims that fundamental particles 'jump' orbits without passing through the intervening space. If one holds that fundamental particles have thisness arising from the matter of which they are made,[10] one holds that identity is preserved over the 'jump' and so that matter can 'jump'. Physical theory however gives no reason to suppose that fundamental particles can 'jump' far enough to allow large-scale objects (which are composed of fundamental particles) to 'jump', and in that case for them spatio-temporal continuity would be very strong evidence of sameness of matter.

Even if material objects do have thisness, further properties could still play an essential part in individuating objects of a given kind. One could have an essential kind such that particular substances of that kind were individuated in part by further properties, even though these did not suffice to individuate. One could invent a new concept of 'desk' such that, although the essential properties of 'desks' were the same as at present, a desk had to preserve its colour in order to be the same desk. To be a certain desk, a desk would have to remain red; if you painted the red desk brown, you would be destroying the old desk and making a new one—even if there was more to being the same desk than having all the same properties. Spatio-temporal continuity could play this role of neces-sary but not sufficient individuating property, even if material objects do have thisness—but I do not think that it would be natural for us so to regard it. In general, I suggest, our conceptual systems are such that we regard the further properties by which we pick out substances of a kind as the particular substances they are either as jointly sufficient to determine identity, or alternatively as evidence of an identity determined in some other way. Yet, as we saw in Chapter 1, we can describe the history of the world equally well with very different schemes of classifying material objects, since they are impure substances. A full history of the world must however trace the continuities of pure substances, and in particular of souls. In consequence the criteria of their individuation—what makes a soul the individual soul it is—are not determined by arbitrary choice. If something is a soul (whether of a human or many another animate

---

[10] For the reasons given in Additional Note 2.

being), and souls have thisness, there are not further properties required to individuate. The particular soul that is me could have had an entirely different mental life (i.e. a quite different series of monadic mental properties could have been instantiated in it) and quite different relations to other things (e.g. it could have been connected with a different body), and yet been the same soul. The same kind of thought experiment that suggests that another soul might have been connected to my body and lived my mental life suggests that that soul might have been you and that I might have led quite a different life. These additional accidental properties of souls do, however, have the role of providing inductive evidence enabling us to identify and reidentify souls, albeit fallibly. It provides the simplest account of human bodily behaviour and mental life— and therefore that most likely to be true—if we suppose that same soul is normally connected to same body, and that similarity of character and memory is evidence of sameness of soul.[11] The fact, for example, that I claim to remember that my body looked like this and I had that experience when I was young is evidence that I have the same soul as (i.e. am the same person as) the person who looked like this and had that experience, but it does not make me that person. These additional properties thus play the same role for souls as spatio-temporal continuity naturally does for material objects, if the latter have thisness.

If however—contrary to all my arguments so far—the souls of humans do not have thisness, then properties will suffice to individuate them. These may be properties of relation to substances of other kinds—souls may be individuated by the bodies to which they are connected; and/or monadic properties and properties of relation to souls having certain monadic properties. In the former case what makes my soul my soul would be that it is connected to the particular body that I call my body. (That in turn may have thisness or be individuated solely by its properties.) In the latter case what makes my soul my soul would be that a certain set of mental properties is instantiated in it, either current beliefs, desires, sensations, etc., and/or continuity of experience with some past soul having certain beliefs, desires, etc. Anyone who had exactly the same monadic and relational properties as I do would be me;

---

[11] See my *The Evolution of the Soul* (Clarendon Press, 1986), ch. 9, for a full account of why such criteria serve as criteria of sameness of soul.

and no doubt some narrower set of properties would suffice to make a substance me. In any of these cases, some form of the principle of identity of indiscernibles would apply to souls—either [B] if they are individuated by their different relations to bodies which have thisness, or otherwise [D].

The Source of Thisness

The history of philosophy since Plato has been dominated by a highly plausible theory of what makes individuals the individuals that they are, which is called the hylemorphic theory. On this theory, individuals are the individuals they are in virtue of the stuff (*hyle*) of which they are made, and the form or nature or essence (*morphe*) imposed upon it. We have already defended this theory as correct for material objects, and its more general applicability is highly plausible. What more can there be to a thing than what it is made of, and what properties are imparted to what it is made of?[12] Suppose now that (despite my doubts) material objects, and (as I claim) souls of human and many other animate beings (and thus the beings of which they are the souls) do have thisness. What more can be said about what this involves? Given the hylemorphic theory, the difference between individuals which have thisness must lie either in their stuff or in their form. On an Aristotelian view, forms are universals—that is, properties in the sense which I defined earlier; ordinary physical matter is the only stuff of which individuals which have thisness are made, and it is that which provides the principle of individuation among individuals with the same form. If the iron spheres differ in thisness, that is because they are made

---

[12] The theory is plausible only as a theory of substances. To my mind the hylemorphic theory has no application to places and times, let alone to the forms themselves. Aristotle seems to have thought that abstract objects are formed of 'intelligible matter'; but since abstract objects do not have thisness, I can ignore this point below when I claim that on an Aristotelian view ordinary physical matter is the only stuff of which individuals which have thisness are made. Or rather it is the only 'prime matter'. One may speak of a substance being made of bits of stuff which already have forms of some sort, e.g. a building being made of bricks; and then the bricks form the matter of the building, which are 'formed' into a shape by the builder. But the bricks themselves are not 'prime matter' for they themselves have a form and matter. Prime matter is, for Aristotle, the unformed stuff underlying all components of wholes.

of different matter. So too, on an Aristotelian view, although two humans may differ in properties other than the form of humanity, what individuates is not these (which are mere 'accidental properties') but the different matter of which each is made.[13] The difference between qualitatively identical chunks of matter is the ultimate intrinsic difference.

But given my earlier arguments to show that what makes two humans different is an essential immaterial part, the soul, then if we wish still to preserve the hylemorphic theory, in order to apply it to an immaterial individual such as the soul, we shall have to understand it in a more liberal way than the normal Aristotelian way. We shall have to allow either a different kind of stuff from physical matter or a different kind of form from universals. We may allow that stuff individuates, but say that the stuff of which souls are made is not physical matter but spiritual matter (or soul-stuff). The difference between two humans will then lie in the different soul-stuff of which they are made. Bonaventure taught that the human soul was an immaterial substance, consisting of spiritual matter informed by a form;[14] and that embodied humans consisted of such a soul united to a human body.

A hylemorphic theory does, however, leave open the possibility of a quite different account of thisness. Perhaps forms are not always universals, but may be individual essences. Maybe there is an essence not just of humanity or being a philosopher, but of Socrates. 'Thisness' is the literal English translation of *haecceitas*, the word that the fourteenth-century philosopher Duns Scotus introduced into philosophy; that word is sometimes most unliterally translated 'individual essence', and Scotus has been held to have introduced into philosophy the notion of individual essences. Maybe in effect he did, but the phenomenon of *haecceitas* to which he drew attention is to be distinguished from the account of it in terms of individual essence.

Scotus certainly taught that ordinary matter was too undifferentiated a thing to be the principle of individuation; and while he may, like Bonaventure, have taught that humans were made of

---

[13] 'When we have the whole, such and such a form in this flesh and these bones, this is Callias or Socrates; and they are different in virtue of their matter (for that is different), but the same in form (for that is indivisible),' Aristotle, *Metaphysics*, 1034^{a}5–7.

[14] St Bonaventure, 2 *Sentences*, 17. 1. 2, *responsio*.

soul-stuff as well as physical matter, and that angels were made of soul-stuff, he did not think that any kind of stuff sufficed to individuate.[15] For him stuff is too undifferentiated a thing to individuate. He says that neither stuff, nor form, nor the composite individuates;[16] and I am interpreting his claim that form does not individuate, as the claim that no properties (in my sense) individuate. The *ultima realitas entis* (ultimate reality of a being) which does individuate is a particular restriction on the specific form;[17] and I shall call that restriction the 'individual essence'. If we assume—which is disputable—that Scotus held a hylemorphic theory, then it is the union of the individual essence with stuff that brings into being particular individuals. Thus the essence of Socrates is a particular restriction on the form of humanity or a wider form such as the form of animate being—it is a particular way of being human (or animate)—and its union with stuff gives rise to Socrates. Such individual essences are not properties in the sense which I distinguished earlier, for individual essences are not universals.

I find the individual essence account implausible for material objects; but, if we allow that they have thisness, more plausible for

---

[15] Duns Scotus discusses the question of what is the principle of individuation—what makes a thing 'this' and not 'that'—among other places, in *Ordinatio*, 2. d3. p1 (vol. vii of the edition of the works of Scotus, published by the Scotistic Commission, Vatican City, 1950–   ). Q5 denies that stuff (*materia*, which covers both physical matter and other stuff) individuates. For commentary including discussion of whether he was committed to 'spiritual matter', see F. Copleston, *A History of Philosophy*, ii. *Augustine to Scotus* (Burns & Oates, 1964), 279, 513 f; and Allan B. Wolter, 'Scotus' Individuation Theory', in his *The Philosophical Theology of John Duns Scotus* (Cornell University Press, 1990).

[16] See *Ordinatio*, 2. d3. p1. q5–6. n. 187. Part of his reason for denying that stuff individuates seems to be that that would leave us with the problem of what individuates stuff, i.e. makes the difference between this chunk of stuff and that. That is so, but one can simply hold that the latter distinction is ultimate and provides the basis of the distinction between substances. See Wolter, 'Scotus' Individuation Theory', 88 f.

[17] In *Ordinatio*, 2. d3. p1. q5–6. nn. 167–77 he explains that individual difference arises from a contraction of the specific form, like the way in which a generic form is contracted to a specific but unlike it in that what we are left with is no longer a universal. He seems unclear however whether that with which we are left can exist or in some sense be, without being united with matter, i.e. whether the essence of Socrates can exist without Socrates. I am interpreting him as supposing that it can, at least in the fictional way in which a universal exists without its instances and possibly (see later) in the real way in which substances exist without inessential parts. Elsewhere he claims that the distinction between the specific human nature and a *haecceitas* is a purely 'formal one'; not even God could separate them. That naturally fits his view that *haecceitas* arises from a modification of the form. On this see Copleston, *History of Philosophy*, ii. 512, and the passages which he cites.

souls. Applied to material objects, which are made from physical matter alone, it would have the consequence that this particular desk of mine, instead of being made in the way it was at the time it was from the matter it was might have been made from quite different matter somewhere else. Yet it seems absurd to suppose that two desks made of different matter could have anything in common beyond their universal form, which made them the same desk. If material objects have thisness, we need a 'thick' enough doctrine of matter to allow matter to provide the criterion of individuation. If animate beings have a thisness that is independent of the physical matter of which they are made, and arises from a difference in souls, then it might seem possible for soul-stuff to provide individuation. But even if we could make sense of a 'stuff' which was not spatially extended, it does seem to be of the essence of 'stuff' that it is divisible and combinable into chunks of different sizes; and that it does not come into being or cease to exist in the natural course of things—it continues to be, informed over time with different forms. So an account of the nature of animate beings which was grounded in a stuff with these properties would have to allow the possibility of fission and fusion of animate beings, embodied or disembodied, on a massive scale—disembodied humans could all be fused into one superhumanity, in the way that many guns could be melted down to make a supergun.

For the reasons which I gave in Chapter 1, I can give no sense to the application to animate beings of the notions of fission and fusion. Hence I can see no grounds for supposing that souls are individuated by soul-stuff. But individuation by individual essence would have obvious application. My earlier discussions show that we can make sense of the same animate being animating quite different physical matter, as we cannot make sense of similar stories about desks; and if we rule out soul-stuff as the principle of individuation, the obvious thing to say is that *haecceitas* is a restriction on the form. A form with its peculiar restriction can be imposed on different stuff. If we allow the logical possibility of the disembodied existence of animate beings, and continue to hold a hylemorphic theory, then that existence must consist in the instantiation of the form in soul-stuff. But the soul-stuff would not provide the principle of individuation; it would be an undifferentiated soul-stuff which would not therefore allow the possibility of fission or fusion of individuals. Soul-stuff informed by the individual essence of Socrates would be Socrates; soul-stuff not so informed would not be Socrates—there would be no scope for intermediate positions. Individual essences, unlike stuff, cannot be split or combined.

A hylemorphic theory has its natural application to inanimate material objects, where we can actually observe the matter of one substance being re-formed into the matter of another. If we extend it to souls we have to postulate a soul-stuff, whose existence we have no reason to postulate other than to preserve the hylemorphic theory. It does for this reason seem, despite the above insights of the 'individual essence' variant of hylemorphic theory, that it would be better to say that the hylemorphic theory does not apply to souls. Can we in that case say anything more useful about what the thisness of souls consists in? I suggest that we should seek a more general way of bringing out why souls cannot be split or combined, or become anything other than souls. It is easy to do this, while preserving the hylemorphic theory for material objects (if they have thisness) if we say that souls are individual essences—from which the above two characteristics of souls follow—which can exist on their own, without being united with stuff (exist, that is, not in the fictional sense in which forms or universals are sometimes said to exist—see Chapter 1—but in the full-blooded sense in which live humans exist).[18] They may in principle go in and out of existence, without this involving the uniting or separation of a form with anything. An alternative reading of Scotus allows us to attribute this view to him.[19]

It follows from all this, that even if we allow that material objects have thisness, that the thisness of souls and material objects will arise in quite different ways. (Note that in arguing for the thisness of souls, I have been arguing for the thisness of the souls of humans and many other animate beings. I have not been arguing for the thesis that every soul, in the sense of substance in which mental properties inhere, has thisness. There may be kinds of souls which do not have thisness. I shall need to explore that possibility in Part II.)

---

[18] My adopting this way of speaking represents a change of way of putting things from earlier writings of mine—e.g. *Evolution of the Soul*, but no change in my main thesis that souls are the essential parts of humans and can exist without bodies.

[19] See Additional Note 3.

3

Causation

A Basic Category

Substances cause other substances to begin, continue, or cease existing; or to gain or lose properties. They cause or,—to use a synonym—bring about events, that is. They cause because among their properties are causal powers. The stone, when dropped on a plate, causes the plate to break in virtue of having the power to break objects up to a certain level of fragility, and it has that power whether or not it is exercising it. Material objects have liabilities to exercise their powers under certain conditions. The stone has the liability to exercise that power to break objects when dropped from a certain height; this liability is among the properties of the stone. In virtue of having the liability, the stone cannot but exercise its power to break the plate, when dropped from the height. Some substances may not, however, be so confined; within limits, human souls may choose when and where to exercise their powers; and, I believe and have argued elsewhere,[1] nothing causes them to choose as they do. We have libertarian free will.

The distinction between cause and condition is, I suggest, an arbitrary one. Lighting a match in the presence of hydrogen causes an explosion. But is it the match which causes the explosion under the conditions of being lit in the presence of hydrogen, or the hydrogen which causes the explosion under the condition of being in the presence of a lighted match? Although it might seem that one of these accounts could be true and the other false (in the sense that only one of the substances involved was exerting an active influence), there seems little obvious content to such a distinction, and so no reason for denying that all the substances whose causal operation is severally necessary (under those conditions) and jointly sufficient for the production of the effect are involved equally as causes. I

[1] See my *The Evolution of the Soul* (Clarendon Press, 1986), ch. 13.

understand by a full cause one whose active causal operation is sufficient for the production of the effect; and by a partial cause one which is a necessary part of a collection of substances whose active causal operation is sufficient for the production of the effect. (Sometimes an event may have more than one full cause in that each of two or more causes would have caused the event even if the others had not been present. Such an event is said to be 'overdetermined'.) So in my example each of the substances involved, the match and the hydrogen, are partial causes; taken together they form a full cause. But we may speak casually of the match causing an explosion given the presence of hydrogen, if our interest is in matches rather than hydrogen or, *mutatis mutandis*, the other way round. They exercise their causal powers when properties are instantiated in them—for example, the match exercises its power when it is lit. When the relevant properties are instantiated, each of the relevant substances exerts causal power: together, they exert enough causal power to cause.

Many substances have exactly the same powers as each other. To put the point on the (strictly false, but approximately true) assumption that Newton's laws are the true laws of nature—every material object has the power to attract every other material object in the universe with a force proportional to mm'/r^2 (where m is the mass of the first body, m' of the second, and r is the distance between the two); it also has the liability always to exercise that power when there are other material objects. But different kinds of body differ from each other in their causal powers, and have (among other powers) a more determinate form of the power of gravitational attraction. Thus (measuring mass in terms of Mev/c^2, the mass equivalent of an energy of 10^6 electron volts), each proton (defined as a body having a mass of 938 Mev/c^2 and a certain positive electrostatic charge) has the power to attract gravitationally each other material body in the universe with a force of $938m'/r^2$ (where m' is the mass of the other body and r the distance between them): and so on. Given that the true laws of nature are slightly different from Newton's laws, the gravitational powers that all material objects have are slightly different from those that I have just stated, and those that bodies of different kinds have are codified by more determinate forms of the true laws. All material objects are composed of fundamental particles of a few basic kinds, each with the same set of powers. In consequence no doubt of the powers of their component particles, all larger substances have determinate sets of powers, each set for each kind of substance, kinds being defined by other properties of the substance. A car of a certain construction has the power to travel 60 m.p.h., and the liability to exercise that power when its engine is started, its clutch connected, and its accelerator pressed. And all other cars of exactly the same construction have the same powers and liabilities to exercise them.

The liability of a substance to exercise its causal powers may be only a probabilistic one. It may, that is, have an inclination or propensity (of a strength measured by a certain degree of physical probability[2]) to exercise its causal powers under certain circumstances, rather than a liability inevitably to do so. If Quantum Theory shows—as I believe it does—that nature on the very small scale is not deterministic, then what that amounts to is that material objects have liabilities to exercise their causal powers with different degrees of probability under different circumstances. An atom of radium having a half-life of 1,700 years is it having the causal power to decay and produce the products of decay, and a liability to exercise that power with a probability of $\frac{1}{2}$ within 1,700 years. A photon travelling towards a screen with two slits in it and a probability of passing through each of $\frac{1}{2}$ has the causal power to pass through a given slit and an inclination of physical probability $\frac{1}{2}$ to exercise that power. This indeterminism is, however, in general, only of any significance on the very small scale. In general, medium-scale objects have liabilities to exercise their powers under (and only under) certain conditions with physical probabilities of virtually 1.

In a case where a cause C produces some effect E only because some substance S which has the causal power to prevent the effect

---

[2] It is very important to distinguish 'physical probability' which is a measure of the strength of an inclination of a substance to produce an effect, from probabilities of two other kinds. First, there is statistical probability which is a measure of the proportion of substances or events with one property which also have some other property—e.g. of inhabitants of Pennsylvania who are registered Republicans, or *a* toss of a coin (or this coin) being heads. Secondly, there is epistemic or inductive probability which is a measure of the strength of support which some evidence gives to a hypothesis. In this sense we talk of the probability on the evidence of its past performance that the next toss of this coin will be heads, or the probability on the evidence available today that Quantum Theory is true. (This latter 'probability' may not, of course, be susceptible of an exact numerical measure.) For these distinctions see, among other places, my *An Introduction to Confirmation Theory* (Methuen, 1973), chs. 1 and 2.

from occurring and no liability not to exercise that power, does not do so, we may say that *S* permits (or allows) the effect to occur and speak of *S* as a permissive cause. Suppose that the decay of a radium atom would trigger some mechanism which prevents the ignition of a match from having its normal effect of causing an explosion, and there is no natural necessity for the atom not to decay (it is not fully caused not to decay), but whether it does is a matter of physical probability, then I shall say that the atom is a permissive (as opposed to active) cause of the explosion. The main use for such talk of permissive causes will arise when we consider intentional causation.

The empiricist tradition of the past 200 years has sought to follow Hume in his claim that causality is not an ultimate relation between things, but is reducible to something more basic. It regarded causation as a relation between events; and it normally sought to analyse that relation along the lines provided by one of Hume's two main suggested definitions[3] in terms of patterns of regular succession between similar events. A simple Humean 'regularity' analysis is this: to say that event α caused event β is to say that α belongs to a type of event A, and β belongs to a type of event B, and events of type A are always followed by events of type B—for example to say that the ignition of the gunpowder caused the explosion is to say that the first event was of a type 'ignition of gunpowder under such-and-such conditions of temperature and pressure'; and the second event was of type 'explosion', and always events of the first kind are followed by events of the second kind.

The empiricist programme for reducing causation to patterns of regular successions of actual events has run into such difficulties, especially in recent years, that perhaps the majority of philosophers have now abandoned it. One difficulty is that there are regular successions which are clearly not causal. One clock pointing to the hour may be followed regularly by a different clock striking the hour; but that does not mean that an event of the first kind causes an event of the second kind. The regularities have to be those of laws of nature, which state a physically necessary connection between events and thus have the form 'event of type A is followed of physical necessity by event of type B'. Necessary connections generate counter-factuals, i.e. conditionals about what would happen under various unrealized circumstances such as 'if the event of

---

[3] See Additional Note 4.

type A had not happened, the event of type B would not have happened'.

But even a physically necessary connection is insufficient to guarantee causality. Maybe it is physically necessary that (in the right conditions) a fall of the barometer is followed by rain; but the former does not cause the latter. Rather a fall of the air pressure causes, by different routes, both the barometer fall and rain. The event of type A must not merely guarantee that the event of type B will occur of physical necessity; but must physically necessitate it. But 'physically necessitate' is a philosopher's term for the more ordinary language term 'cause'. So the empiricist programme has analysed α causing β in terms of events like α causing events like β. Cause cannot be analysed away. Causation is a fundamental feature of the world; and the category of causing cannot be analysed in terms of any more fundamental categories.

The empiricist programme represented causation as a relation between events; I have represented it as a relation between a substance and an event. For the empiricist the cause α is always an event—for instance, S being ϕ at t_1 (or S coming into existence, or ceasing to exist). My rival account is that it is always some substance S that does the causing at some time t_1. It may do so because it has some property ϕ at that time (or comes into being or ceases to exist then) and has a liability L to exercise its power under those circumstances, or it may be able to do so without having a liability to do so. An event causing another event can always be represented as a substance, namely, the substance involved in the first event, causing the latter, in virtue of its properties (or existing, or coming, or ceasing to exist); the motion of the brick causing the breaking of the window can be represented as the brick in virtue of its motion causing the breaking of the window. But, I shall now argue, the translation cannot always be done the other way round. If that is correct, then the account of causation as effected by substances will be shown to be the more fundamental. Although causation by substances is, I shall argue, the fundamental notion, one can of course often talk loosely and colloquially about causation by events and I shall sometimes do so, when nothing turns on what is the nature of the cause.

That a substance may exercise causality without its doing so being merely a matter of any other property (monadic or relational) being instantiated in it is brought out, as well as by cases

of physical indeterminism in the behaviour of material objects such
as the photon, most clearly in the case of intentional causation,
where the substance is a person (or more generally an animate
being) who brings about the effect, in virtue of his causal powers
simply because he purposes to do so. But, it turns out, his purposing
just is his (intentionally) causing.

Intentional Causation

Persons perform intentional actions, that is, they do actions which
they mean to do. They often do one action by doing another action
or actions. I open the door by turning the handle and pulling. I kill
you by shooting at you, insult you by saying 'you are a fool', walk
from P to R (along a route through Q) by walking from P to Q and
then from Q to R. An action is often said to be a mediated action
if one does it by doing something else, a basic action if one does it
not by doing anything else. But these notions are ambiguous and
we need some more precise distinctions. We need, to start with,
the distinction which I shall call the distinction between the causally
basic and the causally mediated.[4] I shall say that when I do A
intentionally and intend thereby to cause some event β, bringing
about which constitutes doing B, then doing A is causally more
basic than doing B. When I kill you by shooting at you, shooting is
causally more basic than killing, because I shoot at you intending
thereby to cause your death, and my bringing about your death
constitutes killing you. When I open the door by pulling the handle,
pulling the handle is causally more basic than opening the door,

---

[4] The two influential modern writers who have introduced and developed a
distinction between basic and mediated actions are A. C. Danto (see his 'Basic
Actions', *American Philosophical Quarterly*, 2 (1965), 141–8) and R. M. Chisholm
(see his 'The Descriptive Element in the Concept of Action', *Journal of Philosophy*,
90 (1964), 613–24). The words 'basic' and 'mediated' are Danto's; Chisholm contrasts
making things happen 'directly' and 'indirectly'. Annette Baier pointed out in her
'The Search for Basic Actions', *American Philosophical Quarterly*, 8 (1971), 161–70,
that they make slightly different distinctions from each other, and that there are
also many other similar ways of making a distinction which might be confused
with theirs. She calls Danto's sense of 'basic', 'causally basic', and Chisholm's
sense, 'instrumentally basic'. My accounts of the causally basic and the instrumentally
basic take off from hers, but are not quite the same as hers, since she confines basic
actions to 'mere bodily movements'.

because I pull the handle intending thereby to cause the door being open, bringing about which is opening the door. An action than which none is causally more basic is a causally basic action *simpliciter*; all other actions are causally mediated.

I distinguish the causally more basic from the compositionally more basic. Doing A is compositionally more basic than doing B if to do B, you need in addition to doing A to perform some other intentional action C as well, such that as well as doing C you need to do A in order to do B. Opening one door is compositionally more basic than opening both doors; walking from P to Q is compositionally more basic than walking from P to R via Q. With the compositionally mediated, the filling that turns the more basic action into the more mediated action is another intentional action; with the causally mediated, the filling that turns the more basic action into the more mediated action is a series of events caused by the basic action.

There is no very natural sense to the compositionally basic *simpliciter*, that is, compositionally most basic action. Almost any intentional action consists of two part-actions—my walking across the room consists in my walking the first half of the way and then walking the second half of the way. However, the focus of one's activity, what one sees oneself as most readily and naturally up to, may be an action at a certain level of compositional basicality. Although I am writing (intentionally) the word 'action' by writing intentionally 'a' and then 'c' and so on, I am only doing the latter almost unconsciously in the course of doing the former. The former is the focus of my activity. Likewise the focus of one's activity may be an action at a certain level of causal basicality, not necessarily the most basic. I write the word 'action' by moving my hand which grips my pen in certain ways, now up, now down; but again I am only doing the latter almost unconsciously in the course of doing the former. I term an action instrumentally basic if the subject is doing that action easily and naturally without following some recipe of doing some other action or actions which will achieve it; an action is instrumentally mediated if I am setting about performing that action by doing other actions, compositionally or causally more basic.

Causally basic actions are always purposings, and purposings are always causally basic. I use 'purposing' in the sense defined in Chapter 1; but I shall instead for the next few pages, for ease of exposition, use 'trying'. I thus use 'trying' in an extended sense to describe the intentional component in all intentional actions which operates even when performing the action is easy, as well as when it is difficult or the agent's attempt to perform the action fails. Trying to move my hand is an intentional action—I mean to do it. Yet I do not do it by doing any more (causally) basic action which causes it to be the case that I try; I just try. (To try to try to do x is to try to do x.) But by trying to move my hand, I move my hand. Moving a part of one's body is typically, after trying, the next (causally) most basic action which humans do. Of course certain events need to happen in my body, caused by my trying, in order that my trying may be efficacious—for instance, a nerve impulse has to be transmitted down my arm—but they are not events which I bring about intentionally, and so bringing them about is not an intentional action. There is (normally) nothing causally more basic than moving one's hand except trying to move one's hand. There are exceptions—one may sometimes move one part of one's body by moving another part, as when one moves a paralysed hand by grasping it with the other hand and moving that. And there are actions which one can do by trying that do not involve intentionally moving a bodily part—as when one performs a piece of mental arithmetic. But the normal story for humans is that one tries to move a bodily part, and thereby moves that part, and thereby effects changes in the world outside one's body. When we move parts of the body very easily and naturally, so that we would not in the ordinary sense be said to be 'trying' to do so, trying (i.e. purposing) to move the body is instrumentally less basic than moving it. However, trying (i.e. purposing) to do x is always causally more basic than doing x. All I can do to move my hand is to try; that will normally cause a brain event and the brain event will cause the hand motion—after I try nature takes over and does the rest. Sometimes of course I fail to perform the instrumentally basic action which I am trying to perform, for instance, if I am suddenly paralysed. But there is no other way by which I can effect any result except to try.

To try to do x is to do whatever one believes will make success (i.e. actually doing x) more probable than it would otherwise be. Often there is a recipe for success, in that there are one or more instrumentally more basic actions than doing x, doing which will make success more probable than it would otherwise be. For any long-term or complicated action there will always be such a recipe, and to try to do the action will involve following what the subject believes to be such a recipe. A recipe for passing some exam would be, say, reading books, taking notes, going to lectures. To try to pass the exam involves trying to read books, take notes, go to lectures. The latter tryings are instrumentally (though not caus- ally) more basic than trying to pass the exam. And maybe for some of us, there are tryings instrumentally more basic than trying to go to lectures etc., that is, recipes which the subject can try to follow to try to get to lectures, such as trying to get out of bed when the alarm clock goes off. But in the end there is a trying which is in- strumentally basic—because that is the trying which the subject is easily and naturally performing, not performing via trying to follow some recipe.

Typically those tryings will be tryings to do the actions which are causally next most basic after tryings, for instance, tryings to perform bodily movements. For such instrumentally basic tryings, which I shall in future call just basic tryings, there is no recipe; you just try. There is (normally) no way to try to move your hand (without moving another limb); you just try. Certainly which tryings are basic may vary with persons and time. If I try to hit the ball over the net as a basic trying and fail, someone may give me a recipe for success—do not look at the ball as you hit it but look at where you want it to go, try to hit the ball over the net by trying to hit the ball while looking at where you want it to go. When I try to follow the recipe, trying to hit the ball over the net has ceased to be a basic trying. But at any one time for any one person there is a set of actions that he has no recipe for performing but that he can try to perform not by following any recipe but just by trying. There must be such—for if there is a recipe for trying to do x, the recipe will consist of trying to do y or z; and although there might be recipes for the latter tryings, the series must come to an end some- where, with basic tryings. For otherwise there would be no way of grasping what the recipe was telling one to do. Without such basic trying we can do nothing. We cannot make a difference to anything without moving our fingers or lips or conjuring up thoughts, and typically the only way to do so is just to try (in a basic way).

Now it cannot be merely an empirical discovery that such basic tryings are causally influential, but it is an a priori presupposition of acting at all that in general they are. For trying to do an action is simply initiating whatever causal chain, the agent believes, would make the relevant effect more likely to occur than it otherwise would be. We could not try to do anything unless we believed that our trying was causally influential, although not necessarily in the end effective (because other partial causes necessary for the effect are not in the right state—e.g. my nerves are not in the right condition for my trying to move my hand to cause my hand to move). I could not try to lift a weight unless I believed that what I was doing was making some difference to whether or not the weight rose in the air. Nothing would count as trying unless I believed that with regard to it; and in order to believe that of any trying (e.g. to pass an exam) I have to believe it of the basic tryings by means of which I try to do other things.

It is logically possible that we are mistaken in supposing that our basic tryings are causally influential—maybe they are mere epiphenomena of what is happening in our brains and make no difference to what is happening. But if we thought that, there would be nothing we could do that would constitute trying; and so we would cease to try and so to act. If we are to act, we must believe that our tryings (including our basic tryings) are causally influential. Yet since our basic tryings do not consist in performing any other action, such as bringing about some intermediate state of affairs, we must regard such trying simply as intentionally exerting causal influence. To try basically is to exert causal influence; it is to pull the causal levers themselves, not to do something else which in turn pulls the causal levers. When agents purpose (to revert to my technical term) that does not consist in their being in a state which makes them liable to exert their causal powers; their purposing is their exerting causal power, and so, given the necessary co-operation of other causes, causing the purposed effect. Purposing being a mental event, agents are aware of themselves as causing; they would be so aware of themselves even if they were not always liable (i.e. predetermined) to exercise their causal powers, or even inclined with a definite degree of probability to exert their causal powers, when they do (as indeed I believe they are not so predetermined always).

Since persons are substances, it follows that causation can be exercised by substances even if there is no necessary liability to exercise it; substances do not always exercise causality in virtue of being in some state, and so causation cannot always be represented as a relation between events. The fundamental causal notion is of substances, not events, causing events; and some substances cause events intentionally, by bringing them about when they mean so to do.[5]

It is in virtue of exercising causal power ourselves, and being aware of ourselves as doing so, that we acquire the concept of causation. Having done so, we can then recognize ourselves not merely as acting causally but as being acted upon causally—we can feel our bodies resisting pressure (i.e. the exercise by other objects of causal power upon our bodies) in the way that material objects resist our pressure (i.e. the exercise by us of causal power upon them). But when we are acted upon by sticks and stones, there are no grounds for attributing intentionality to the causing substances and hence we derive a notion of non-intentional causality, which we then attribute (as an explanation of their behaviour) to substances that we observe interacting with other substances. For example, feeling weights exercising causal powers on us—for instance, when we hold them in our hands and have to exercise causal power ourselves to oppose their exercise of causal power to pull down our hands, we attribute causal power, to compress or move downwards, to the weight. When we hold the same weight we feel the same causal power. We thus attribute continuing constant causal powers to weights. Such attribution enables us to explain goings on outside ourselves—for example, that a spring is extended when a weight is hung from it, because the causal power to move downwards exercised by the weight is not fully opposed by any exercise of causal power by the spring until the spring is extended. More generally, in view of the constancy of the causal powers of the material objects that exert such powers on us, and the regularity with which they exert those powers under specifiable conditions, we suppose that material objects generally have fairly constant causal powers and fairly constant liabilities to exercise them, and find that on this supposition we can account simply for much of the observed behaviour of material objects.

There is a distinction, of which agents are aware in themselves, between intentionally bringing about some effect and intentionally permitting it to occur; between intervening in nature and allowing nature to take its course; between exercising active causal influence

[5] That our causing is part of the content of what we experience when we act is very well argued in J. R. Searle, *Intentionality* (Cambridge University Press, 1973), chs. 3 and 4.

and refraining from doing so. Given that the agent is not under any natural or causal necessity to refrain, his refraining constitutes him as a permissive cause of the effect which he allows to occur. (Since, as will be shown at the end of this chapter, rational considerations—an agent's awareness of what is the best action to do—may (in so far as he is free from contrary causal influence) make it inevitable how he will act, this definition of a permissive cause has the consequence that such a cause may permit inevitably. What it rules out from being a permissive cause is something that has a blind liability not to act in the relevant circumstances. The point of this distinction is that a substance of the latter kind is simply not involved in some causal process; whereas an agent who deliberately chooses not to interfere is involved, in virtue of his non-interference arising from his perception of the situation.)

Causal Powers versus Laws of Nature

Until the sixteenth century, scientists and philosophers talked about the causal powers and liabilities of material objects rather than of their conformity to 'laws of nature'. Given the fundamental nature of the notion of causation, a notion to which we have access as soon as we perform intentional actions, it is to be expected that talk of laws of nature is analysable in terms of causation rather than vice versa (as in the empiricist programme).[6] To say that it is a law of nature that events of type A are followed by events of type B, is just—if for the moment we talk of events as doing the causing—to say that events of type A cause events of type B, or that whatever causes an event of type A also causes an event of type B. Now of course the natural world is full of regular causal successions. If an event α causes an event β on some occasion, there will normally be descriptions of α occurring on that occasion, as an event of type A, and of β as an event of type B, such that events of type A normally cause events of type B. If some ignition of gunpowder causes an explosion today, then under the same conditions of temperature and pressure an ignition of gunpowder will cause an explosion tomorrow. Causation is often predictable. And it was this predictability which

---

[6] See Additional Note 5.

led to the hypostatizing of laws of nature, or what I may call the 'invisible grid' model of nature. On this model, the world is supposed to be covered by laws of nature of the form 'event of type A is followed of physical necessity by event of type B', and then if an event of type A happens, the laws take over and bring from it an event of type B. Thus one might picture space as, as it were, filled by the law of gravity; then if you drop a coin from a tower, the law takes over and brings it to the ground.

Given that causation is by substances in virtue of their causal powers, we do not need to hypostatize the invisible grid of laws of nature. But the account of causation in which laws of nature are fundamental might seem to have the advantage that it was explicitly committed to predictable regularity.[7] If the world was full of laws of nature determining that events of certain types would be followed by events of certain other types, then whenever an event of one type happened, one could predict that an event of a certain other type would follow it. But the substance model is not as such committed to predictable regularity. A substance could cause an event without similar substances causing similar events in similar circumstances;[8] and indeed I believe that human beings do cause without their causation being of a totally predictable kind. But in general nature is highly predictable, and we need to add something to the substance model to explain why. We have to say, as we saw earlier, that as a matter of fact all substances which are material objects have in common certain causal powers, for example, the power of

[7] By 'predictable regularity' I mean regularity in the behaviour of the world such that an investigator observing patterns of regular succession in some segment of it can infer with a high probability how things will be in other segments, and such predictions are very often fulfilled. I assume that the regular successions are an objective feature of the world, and that there are objective standards of probability determining what they render probable. Some philosophers would deny these assumptions about objectivity, claiming only that there was coincidence between the regularities which *humans* observe and the standards of probability which they use, and the way the world is. It does not affect the present issue which of these accounts of the order in nature we adopt.

[8] Elizabeth Anscombe argued that there was no good reason to believe that 'any singular causal proposition implies a universal statement running "always when this, then that" '. (See her 'Causality and Determination', Inaugural Lecture at Cambridge, reprinted in E. Sosa (ed.), *Causation and Conditionals* (Oxford University Press, 1975), 81.) D. M. Armstrong in his *What is a Law of Nature?* (Cambridge University Press, 1983), 95, accepts the logical possibility of 'causation without law', but doubts whether it ever or often occurs. But the logical possibility is enough to show that it is not of the essence of causation to be lawlike.

(gravitationally) attracting every other material object in the universe with a force proportional to mm'/r^2, where m' is the mass of the other body and r its distance away) and a liability always to exercise those powers when there are other material objects. Further, such material objects fall into a few determinate kinds in virtue of having (among other properties in common) more and more determinate causal powers in common—for instance (to use a different example from the one used earlier) each electron (defined as a body having a mass of $\frac{1}{2} Mev/c^2$ and a certain power of electrostatic attraction for protons) has also the power to repulse (electrostatically) each other electron with a force of e^2/r^2, and the liability always to exercise that power when there are other electrons (where e is the charge on the electron, measured by its attractive power, and r the distance form the other electron). Objects with the same other properties typically have the same causal powers and the same liabilities to exercise them (e.g. under very general or narrowly specific conditions).

It might seem that this is an *ad hoc* addition to the substance model of causation, which would give an advantage to the laws-of-nature model from which predictable regularity is apparently a natural consequence. But the appearances that I have described above are misleading. Predictable regularity of the kind observable in our universe is not a natural consequence of the laws-of-nature model. For the world could be filled with an infinite number of laws of nature, each of a very specific kind—for instance, laws laying down that all square objects of between 2 and 2.0001 metres are at each moment of their existence followed by a green flash at the same place two seconds later, and all square objects of between 2.0001 metres and 2.000163 metres are at each moment of their existence 2 million miles away from the location of a round object of 9.0163 metres diameter exactly one second earlier. There could be as many laws of nature as there were events in any way distinct from each other. Unless the universe were totally symmetrical or infinitely recurrent in space, or eternally cyclical in time, then every event would be in some way distinguishable from each other event; in that case such specific laws of nature would make the world utterly irregular and (from mere observation of the events) utterly unpredictable. Predictable regularity arises not from laws of nature as such but from the existence of only a few simple laws of nature which have consequences for very many events. Whether the fundamental causal factors are laws of nature or substances, predictable regularity is a further striking feature of the universe beyond the mere fact of the universe being largely deterministic crying out for further explanation, an explanation which, I argue elsewhere,[9] can be provided by the operation of one substance, God. The earlier argument for the primacy of causation by substances remains unaffected by this objection. I conclude that talk of laws of nature is to be regarded simply as talk of regularities, but not mere regularities in the patterns of succession of types of events, but regularities in the patterns of which events of which type cause which events of which other type, that is, which substances have which causal powers and the liability to exercise them under which conditions. The operation of Newton's law of gravity is the regularity that each material object of mass m has the causal power to attract any object of mass m' at a distance away of r with a force of mm'/r^2 which it has a liability to exercise when there is any object of mass m' at distance r.

Rational Agency

A purposive agent, one who acts intentionally to endeavour to bring about some state of affairs, will always be inclined to act for the sake of the good, as he sees it.

I shall assume that there are truths about what is morally good and what is morally bad. By the morally good I mean the good overall. All self-indulgence, for example, is good as such—it is good that I shall enjoy food, drink, sex, power, etc. But it is often better that I shall do things incompatible with pursuing these goods. The enjoyment of drink is good but if it impoverishes me and ruins my health it is bad overall—both for prudential reasons (reasons which concern goods for me alone) and for wider reasons (if I am poor and in bad health, I cannot benefit others); and so on.

Among good acts are obligations to others, some of which arise from benefits received from others (we have obligations to our parents, our teachers, our country) and others which we undertake voluntarily (such as keeping promises and paying debts). In general, doing the best act involves fulfilling one's obligations first before

---

[9] See my *The Existence of God* (Clarendon Press, 1979), esp. ch. 8.

undertaking supererogatory good acts. There is a limit to obligations, and we can normally fulfil them all. But there is no limit to supererogatory goodness, the goodness which goes beyond obligation; we can go on and on doing more and more worthwhile acts, acts of benefitting others and creative acts (such as painting a picture, or composing a symphony, which may benefit no one apart from the agent). We are in general[10] culpable, blameworthy for failing to fulfil what we believe to be our obligations, but not praiseworthy for fulfilling them; conversely, we are praiseworthy for doing what we believe to be acts of supererogatory goodness, but not blameworthy for failing to do so. In so far as an action is good, there is reason to do it; and overriding reason for doing the best action or one of the equal best actions. In so far as an action is bad, there is reason not to do it; and in so far as overall it is bad, there is overriding reason not to do it. In general there is overriding reason not to do an action which is wrong (i.e. a breach of obligation). To believe an action to be good or bad is to believe these things about it; and our beliefs guide our actions.

In general, for an agent to have a belief about some action open to him, that it has this or that nature or effect, has no consequences for whether the agent does or does not do the action. Consequences only follow when combined with the agent's purposes. I may believe that saying to you, 'You are a fool,' will cause you hurt. Whether I say it will then depend on my purposes—whether I seek to hurt you or to save you from hurt. If I seek to hurt you, then (other things being equal, that is, given that with my other beliefs it will not impede any of my other purposes) I shall say it; but if I seek to save you from hurt I shall refrain. But to have a belief that there is a reason, and especially an overriding reason, for doing some action, is different. To have the belief that there is a reason for doing an action is to acknowledge that, thus far, it would be sensible, appropriate, reasonable, rational, to do the action, that it is the thing to do. Really to believe that some action would be sensible, appropriate, etc., to do is to acknowledge, to put the point dramatically, the summons of the action to me to do it; and thereby to have an inclination to do the action—other things being equal. I could not recognize R as a reason for doing A unless I accepted pressure

---

[10] For elaboration and qualification of these points about obligation and supererogatory goodness, and the liability to praise and blame, see my *Responsibility and Atonement* (Clarendon Press, 1989), pt. i.

from how I see things to be in the direction of doing A. To admit that R was a 'reason' for doing A but to deny that I had any inclination at all in consequence to do A would be to say something apparently contradictory, and to suggest that, when I said that R was a 'reason', I was using the word in an 'inverted comma sense' and meant something like 'what most people would consider a "reason"'. To recognize a reason for doing A is only to have an inclination to do A—other things being equal. But other things may not be equal. There may be other and better reasons for not doing the action. To believe that there is an overriding reason for doing the action is to believe that, on the balance of reason, it would be sensible, appropriate, reasonable, rational to do the action. I may still not do the action because I may yield to non-rational forces which influence the purposes I form. But to believe that there is overriding reason to do it entails being inclined to do it, and doing it in so far as unimpeded by non-rational forces.

'Reasons', as I have been concerned with them, like more obviously moral terms such as 'good' and 'ought', are action-guiding terms. That is a lesson which the emotivist and prescriptivist moral philosophers taught us. While we have rightly abandoned their view that moral judgements do not have objective truth-value, we must not abandon the insight that mistakenly led philosophers to that view—that to have a moral belief entails having an inclination to action. The view of morality which I am advocating alone takes seriously both the considerations which moved emotivist-prescriptivists and the considerations which moved objectivists to their doctrines. A moral belief is not as irrelevant to action as beliefs that things are square or yellow. There is a difference between moral and non-moral beliefs. One might be able to list all the good-making characteristics of actions and the principles for ranking them, in the way that the utilitarians thought they had done with a slogan such as that 'the best act is that which promotes the most pleasure and the least pain' (to which of course need to be added principles for measuring pleasure and pain, and for weighing them against each other). But even if such an account could be given by non-moral descriptions of what the goodness of actions consisted in, it would still be something quite different to say that an action was good from saying that it satisfied some such description, even if the latter is logically equivalent to (i.e. entails and is entailed by) the former. 'There are 4 apples in the box' is logically equivalent to 'the number of apples in the box is $\sqrt{16}$', but the former means something quite different from the latter. So an action being 'good' means something different from the action satisfying some (highly complex disjunctive) non-moral description, even if the latter entails and is entailed by the former. Belief that the latter holds does not as such incline to action, belief that an action is morally good does.

We humans are moved by reason—in part. Rational considerations affect our choices. But we are also subject to 'desires', non-rational influences that make certain actions easy to do and others difficult. These are forces to which we find ourselves subject, to which we may yield or against which we may fight. The known satisfaction of desire is pleasure, and so there is always a reason to yield to desire; but there is often more reason not to yield to desire, and then we must choose whether to yield to desire or whether to struggle to conform to reason. But in so far as we choose to do one action rather than another, we choose it because it has certain characteristics which provide a reason for doing it, even if not an overriding reason. To 'choose' to do an action for no reason, that is, not in virtue of any characteristic which we believe makes it worth doing (even if only the pleasure of indulging a habit, or of avoiding further mental deliberation) would not really be to choose at all, or therefore to do an intentional action at all. It would simply be for one's body to react. Choice involves believed reason having some influence.

There was a long tradition in Western philosophy from Plato to Aquinas that agents always pursue what they believe to be the best, from which it followed that wrongdoing was the result of ignorance alone. Its Christian exponents did of course have great difficulty in reconciling this tradition with the Christian account of sin. My arguments have the consequence that the tradition gave the correct account only for agents not subject to desire. We humans however are caught between reason and desire, and may choose to yield to desire rather than pursue the best.[11]

An agent subject to no non-rational influences, that is, no causes in any way influencing how he will act, is a perfectly free agent. He will pursue the good without hindrance. He will fulfil all his obligations (as he sees them), and do much good beyond obligation.

[11] For a fuller account of the role of desire in influencing choice, see my *Evolution of the Soul*, ch. 6.

Where there is (he believes) a best possible act open to him, he will do it. Where there are a number of incompatible possible acts open to him, each—he believes—equally good (say, giving all his money to this charity, or alternatively to that charity), he will do one such act, perhaps choosing which of them to do by some non-rational means (e.g. tossing a coin). But what will the perfectly free agent do, if—he believes—there is no best and no equal best action; for each of an infinite number of incompatible possible actions open to him, there is a better, but there is never a best? Clearly only a being to whose powers of some sort there are no limits will be in this situation; we humans are never in this situation—our powers are so limited that for us there is always a maximum to the goodness of any kind that we can bring about. We can always do our best. But suppose that there is a painter, not (in this matter, at any rate) subject to desire who can at a time paint only one painting; but that there are an infinite number of possible paintings (including paintings of any size and colour he chooses) which he could paint, yet for each such—he believes—there is always a better one. How will he act?

I think that that will depend on what further holds with respect to the way in which the infinite number of possible acts are ordered, and the reasons which—he believes—make one better than another. One possibility is that all the possible acts can be arranged in a linear order, like this:

better
$$a \quad b \quad c \quad e \quad f \quad i\ldots$$
$$d \qquad\quad g$$
$$h$$

At some points on the line there may be a finite number of equally good acts (as are f, g, and h in my diagram) but each act will have a better; and I suppose, the reason why each act is better than its predecessor is the same reason. Suppose that the goodness of a picture was merely a matter of the size of the picture, and that the painter could paint a picture of any (finite) size. Then he would have no reason for painting a picture of any one size rather than any other. Of whichever size he painted the picture, it would be a good picture but less good than an infinite number of pictures that he could paint; and for just the same reason as it was better than the other possible pictures—its size. There would be no overriding reason for painting a picture of any particular size. But there would still be overriding reason for painting a picture, and so overriding reason for painting a picture that was not as good as some picture that he could have painted instead. For if he does not paint there is a certain kind of goodness which is not brought into being, and there is overriding reason for bringing that kind of goodness into being.

To refine the suggestion of the last sentence—if the infinite number of incompatible good actions open to an agent, each less good than some other, can be divided into kinds by the kind of reason which make them good, and there is a best kind, but not a best of that kind, then there is overriding reason to do an action of the best kind rather than of any other kind, but no overriding reason to do one rather than another action of that kind. If the choice is between painting nothing (the null action, as it were), and painting something, then all actions of the latter kind are good for a kind of reason for which the null action is not good—they involve bringing about a painting. Hence there is overriding reason to paint something rather than nothing; but no overriding reason to paint one painting rather than another. Or suppose, the painter believes, all acts of painting in colour are better than all acts of painting in black and white but there is no best act of each kind. Then he will have reason for doing an act of the former kind which is not bettered by a reason for doing a better kind of act; and so his pursuit of the good will lead him to do it. But for acts and kinds of act where there is no maximum, perfect freedom will not lead an agent to do one act rather than another.

A perfectly free agent will pursue the good as he sees it without hindrance and I have analysed what this involves. Suppose now that he has true beliefs about which actions are good and bad, and better or worse than others. Then he will pursue the good as it is without hindrance. Such an agent is surely perfectly good—for there can be no better agent than such a one. He does what is good for the reason that it is good, strives to do the best in so far as that is available to him, and no other motives influence him. Yet note a paradoxical consequence—if there are an infinite number of incompatible actions open to a perfectly good agent, each not as good as some other action, the agent will inevitably do an action less good than one which he could do. And if that is frequently the situation, a perfectly good agent will frequently be doing acts less good than he could do. The paradoxical nature of this consequence arises not, I suggest, from some arbitrary definition of mine, but from the nature of the good.

There is another paradoxical consequence of the results which I have reached in this chapter, whose paradoxical nature arises perhaps more from my definition of 'free' than from the nature of things. An agent is perfectly free, as I have defined the term, if no causes influence how he acts. It may however often be that such an agent has no option as to how to act, because considerations of reason make one choice inevitable. There may be one action which he believes to be the best action open to him, and in such a case he will do it. In virtue of the nature of intentionality, the freedom of an intentional agent is a freedom to act within reason and not against it. An agent is free to the extent to which causes (i.e. desires) do not determine how he will act, although they may exert influence upon him. If he is to act intentionally, he must, as we have noted, see what he does as good in some way although he may yield to desires to do what is other than the best. But sometimes an agent with only limited freedom may also have no option as to how to act. This will arise if he believes one action to be the best available to him, and he has no stronger desire to do any incompatible action. It may seem odd to say that agents are 'perfectly free' or have some limited 'freedom', if it is inevitable what they will do. I could have introduced a different terminology for describing this situation, and talked perhaps instead of agents being perfectly or in part 'rational'. But that terminology also has its disadvantages—'rationality' is more naturally thought of as characterizing how we infer, rather than how we act generally; and acting 'rationally' is naturally thought of as being compatible with being caused to act. So, I have adopted the terminology of 'freedom', while warning the reader to bear in mind its oddness in certain respects. It does have the great advantage that saying of God that he is 'perfectly free', as we are naturally inclined to do, does not have the consequence that God may choose to go against reason, and do less than the best when there is a best.

4
Time

First Principle: Events Happen at Periods

I need to argue here for four basic principles about time which are important for my later purposes. The first is that everything that happens, every event that is—including the mere existence of a substance with its properties—happens over a period of time and never at an instant of time, or is analysable in terms of things happening over periods of time. Instants are the bounding points of the periods during which things happen. Among instants are 2.00.00 p.m. on Friday, 3 November 1989, and 7.30.02 a.m. on Saturday, 4 November 1989. Among periods is the period between these two instants. Periods may last for varying intervals such as two hours or three days.

In general our ascription of properties to objects is ascription to them over periods of time—things are green or wet or weigh 10 lb. for periods of time. And normally when we do ascribe properties to objects at instants, our doing so is to be read as ascribing them to objects for periods which include the instant. To say that the object is green at 2 p.m. is to say that it is green for some period which includes 2 p.m. It is difficult to see what would be meant by an object being green at 2 p.m. although it was not green either before or after 2 p.m. It was green for a period of zero duration, and how could that differ from its not being green at all? Certainly, things like winning a race or becoming 60 years old can happen at an instant. But one becomes 60 at an instant if and only if that instant is the bounding point of a period of sixty years during which one has lived. And one wins a race at a certain instant if and only if one has run it for a period ending at that instant and there is a final segment of that period (however small) during all of which one is ahead of the field. These things apparently happening at an instant are thus analysable in terms of things happening over periods of time. The same applies to talk in a scientific context of instantaneous possession of a property by an object, when it does not possess that property before or after the instant in question. Such talk is introduced by a special definition in terms of limits. We say that a particle has instantaneous velocity of 10 ft./sec. at 2 p.m. if, as we take smaller and smaller periods of time beginning at 2 p.m. and measure the velocity (ratio of distance covered to period of time) over those periods, it gets closer and closer to 10 ft./sec.; *and* also, as we take smaller and smaller periods of time ending at 2 p.m., and measure the velocity over those periods, it gets closer and closer to 10 ft./sec.[1] But since 'instantaneous velocity' is introduced by such careful mathematical definition, the obvious thing to say is that that is what instantaneous velocity is. It is not a velocity possessed at an instant discovered via study of limits, but rather a limit of velocities possessed over series of periods bounded by that instant. That that is the right thing to say is brought out by the fact that where velocities from above converge on a different limit from velocities from below, not merely does physics not ascribe an instantaneous velocity, but it provides no grip as what would be meant by a claim about it.

Any period of time during which an event occurs is infinitely divisible in thought—we can consider $\frac{1}{2}$ of the period, $\frac{1}{4}$ of the period, $\frac{1}{8}$ of the period, and so on *ad infinitum*. Hence any period of time is composed of an infinite number of smaller periods. In that sense[2]

---

[1] More formally,

$$\lim_{t \to t_2} \frac{s_2 - s}{t_2 - t} \to 10$$

for $t < t_2$; and

$$\lim_{t \to t_2} \frac{s - s_2}{t - t_2} \to 10$$

for $t > t_2$ (when $t_2 = 2$ p.m., s_2 is the distance covered at t_2 since some arbitrary origin, s is the distance covered at t since the origin, distance is measured in feet and time in seconds).

[2] Philosophers and scientists sometimes raise the question of whether space and time are 'continuous' or alternatively merely 'dense' in a different sense. This is the question of whether the instants which lie within some period of time form a set which is dense but not continuous (i.e. one which can be put into one–one correlation with the rational numbers, fractions in which both numerator and denominator are natural numbers) or one which is continuous (i.e. can be put into one–one correlation only with the real numbers, the rationals plus the irrationals lying between them such as $\sqrt{2}$ or π). The only factual issue is whether any event can begin at an instant distant a real non-rational number of seconds from when another one ended, or whether all events occur at temporal distances measurable by rational numbers of

I shall say that time is a continuum. To say that is not to make any claim about how things behave in the natural world, for example, it is not to rule out the possibility of all change in the natural world being staccato—objects always remaining unchanging for some very small period and then changing to another distinct state without passing through intermediate states. It is only to say that any period consists of smaller periods, even if some of them are too small for any object to change during them more than once. The very concept of a period during which something remains changeless, or alternatively changes, involves it consisting of more than one smaller period during which things remain changeless or are different. A 'period' which did not contain smaller periods would be really not a period, but an instant. It is a mistake to think of a period of time as (in any natural sense) composed of instants—for example, the hour between 2 p.m. and 3 p.m. as the collection of the instants between 2 p.m. and 3 p.m. Instants are boundaries of periods and have no duration. And things that have no duration—even an infinite number of them—put together, do not make a thing with duration. A period is only composed of instants, in the sense that instants, indeed an infinite number of them, lie between its bounding instants.

Ancient and medieval thinkers were unable to deal with the continuities of space and time in a coherent mathematical way.[3] The invention in the seventeenth century of the differential calculus, and in the nineteenth century of transfinite arithmetic provided the mathematical apparatus. But there always remained the danger of misdescribing that apparatus, by thinking of the 'instantaneous velocities' of the calculus as velocities, or of the points or instants which formed infinite sets as very small places or periods. 'Instantaneous velocities' are not velocities, but limits of series of velocities—as Berkeley pointed out in his 'demythologizing' account of the calculus in *The Analyst* (1734)—and points and instants are not places and periods, but boundaries thereof.

seconds alone. If the former holds, we must regard time as continuous in this mathematical sense. If not, we can regard time either as continuous or as merely dense; nothing factual is at stake, nothing except convenience turns on which mathematics we use.

[3] For a detailed history of their attempts to deal with continuity, see Richard Sorabji, *Time, Creation and the Continuum* (Duckworth, 1983), esp. pt. 5.

Second Principle: Metric and Laws of Nature

The second principle is that while time has a topology, independently of whether there are laws of nature, it has a metric only if there are laws of nature, and indeed ones that attain a unique simplest form on the assumption that some periodic process measures intervals of equal time. (Talk of laws of nature is to be understood as analysed in the previous chapter.) Topology is concerned with the ordering of events, metric with the size of interval between them. So, I claim, whether an event E_2 occurs after or before an event E_1 is independent of whether there are laws of nature;[4] but whether there is a truth about how much later or earlier than E_2 E_1 occurs— for instance, one hour or two hours—depends on whether there are such laws of nature. For statements about length of temporal intervals are statements about what would be measured by clocks. We regard some periodic mechanism as a clock because it coincides in the periods it measures with those of many other mechanisms that are or could be constructed (i.e. their periods are linearly related), and because when the durations of events are measured by those mechanisms, laws of nature which predict their occurrence take a unique simplest form. Pendulum clocks, the daily rotation of the Earth on its axis (or of the revolution of the Sun about the Earth, according to pre-Copernican astronomy), the annual revolution of

---

[4] I ignore the special and general Theories of Relativity which are normally supposed to show 'the relativity of simultaneity'—that whether an event occurs before, or at the same time as, or after another event is relative to the frame of reference (i.e. solid body) in relation to which we make our measurements. I ignore them because I do not think they make any great difference to the issues. First, because the Theories of Relativity are perfectly compatible with the view that there are truths about which events are 'absolutely simultaneous' with which (i.c. that there is a unique frame of reference in which measurements of simultaneity are correct)—the so-called 'relativity of simultaneity' being a limit on our knowledge of simultaneity (our ability to discover that true frame), not a limit on its existence. On this, see my *Space and Time*, 2nd edn. (Macmillan, 1981), 181–202. And secondly, because even on the normal interpretation of Relativity Theory, 'the relativity of simultaneity' only applies between events that are not causally connectible (i.e. are so far away from each other in space that no signal is fast enough to travel from one to the other). All events E_1 and E_2 that are causally connectible are such that if E_1 is earlier than E_2 in one frame of reference, it is earlier in all frames. Pairs of causally connectible events (and most pairs of events are causally connectible) are such that one is absolutely before the other or the other absolutely before the one—even on the normal interpretation of Relativity Theory.

the Earth about the Sun relative to the 'fixed stars' (or vice versa) were regarded as (approximately accurate) clocks because their periods were linearly related—that is, if a pendulum ticked a certain number of times while another pendulum ticked once on one occasion, it did so on every other occasion when the latter pendulum ticked once; and if it ticked a certain number of times during one daily rotation of the Earth, it ticked that number of times during another rotation; and so on. If you assume that the periods measured by such clocks (e.g. each tick of a given pendulum; or each rotation of the Earth) are approximately equal, and measure the durations of events on that assumption, then relatively simple postulated laws of nature (e.g. Newton's laws) are confirmed by observation of those events (and simpler laws than you would get if you measured the duration of events on some other assumption—e.g. that the hand of a medieval town-clock rotated with uniform velocity, or that a falling weight fell equal intervals in equal times.) Today we have developed atomic clocks whose periods we judge to be equal to a much higher degree of approximation than the periods of pendulums or the Earth, but the criteria for adopting them as such are the same.[5]

Yet time has a metric only under the stated conditions that there are laws of nature governing events in the universe, which take a unique simplest form[6] on the assumption that certain periodic processes which coincide with each other are true clocks. If there were two kinds of periodic mechanisms which could be constructed, such that clocks of one kind kept time with each other but not with clocks of the other kind, (the scale of intervals measured by the one might be related non-linearly to the scale of intervals measured by the other),[7] and clocks of one kind enabled laws of one kind of event to reach their simplest form, and clocks of the other kind enabled laws of a different kind of event to reach their simplest form, the only truth about the interval between two events E_1 and

[5] For a fuller account of the criteria for regarding a clock as a true clock, see my *Space and Time*, 2nd edn., 177–80.

[6] Of course the unique 'simplest' form might be fairly complicated, but be all the same the simplest form compatible with observations.

[7] Two scales are related non-linearly, e.g. asymptotically, if an interval measured by one mechanism coincides with an interval measured by the other mechanism on one occasion but on another occasion is some multiple (determined by a stated formula) of the interval measured by the other mechanism. E. A. Milne once suggested that dynamic and electromagnetic processes were best measured by temporal scales which were related to each other non-linearly. See his *Kinematic Relativity* (Clarendon Press, 1948), *passim*, and esp. 224 f.

E_2 would be that it was (say) one hour by one sort of clock, and two hours by a different sort of clock. *A fortiori*, if there were no periodic processes that existed or could be constructed to keep time with each other, and to measure the durations of events in such a way as to confirm natural laws, then time would not have a metric—there would in general be no truth about whether an event E_1 lasted longer or shorter than another event E_2. (There would only be such a truth if one event began simultaneously with or after the other event and ended simultaneously with or before the other event, i.e. the duration of the one coincided with or included that of the other.)

The view that there are truths about temporal interval that hold quite independently of how clocks behave was expounded most famously by Newton, when he wrote that 'absolute, true, and mathematical time, of itself and from its own nature, flows equably without relation to anything external'.[8] But if one supposes that there is a truth about temporal interval independent of what would be measured by clocks, one needs an explanation of why it is in our universe that clocks measure intervals correctly and it is hard to see what such an explanation would be like—time is not a substance which can influence the behaviour of clocks. Yet if one denies that there is any reason to suppose that clocks do measure intervals correctly, one loses one's grip on the notion of a temporal interval—it is no longer clear what one is saying when one says that two intervals are of equal length. It follows from this line of argument that if there were no laws of nature, and so no periodic mechanisms that kept time with each other, there would be no content to the notion that some interval had any definite length at all.

Periods of time are the periods they are in virtue of the actual or possible events that end or begin when they begin, or end or begin when they end; and instants are the points of time that are the boundaries of such events. By a 'possible event' I mean some event of a specified kind, picked out by a uniquely identifying description, that would be brought about in virtue of the laws of nature if some earlier event of a specified kind, picked out by a uniquely identifying description, had happened at some earlier period of time—as dated by an actual event; or that would have brought about some later event at a time dated by an actual event. Thus one possible event is the first explosion that would have happened if I had lit a certain fuse with a certain set-up at the same time as a certain man

[8] I. Newton, *Principia*, scholium to def. 8.

walked out of the door. Or another possible event is the minute hand of this clock pointing to 12 for the second time if I had started the clock going when John started to run the race.

We normally pick out periods of time by their relations to actual events—the period from the end of this event to the beginning of that event, or from when the clock-hand pointed to 2 until it pointed to 4. But some have argued—rightly, it seems to me—that there could be a universe in which nothing changed for a period of time of definite length, or there could even be a universe empty of matter for such a period of time. Sydney Shoemaker described a thought-experiment in which there is a universe which has three parts, A, B, and C, observable from each other.[9] Observers on B and C observe over a period of some fifty years that A 'freezes' for a year every three years (i.e. everything on A remains totally changeless); observers on A and C observe that B freezes for a year every four years; and observers on A and B observe that C freezes for a year every five years. They therefore all extrapolate from their observations over the limited period to reach the generalization that these freezings happen outside that period and hence conclude that every sixty years the whole universe (including the observers) freezes for a year. And what content is there to the supposition that this static period when all clocks have stopped lasts for a year rather than for any other length of time? The content is the consequence that if some clock had been preserved from the freezing process (e.g. a clock on A if A had not been frozen three years before) that is the length of time it would have measured. Hence the frozen period consists of two $\frac{1}{2}$-years, the boundary instant separating them being the instant by which a clock exempt from freezing would have measured $\frac{1}{2}$ year. We can therefore refer to such periods, picking out the beginning or end thereof by the (beginning or end of the) 'possible event' of when a clock would have pointed to some figure if we had managed to exempt it from the freezing process. Since laws of nature operate during such a period, the description 'instant at which a clock would have measured $\frac{1}{2}$ year' picks out a definite instant.

---

[9] S. Shoemaker, 'Time Without Change', *Journal of Philosophy*, 66 (1969), 363–81. (Repr. in R. le Poidevin and M. MacBeath (eds.), *The Philosophy of Time* (Oxford University Press, 1993).) The extension to a world temporarily lacking any physical objects was made by W. Newton-Smith, *The Structure of Time* (Routledge & Kegan Paul, 1980), ch. 2.

But now suppose a universe in which there are no laws of nature. There will then be no content to talk of periods of time located by their relation to possible events; for 'the instant at which such and such would have begun or ceased to happen if initial conditions had been different' picks out no definite instant rather than any other. Even if it were true that if certain initial conditions had occurred, so-and-so would have happened (e.g. because God would have brought it about directly), there would be no truth that so-and-so would have begun/ceased to happen at this instant rather than that instant of the actual temporal continuum in which there are no laws of nature and the initial conditions did not occur. For instants are the instants they are in virtue of their temporal distance from events[10]—there is nothing intrinsic to the instant which is 3 p.m. independent of its temporal relations to other things; neither periods nor instants have thisness. Nor can an instant be the instant it is in virtue of the other instants to which it is contiguous—for in a temporal continuum, between any two instants, there is always another one. Yet in the absence of laws of nature, there will be no temporal distances and so talk about the instant (of actual time) at which some possible event would have begun/ended is empty. So we could only pick out periods of time by their temporal relations of before or after to actual events—'the period between E_1 and E_2', or 'the period before E_1'. So if there were no God and the universe had a beginning, then before then there would be no substances and hence no laws of nature; and then although one could talk of the time before there was a universe (and I think that we must be able to do this—for, as I shall argue later, something can only have a beginning if at an earlier time it was not) one could not distinguish any one such period from any other. And by 'one could not distinguish' I mean—in virtue of my earlier argument—that there would

---

[10] That instants are the instants they are in virtue of their temporal distance from actual events is a thesis argued by Graeme Forbes, 'Time, Events and Modality' in le Poidevin and MacBeath, *Philosophy of Time*. He advocates a theory of an instant as constituted by the events that actually occur at it, or occur in a possible world which branches from the actual world (i.e. has the same history as our world up to a certain instant) at the same temporal distance from the branching point as the actual events; and the branching point is identified by the events that actually occur at it. Forbes's theory seems to me basically correct, though I would need to express it somewhat differently in view of my first principle of this chapter that events occur over periods and not at instants. Forbes goes on to draw the conclusion, to my view correct, that instants cannot be the same as instants of our world, in a world which does not branch from our world.

be no difference between them—every period ending with the beginning of the universe would be identical to every other. There is no content to the period of an hour before the beginning of the universe distinct from the period of half an hour before that beginning in the absence of laws of nature determining how clocks would have behaved.

The Greeks[11] generally saw a close connection between time and change. Time, claimed Aristotle, is not the same as change but it cannot exist without it.[12] This led the Christian Fathers and in particular Augustine[13] to hold that time began when the universe began (a finite number of years ago); and the scholastics followed them in this. Yet the Greeks seem much less committed to a connection between time and measurable change; time might perhaps exist without the normal processes of regular change by which it is measured (the revolution of the heavens daily round the Earth, and the annual revolution of the Sun relative to the stars).[14] And the scholastics, too, sometimes seem to allow the possibility of there being time with a topology yet lacking a metric. For when they discuss the life of the angels, they sometimes allow the possibility that they might have come into existence before the physical universe with its regular motions (of the heavens about the Earth, or something else). For unlike God, the angels came into being and performed successive acts—yet these might have pre-existed any regular motions.[15]

---

[11] For exceptions, see Sorabji, *Time, Creation and the Continuum*, 81 f.

[12] *Physics*, 218ᵇ.

[13] *Confessions*, 11. 10–14 and *De Civitate Dei*, 11. 5–6.

[14] See Sorabji, *Time, Creation and the Continuum*, ch. 6.

[15] See Thomas Aquinas, *Summa theologiae*, 1a, 63. 6 ad 4, (Blackfriars edn., 1968, ix, trans. Kenelm Foster OP), 'Angels are in no way contained by the heavenly motion which is where the measure of continuous time begins; so that if we speak of time in the angels, we can only mean a succession of acts of mind or will.' The scholastics spoke of the angels as existing not in 'eternity', where God alone dwelt; nor in time, in which all mundane things lived; but in some intermediate duration, the *aevum*. They had no agreed account of how that differed from time, but the cited passage suggests the view that it had a topology but no metric. Suárez hints at a similar idea when he writes that to say that one angel lasted longer than another is to say nothing more (*nil amplius*) than that the one began before or ended after the other, or to compare their duration with events in our time (*Disputationes Metaphysicae*, 50. 5. 28), i.e. presumably to say in the case of those comings-to-be or ceasings-to-be that occurred simultaneously with events on earth, that they lasted as long as certain events on earth; there was no intrinsic time internal to the angelic events themselves.

Third Principle: Causal Theory of Time

My third principle—to put it fairly loosely to begin with—is that a period of time is future if it is logically possible that an agent can now causally affect what happens then; and a period of time is past if it is logically possible that an agent acting then could have causally affected what happens now. To put it more precisely—the future at an instant *t* is any period such that it is logically possible that an agent can causally affect (the whole of) it by an action beginning at *t*; the past is any period such that it is logically possible that by acting during it an agent can causally affect (the whole of) any state of affairs beginning at *t*. To say that it is logically possible that an agent could have causally affected some state of affairs is to say that he would have causally affected it if he had chosen and were in some logically possible way a lot more powerful than he is. It is logically possible that I now cause the sun to disappear instantaneously, because if I had power to make things disappear, and had that power to a great degree, and could propagate my causal influence faster than light, and had chosen to do so, I would have caused the sun to disappear instantaneously.

The present instant is the boundary between past and future. Our use of 'present' (alias 'happening now') with respect to events which last for a period of time is loose and context-dependent, and may need separate explication for each context of use. But roughly—events which last for a period are present if the period includes or terminates with the present instant or is fairly close to it—given that the period is fairly short relative to other periods relevant to the context of discussion. The movements of walkers that I watch from the window are, for most contexts of discussion, present events, loosely speaking; even if strictly speaking they are very slightly past. But in a context where we are talking of the physiological processes which produce my 'present' perception of them, we would say that the movements perceived are no longer present. My present action of writing this sentence includes (at this stage) both elements which (strictly speaking) are past, and elements which (strictly speaking) are future.[16]

[16] Where we do think of the present as an extended period, to avoid contradiction, we must think of the past as ending at the instant at which that extended period begins, and the future as beginning only at the instant at which the extended period ends. See Sorabji, *Time, Creation and the Continuum*, 14.

Causation in a circle is not logically possible. If A causes B, B cannot cause A (or cause anything which by a longer circle causes A). For what causes what is logically contingent—'anything can produce anything', wrote Hume.[17] Let us put the point in this way: a sufficiently powerful being could, it is logically possible, alter the laws of nature in such a way that some event had, instead of its normal effect at a certain time, one incompatible with that normal effect. So if causation in a circle were logically possible and A caused B and B caused A, a sufficiently powerful being at the moment of B's occurrence could have altered the laws of nature so that B caused not-A; in which case A would have (indirectly) caused A not to occur—which is absurd. So since manifestly the future is causally affectible, the past is not. It follows that backward causation is impossible—causes cannot be later than their effects. It follows too that simultaneous causation is impossible. For if simultaneous causation were possible and A caused B simultaneously, and B caused C simultaneously, then, by Hume's principle cited earlier, it would be logically possible that B could have had, instead of its normal effect, not-A. That logically impossible conjunction of causal sequences is, given Hume's principle, only rendered impossible if we suppose simultaneous causation itself to be impossible.[18] Hence, given that causes and effects are events which last for periods of time, any effect (which has a beginning) must begin at an instant later than its cause begins; and any effect (which has an end) must end at an instant later than its cause ends.[19]

If follows therefore that the past is not merely the period in which events can causally affect us but a period, events in which

---

[17] *Treatise of Human Nature*, 1. 3. 15. There is however a subsequent sentence limiting the possibility of causation to objects that are 'not contrary' to each other; but even that could not be deployed to rule out A causing B, and B separately causing not-A.   [18] See Additional Note 6.

[19] Every event that has one full cause in the sense of an event that physically necessitates its occurrence in all its detail will have infinitely many such. For if E has one such full cause C, it has also as full causes all events that are later parts of C and that begin before E does, and given a temporal continuum (which time must be—see above), there will be infinitely many such; and, if there are events that include C as later parts (as normally there will be) they too will be the causes of E. So if there is an effect E that depends on its cause C not merely for its coming into existence, but for its continuing in existence at every period of its existence (as might be the case with the motion of my pen in my hand depending on the motion of my hand as I write), this will be by each segment of E beginning at time t and ending at a time t' having as its full cause every segment of C beginning earlier than t and ending at t'.

are beyond our power to influence—for reasons of logic. Could there be any period of time, events in which are beyond our power now to influence for reasons of logic, and that is also such that events in it could not affect us now also for reasons of logic? It is sometimes suggested that there could be separate time series all periods of which are neither before nor after nor simultaneous with any period of our time. I can give no content to such a possibility— for what possible logical constraint could there be on the propagation of causal influence from A to B, except that B was already causally fixed at the time of the occurrence of A in virtue of the possibility of the propagation of causal influence from B to A? But even suppose that such separate time series were logically possible, we could have no knowledge of any time series other than our own. For the only way in which we can have knowledge of anything logically contingent is by it causally influencing our mental states (directly or via intermediate effects), or our mental states causally influencing it, or by a cause of it also causally influencing our mental states—as when we infer the future rain from the fall of air pressure which causes us (when we look at the barometer) to see the barometer fall and also causes the rain. All such events of which we learn are linked to us by a chain of causes and effects and are thus located within our time series, and so, if future, are causally affectible and, if past, able causally to have affected us. Events in other time series would, if there could be any such, by definition of 'time series', lie beyond our power to influence them or their power to influence us, and so be unknowable.[20]

---

[20] The argument in the text is an argument to show that we could not have knowledge of events in a separate time series disjoint from our own (i.e. a series of periods, none of which are temporally related to, i.e. before, after, or simultaneous with, any periods of our time series). But might we not have knowledge of events that (via relations of possible causation) were temporally related to some event in our time series, and yet were not temporally related to each other? Could there not be fission or fusion of time series, of which we could learn? No. We could learn of two events, E_1 and E_2, both earlier than (or both simultaneous with or both later than) some event in our time series, between which there were no actual causal relations and between which it might be physically impossible that there be causal relations. But again, how could causal relations between them in either direction be logically impossible except for the reason that they are simultaneous with each other, and so (it is logically possible) each could have causal relations with each event earlier or later than E_1 or E_2? This argument against the possibility of knowledge of events of divided time series, unlike the argument against the possibility of knowledge of separate time series, falls back on the difficulty of giving sense to that of which we are supposed to have knowledge. But that, I suggest, remains a very

So the future just is the causally influenceable, the past the causally uninfluenceable. The present—to speak strictly—is simply an instant dividing them. When the question is asked whether an effect can precede its cause, it is often supposed that we have a conception of past and future on the one hand, and of causality on the other and the question asks whether they have always to be instantiated in one alignment, whether time and causation always have to have the same direction. But I deny that we have such an independent grasp on conceptions of the past or future, for the question to be raised in this way. The most primitive concepts that we acquire are the concepts of the world being this way rather than that (the concept of a logically contingent event), and the concept of an ability to make it this way rather than that (the concept of causation analysed in Chapter 3). We then divide events up into those that we can, or could if we were powerful enough, make—that is, cause to be—this way rather than that; and those that—because they could have caused us to be this way rather than that—are such that, however powerful we were, are beyond making this way or that. The former are future, the latter are past. It is in this way, I suggest, that the concepts of past and future are connected to the rest of our conceptual scheme.

It might be suggested that our concepts of the past and future are connected to the rest of our conceptual scheme, not via the logical possibility or impossibility of causation, but in a different way via the concepts of (personal) memory[21] and perception. An event is past if we now remember it or if we now perceive it. But a perception of an event perceived or a personal memory of an event remembered must be caused by the event perceived or remembered. The points are logical ones; nothing would count as a 'perception' or 'memory' unless these causal relations held. This basic tenet of the causal theories of perception and memory is surely correct. So the concepts of perception and memory only link us to

strong argument. For a more detailed argument as to why any evidence apparently supporting the occurrence of divided time series could always be more plausibly interpreted in a different way, see my *Space and Time*, ch. 10.

[21] I understand by a 'personal memory' roughly a memory of what one has experienced oneself based on the previous experience of it. This definition is due to N. Malcolm, 'Three Forms of Memory', in his *Knowledge and Certainty* (Prentice-Hall, 1963), 215. Most uses of 'memory' and cognate words have such a sense. My memory of going to London when young or having toast for breakfast this morning are personal memories. My memory that $5 \times 7 = 35$ is not.

the concepts of past and future via the concept of causality. To label something a perception or memory is already to have built into it the causal fixedness of what it delivers.

Alternatively, it might be suggested that our present experiences provide us with our concepts of past and future. Our 'present' conscious experiences are not (by my first principle) instantaneous static experiences, but extended and often changing experiences. I experience change of pattern in my visual field, change of thought as I make an inference. My every experience is a temporally extended experience, and so contains parts which I recognize as more past than other parts. That is enough, the argument might go, to give us the concept of the past as a whole—the past is whatever is 'in the same direction' as 'the more past' parts of my present experience; the future is whatever is 'in the other direction'. The trouble with this suggested way of access to the past is that it assumes that an experience being present is something of which we can get a grasp without bringing in the concept of causation. I do not think it is. In talking of a 'present' extended experience we are talking of an event that happens over a period of time. And how am I aware of it? In what does my awareness of it consist? How is the coincidence between what is going on and my belief about what is going on sustained? Clearly what is going on causes me to be aware of what is going on. And because I think this about it, I regard my experience as now unaffectible by anything I or anyone, however powerful, might do; and so I regard the 'specious present' of my experience as, strictly speaking, past. If I believed that some other mechanism (e.g. causation by a common cause; or some sort of non-causal awareness) was responsible for sustaining the coincidence, the question would arise why I should regard 'what is going on' as happening in the specious present, rather than yet to happen; and any satisfactory answer thereto would, I suggest, involve some sort of causal story. A present experience is—to speak strictly—one most recently past, and I can have no grasp on that notion in order to use it for other purposes, unless I have already understood it via the notion of causality.

So, I claim, the concepts of past and future cannot be connected to the rest of our conceptual scheme unless we understand the past as the logically contingent that is causally unaffectible, and the future as the logically contingent that is causally affectible. Unless we suppose that, any grasp we might have on the concepts would be utterly mysterious and irrelevant to anything else. Although most philosophers have claimed that backward causation (an effect preceding its cause) is logically impossible, they have had considerable difficulty in explaining why this is so. My answer is that the past is constituted as such by its causal fixedness. That answer was also that of Leibniz.[22]

Although most philosophers have denied the logical possibility of backward causation, a significant minority (especially philosophers of the last forty years much influenced by science) have allowed its logical possibility. Such philosophers have tried to substantiate their claim by telling us imaginary stories, claimed to be coherent, that would be most naturally interpreted as stories of worlds in which the evidence suggests that some causes follow their effects. I suggest that when any of these stories are spelled out a little more fully, the evidence cannot be interpreted in that way.

Michael Dummett, among others, has suggested that the following would be evidence of backward causation of a past F by a later B:

1. The performance of B approximates, in our experience [e.g. presumably because of similar patterns of events in the past], to being a sufficient condition for the previous occurrence of F . . .
2. We can find no ordinary causal explanation for the occurrence of F . . .
3. So far as our experience goes, B is an action which it is in our power to perform if we choose.[23]

It might seem that we could never be in a position where we had substantial evidence of this kind, for if our evidence ever began

---

[22] 'When one of two non-contemporaneous elements contains the ground for the other, the former is regarded as the antecedent, and latter as the consequent', G. W. Leibniz, *The Metaphysical Foundations of Mathematics*, extract trans. in P. P. Wiener (ed.), *Leibniz, Selections* (Scribner's, 1951), 201. For commentary see Bas van Fraassen, *An Introduction to the Philosophy of Time and Space* (Random House, 1970), ch. 2. Leibniz unfortunately spoils his account by supposing that any collection of events that are compatible with each other is a state of the world, i.e. a collection of events simultaneous with each other. But that would *seem* to have the consequence that all logical possibilities must eventually occur—an utterly unwarranted claim.
[23] Michael Dummett, 'Causal Loops', in R. Flood and M. Lockwood (eds.), *The Nature of Time* (Blackwell, 1986), 148. (The position for which he argues here is similar to that for which he argued in 'Can An Effect Precede its Cause?', *Proceedings of the Aristotelian Society*, 28, suppl. vol. (1954), 27–44; and 'Bringing About the Past', *Philosophical Review*, 73 (1964), 338–59, repr. in le Poidevin and MacBeath (eds.), *Philosophy of Time*.

to look like this, we could easily make the balance of our evidence very different by performing a 'bilking experiment'. Wait until an F-type event has not occurred, and then try to bring about a B-type event. If you cannot, that suggests (3) is false. If you can, that suggests (1) is false. But this description of the 'bilking experiment' assumes that we can know 'whether or not F had occurred independently of our intentions'.[24] Yet suppose we find that the performance of B 'increases the probability that any report we have that F did not occur will be found to be in error'.[25] Then we would indeed have evidence of backward causation, suggests Dummett.

Our grounds for believing that a past action has a future effect is that before the action our evidence suggests that one thing is going to happen in future, and after the action our evidence suggests that a different thing is going to happen. Analogously any defender of the claim that there could be evidence that an action had had a past effect must claim, as Dummett does, that the action produces changes in the evidence about what happened in the past. Otherwise there would be no ground for supposing that the action had any effect in the past at all. Now I shall urge that no change in the evidence could possibly substantiate the claim that someone had affected the past.

For suppose, as Dummett suggests, that an action B, at t_2, a period subsequent to t_1 had the result that the evidence about what happened at t_1, was different subsequently to t_2, including, let us say, at t_3, when we are assessing the effect of our action, from what it was at t_1 and up to t_2. The evidence at t_1 and up to t_2, and the evidence from t_2 to t_3 suggest different occurrences at t_1

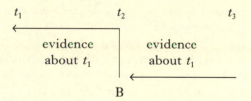

The question then arises as to which evidence shows what really happened at t_1? Clearly the earlier evidence must do so, for that is continuous with the actual event. What happened is what the best

---

[24] Dummett, 'Causal Loops', 149.   [25] Ibid. 150.

evidence available at the time showed.[26] Then the way for a believer in backward causation to construe the other evidence (that available between t_2 and t_3) is not as evidence of what did happen, but as evidence of what would have happened if B had not been done; and that involves a whole causal process running backwards from t_3 to t_2, t_2 to t_1. So it is no good, contrary to Dummett, to think you can overrule the bilking experiment by finding different evidence after t_2 to show that F happened after all. The evidence will not show that.

Dummett's experiment failed to show what he wanted to show, because he tried to introduce a tiny bit of backward causation in a basically forward-moving world. B was supposed to cause F without being linked to it by a causal chain, yet there was supposed to be a stream of evidence connected in a causal chain emanating from F in a later direction; and B was supposed to be uncaused by anything later. If Dummett really wants backward causation, he has got to suppose a situation which is the mirror-image of our world of forward-moving causation. All causes occur later than their effects and are in general linked to them by causal chains. Before an event happens you cannot prevent it from happening, but you have much evidence at most times about what will happen. After it has happened however, you can affect whether or not it happens. F happens at t_1. If B causes F and is later than it, however powerful you were, you could not at t_1 (for reasons of logic) stop B happening —contrary to Dummett's (3). However, once B has happened, you can *then* stop it happening. And so on. That world does not run into the problems of internal consistency that Dummett's world runs into. It is still incoherent, if you take the 'later' and 'earlier' in the description of it as having the same meaning as in ours; for the meaning of these terms, as we use them, is such as to allow the logical possibility of a cause having a later effect. But if you let such terms acquire their meaning from the description of the imaginary world alone, then that world turns out to be the same as ours—its 'later' is to be read as our 'earlier', etc.

---

[26] Unless an event had some effects in its neighbourhood (it could be seen, heard, touched, it left traces, or something), it would not count as happening at that place and time. 'Events are wherever in spacetime their immediate effects are', D. H. Mellor, *Real Time* (Cambridge University Press, 1981), 183. Mellor's whole argument, in ch. 10 of his book, that there cannot be exceptions to the normal direction of causation, is similar to my own in this section.

More generally, there cannot be, not merely cannot be evidence for, a few causal processes flowing in a different temporal direction from the majority of such processes. It is sometimes suggested that we could give content to 'earlier than', 'simultaneous with', and 'later than' from the normal direction of causal processes; we would call the causes in this normal stream 'earlier' than their effects. But, the suggestion goes, there might be a minority stream in which causality acts backwards; simultaneous events Q and R belong to a normal causal stream and cause A and events simultaneous with it, and thus are earlier than it, but there is an odd event P simultaneous with Q and R caused by A.

But, then, I ask, what content is there to this claim of the simultaneity of P with Q and R? Simultaneity is the limit of priority and posteriority, in the sense that if Q and R are simultaneous, any event which is earlier than Q is earlier than R and conversely (whence it follows that any event which is later than Q is later than R and conversely). Since Q and R are normal events from a causal point of view, it follows from their simultaneity that a powerful enough agent (if one existed or came into being) could use the occurrence of Q to interfere with any effect of R, and the occurrence of R to interfere with any effect of Q, that is, could arrange the world so that the occurrence of Q had a train of effects stopping the effects of R which would otherwise occur, and vice versa. But then what would the simultaneity of P with Q and R amount to? There would be no content to it if a powerful enough agent could not use P to interact with the causes or effects of Q and R. But if a powerful enough agent could make P interfere with the effects of Q and R, then the agent could ensure that among those effects was the non-occurrence of A, the action which was allegedly the cause of P. And that, of course, as we noted earlier, is impossible; no event can have among its effects the prevention of its cause—no man can kill his mother before she gives birth; and no agent could be powerful enough to make him do so.

More generally, if someone says that there are causal processes operating simultaneously in a contrary temporal direction to other processes, the question is—can they (logically) interact with each other or not? If they can, there is the possibility of an event preventing the occurrence of its cause and so its own occurrence; if they cannot there seems no content in the claim that the processes are simultaneous. I conclude that all causal processes must operate in the same temporal direction, and since some causes are earlier than their effects, all must be. The logical impossibility of backward causation is explained by the causal theory of time—the later just is the causally affectible.

Both memory and perception must be of things past. But there is a contingent distinction in the kind and method of awareness we humans have of things past which leads to a natural distinction between perception and memory. Those experiences of a kind which arise by an immediate causal chain from an event through sense organs to the brain, and which normally give us very reliable information about the nearby state of the world so little-out-of-date as to enable us to cope with our nearby surroundings fairly effectively, experiences unavoidable if our organs are operative and we direct them aright, we call perceptions. (Occasionally of course experiences of this kind are of things as they were a long time ago—as when we look at the stars. But those are exceptions.)

Memories, by contrast, are not constantly before us; they come to us erratically, it is only partly under our voluntary control whether we have them or not, they are available to us because we have in our brains stored traces of effects of immediate causal chains from the states of affairs remembered. We do not have memories of all the events of our past, and those we do have are not totally reliable. They often have much less sensory (as opposed to cognitive) content than do perceptions. These differences between perceptions and memories in humans clearly have their source in the different brain structures which mediate our experience of the world. Individuals of a very different kind from ourselves might not have a similar twofold scheme of awareness of the past.

Fourth Principle: Indexical Facts

The fourth principle is that there are temporal truths or facts of two kinds, non-indexical and indexical; two different kinds of way of picking out events. An indexical expression picks out something by its relation to the speaker's utterance—'you', 'I', 'that over there' are indexical expressions. A non-indexical expression picks something out in a way that can be used by different speakers at different places and times. McTaggart famously distinguished between the

A-series of events and the B-series of events—although, on some accounts of event-identity, they will be regarded not as two series of distinct events, but rather as two different ways of picking out the same series of events, the events which form the history of the universe.[27] The B-series picks out events non-indexically—that is, by their temporal relations (of order—earlier than, simultaneous with, or later than; and of metric—how much earlier or later) to the supposed time of occurrence of some particular event, such as the Birth of Christ or the Founding of Rome; and so dates them by their dates on some calendar so constructed as, say, '21 BC', 'AD 44', 'AD 1991', and so on. The A-series dates events by their temporal relations to the time of the speaker's utterance—for instance, '5 years ago', 'today', 'tomorrow'.

The same period or instant of time can be picked out either indexically or non-indexically—'today' or '22 May 1994' (given that that is today's date). Although it would be naturally described as the same event,[28] that it is sunny in Oxford today and that it is sunny in Oxford on 22 May 1994, there would seem to be two different facts or truths given by the two different descriptions of the event. For clearly what one knows in knowing the one is not sufficient to enable one to infer the other, and conversely. I may know that it is sunny today without knowing the date, or know that it is sunny on 22 May 1994 (e.g. because a reliable source told me) without knowing that it is sunny today (because I am shut in a dark room and do not know the date). From that it seems to me clearly to follow that the facts known are different. Someone could know the whole history of the universe as described by the B-series, without knowing where he was situated in it.[29] It follows from this

[27] J. M. E. McTaggart, *The Nature of Existence* (Cambridge University Press, 1927), vol. ii, ch. 33, 'Time'.

[28] These two descriptions pick out the same event on my favoured definition of event identity, which is that of J. Kim. See e.g. his 'Events and their Descriptions' in N. Rescher (ed.), *Essays in Honour of G. Hempel* (D. Reidel, 1969). On his theory, which Kim puts forward somewhat tentatively in this article, an event is the event it is in virtue of the substances, properties, and times involved in it. So S_1 being P_1 at t_1 is the same event as S_2 being P_2 at t_2 if and only if $S_1 = S_2$, $P_1 = P_2$, and $t_1 = t_2$— even if S_1 and S_2, etc., are described in ways which are not logically equivalent. Since (we are supposing) today is 22 May 1994, the two descriptions in the text pick out the same event.

[29] One does, of course, need a sophisticated philosophical doctrine of what are the facts that are the items of knowledge, in order to make clear what makes two such items of knowledge, e.g. it being sunny today and it being sunny on 22 May 1994, different—and how they are related to each other. Philosophers have had

that there are facts about periods of time that can only be known
at certain periods—for example, that something is happening now
can only be known now, that something is going to happen can
only be known before it happens. My knowledge that it is sunny
today can only be had today.[30] Such facts being facts in which the
periods or instants of time are picked out indexically are called
tensed facts. Similar arguments show that there are facts which can
only be known by certain persons, for instance, the fact which I
describe as 'I am cold' not being the same fact as the fact that
Swinburne is cold, can be known only by me. However, all non-
indexical knowledge (i.e. all knowledge about individuals, times,
and places not picked out by their relation to the knower) can be
had by any person at any period of time.

What is known as the static view of time (alias the 'B-Theory')
holds that, despite the above arguments,[31] the only temporal facts
are non-indexical. Which events are happening now is not, on this
view, a fact distinct from which events are happening in 1994; their
'nowness' is not a matter of how things are, but of how we look at
them, our perspective on them. The many Christian thinkers of
the first thirteen Christian centuries much influenced by Plato's
view that the fundamental things were timeless, tended to think in
this way, though without any very clear definite thesis about the
matter.[32] In the twentieth century a quite different group of thinkers

some difficulty in producing a satisfactory doctrine of this matter. But that difficulty
need cast no doubt on the fact that the two items of knowledge are different. I have
developed my own doctrine of this matter in 'Tensed Facts', *American Philosophical
Quarterly*, 27 (1990), 117–30.

[30] I used to endorse Castaneda's argument on this point, to the effect that, since
if A knows at t_1 that at t_2 B knows that p, A knows at t_1 that p; and since A could
know that B knows on 22 May 1994 that it is sunny then (which he expresses then
by 'it is sunny today'), at any time, he could know at any time what B knows when
he knows that it is sunny then. (See H.-N. Castaneda, 'Omniscience and Indexical
Reference', *Journal of Philosophy*, 64 (1967), 203–10.) I now think that it does not
follow straightforwardly that if A knows at t_1 that at t_2 B knows that p, A knows at
t_1 that p. It all depends whether (in my terminology of Ch. 5) p is a 'sentence',
'proposition', or 'statement'.

[31] My discussion of this issue has been extremely brief. See my 'Tensed Facts'
for reference to writers on the two sides of the controversy.

[32] According to Augustine, 'Whatever reality extended time or duration has, is in
the mind' writes R. A. Markus in his contribution to A. H. Armstrong (ed.), *The
Cambridge History of Later Greek and Early Medieval Philosophy* (Cambridge
University Press, 1967), 404. Calvin Normore in his contribution to N. Kretzmann
et al. (eds.), *The Cambridge History of Later Medieval Philosophy* (Cambridge University Press, 1982), 367, writes: 'When considered against the background of Aquinas'

has tended to think in this way out of a belief that the only truths are the ones which scientists can report and discuss at different times and that can therefore be expressed equally well at different times; this group includes Grünbaum, Smart, and Mellor.[33] The objective fact of the passage of time by contrast has been espoused by Duns Scotus and some later medieval successors and by a number of modern philosophers; their view is sometimes known as the dynamic or A-Theory of Time.[34]

The Nature of Time

Our four principles leave us with the view that time is linear. An event, and so the period at which it occurs, once past is not and never will be future as well. A future event, and so the period at which it occurs, is not also past and never yet has been past. Instants of time are like points, and periods like intervals, on a line that never meets itself. Time has no first instant or period, or last instant or period. For if before any instant in the history of the universe (i.e. the period during which substances exist) there is another period, then time does not have a beginning. It is only initially plausible to suppose that time has a beginning if the universe has a beginning, in the sense that before some instant there were no substances, and then that instant would be the most plausible candidate for the first instant of time. But if we so describe it, it would then follow that although the first substance to exist began to exist,

position, Scotus' discussions of God's knowledge signal the clash of two fundamentally different ways of conceiving the nature of time. The first, which seems to have been Boethius' and may have been Aquinas', conceives the difference between past and future as perspectival rather than ontological. Human beings have relations to past events which differ from those we have to future events, but these differences are grounded in us rather than in the world outside us. The second view, the one for which Scotus argues and the one which seems to be taken more or less for granted in the first quarter of the fourteenth century, sees the difference between past and future as an objective difference, one that exists for God as well as for us.'

[33] A. Grünbaum, 'The Status of Temporal Becoming', in R. M. Gale (ed.), *The Philosophy of Time* (Macmillan, 1968); J. J. C. Smart, *Philosophy and Scientific Realism* (Routledge & Kegan Paul, 1963), ch. 7; Mellor, *Real Time*.

[34] See C. D. Broad, *An Examination of McTaggart's Philosophy*, (Cambridge University Press, 1938), vol. ii, pt. 1, extract in Gale, *Philosophy of Time*; and Gale, *The Language of Time* (Routledge & Kegan Paul, 1968). For Scotus, see n. 32.

there was no time at which it did not exist. Yet to say that something began to exist seems to involve saying that once it was not,
and then it was.[35] Someone might deny that, saying that to say that
a substance S began to exist at *t* entails only that there was no period
before *t* at which it existed—and that leaves open two possibilities:
either there was a period before *t* in which S did not exist, or there
was no period before *t*. But how is the second alternative—S and
time beginning to exist together at *t*, to be distinguished from S
having existed forever? An answer might be that in the former case
(unlike the latter), *t* is at a finite temporal distance earlier than the
present instant. But that answer can only be given if (during the
existence of the universe) time has a metric, and, as we saw, it need
not have one. If it does not have one, one could not distinguish
between a universe that had a beginning and one that did not,
unless the former entails that there was a period of time in which
there was no universe (no substances existed). And since it seems
clear that there is such a distinction to be made (even if time has no
metric), it follows that if the universe had a beginning but the time
of the universe had no metric, there must be a period of time
before the beginning of the universe. But whether or not time has
a beginning cannot depend on what happens later—that the time of
the universe has a metric. Hence time cannot begin with the
beginning of the universe. But before the beginning of the universe,
I argued earlier, one could not distinguish any period of time from
any other, and hence no instant could be picked out at which time
began—in the sense that there would be no content to the claim
that there was such an instant. So whether or not the universe has
a beginning, time could not have; and although one can talk of a
first period of time, it will be a period identified only by its end-
point. And a parallel argument shows that it could not have an end
either. It follows that since (by my third principle) causes must
precede their effects, if the universe had a beginning, that beginning
of existence would be uncaused. Note that I have used 'the universe'
in the preceding paragraph in the most general sense of 'all the
substances there are', and this will include God, if there is a God.
(I shall later need to define a narrower sense of 'universe'.)

---

[35] This argument is similar to an argument going back to Islamic times (see
Sorabji, *Time, Creation and the Continuum*, 237), that if the universe had a beginning
at a certain time, then since it could have begun to exist earlier than it did, there
must be an earlier time during which it could have existed.

Yet time is not a substance and we must not hypostatize it. If substances exist, they exist for periods of time; and talk of time is talk about their existing, while talk of earlier and later is talk of what they cause and are caused by. And time not having a beginning is just the universe not having a beginning, or—alternatively—the universe coming into being uncaused (i.e. with emptiness before it). Time not having an end is just a matter of the universe not having an end, or alternatively having an end followed by emptiness. Time is something involved in the very existence of substances, the necessary framework for them, an amorphous realm of causal possibilities which surrounds actual substances. Since everything that happens, including the existence of substances, occurs (by my first principle) over a period of time, then if—impossibly—there were no time, there would be no substances. However, if there were no substances, there would still be time in a minimal sense that there would remain the logical possibility of the existence of substances; time would be, as it were, the logical substratum for the existence of substances. For if there is still the logical possibility that substances come into being (and there must be that), then since—by my earlier argument—if they did come into being, there would have existed an empty time before that, that empty time must already exist, for their coming into being cannot bring about the empty time; it must already have been there. Yet in an empty time, there would be no difference between any period or instant of time and any other. But once there are substances, which come into being or cease to be or change (as opposed to existing ever-lastingly), then there are distinct periods and instants of time.

5

Necessity

Some things could not but be as they are; other things could have been different from the way they are. Some things can be; some things cannot ever be. Philosophers codify these vague intuitions with their more technical terms—it is necessary that some things are so, whereas it is merely contingent that other things are so; some things are possible, whereas other things are impossible. And then a central metaphysical task is to say what things are necessary, and what things are contingent, possible, or impossible. Yet before we can enter on that enterprise we need to be clear about what is being said when something is said to be necessary or whatever.

I shall take the central notion as the notion of necessity. The other notions can be explained by means of it. The impossible is that which is necessarily not; the possible is that which is not impossible, and the contingent is that which is neither necessary nor impossible. This chapter will seek to distinguish different things which may be meant by saying that something is necessary, and it will go on to urge that the two most ultimate kinds of necessity are what I shall call 'ontological necessity' and what I shall call 'metaphysical necessity', neither of which are at all the same as what many others have claimed to be the most ultimate kind which they have called 'broadly logical necessity'.

We need first to examine the notion of logical necessity, and show that it is not a very deep feature of the world. One reason why it has been supposed to be a very deep feature of the world is because it has been supposed to characterize timeless entities called 'statements' or 'propositions'. I shall argue that such things are merely abstract fictional constructs, like numbers, on which I touched briefly in Chapter 1, that are such that it is useful for certain purposes to talk as if they existed but really they do not. I seek now to bring out both the utility of such talk and its dispensability. I shall then go on to show that logical necessity is at root a feature of actual human sentences and how they are used. It governs language, and not the world. Much of this chapter is thus concerned to establish a negative thesis. I spend so much time on this destructive task because many philosophers of religion have believed strongly in the deep significance of 'broadly logical necessity', and this has greatly influenced their account of God. We need to clear the ground in order to see what is the most ultimate kind of necessity at work in the world.

Sentences, Propositions, and Statements

A type sentence is a combination of words, for instance, 'I am ill,' which may be uttered or written on many occasions by different persons; a token sentence is one particular utterance or inscription of such a type sentence, for example, my saying 'I am ill,' at midday on 31 May 1991. Different token sentences may say the same thing, make the same claim about the world, convey the same information. Hence philosophers often wish to introduce a notion of a statement or proposition as that which a token sentence expresses which has a truth-value (i.e. is true or false), and which may be expressed by different token sentences. But there are different ways of understanding 'say the same thing' that generate different notions of statement or proposition. I suggest that if we are in this way to hypostatize what is expressed, the most useful way to do it is to distinguish between two different things expressed by sentences, which I shall call the statement and the proposition, as follows.[1]

---

[1] My definitions take off from those given by E. J. Lemmon in 'Sentences, Statements and Propositions', in Bernard Williams and Alan Montefiore (eds.), *British Analytical Philosophy* (Routledge & Kegan Paul, 1966), but differ from those that he gives—e.g. his criterion of property identity is that of coextensionality. My concept of 'proposition' is similar to Kaplan's concept of 'character', except (if I understand him correctly) in the crucial respect that a 'character' does not have a truth-value; it is rather what (together with context) gives truth-value to a sentence. (See David Kaplan, 'On the Logic of Demonstratives', in P. French *et al.* (eds.), *Contemporary Perspectives in the Philosophy of Language* (University of Minnesota Press, 1979).) My 'statement' is Bertrand Russell's 'proposition'. I apologize to those familiar with my writing that here, as also in *Revelation* (Clarendon Press, 1992), 9 f., I define a 'proposition' in a way different from that in which I define it in *The Coherence of Theism* (Clarendon Press, 1977), 14. There I defined a 'proposition' as a 'coherent statement', and I used the term in that work subsequently in that sense. The sense here is quite different. Nothing of philosophical importance turns on this change of usage, which is made solely for purposes of simple exposition.

The proposition which a token sentence *s* expresses is that element of claim in what is said which is also made by any other token sentence (whether of the same type or not) which is synonymous with *s*. Two sentences express the same proposition if and only if they are synonymous. 'Rex mortuus est,' uttered by a Latin speaker of the fourteenth century, 'Le roi est mort,' uttered by a French speaker of the eighteenth century, and 'The king is dead,' uttered by an English speaker of the twentieth century express the same proposition.[2] The statement which a token sentence *s* expresses is that element of claim in what is said which is made by any other token sentence *r* which predicates the same properties of the same individuals, at the same times and places (however the individuals, times, and places are picked out), when properties are the same if and only if the predicates which designate them are synonymous. So two sentences express the same statement if and only if they attribute the same property to the same individuals at the same place and time, whatever the way of referring (or 'mode of presentation' to use the technical term) by which those individuals, places, and times are picked out. The three token sentences just cited did not express the same statement, for (we may reasonably suppose) they concern different kings. Whereas, 'I am ill,' spoken by me, 'You are ill,' addressed to me, and 'He is ill,' spoken of me, all spoken at the same time, do all express the same statement (although not the same proposition). So do 'I will go to London tomorrow,' uttered by me on 1 January, 'I am going to London today,' uttered by me on 2 January, and 'I went to London yesterday,' uttered by me on 3 January (given that the reference of 'London' remains the same).

Whether a given token sentence is true or false depends on three facets of the world: (1) the conventions of the language in which the sentence is uttered, or written; (2) the referential context, that is, those circumstances of its utterance that determine the reference of its expressions referring to individuals, places, and times—for instance, by whom it is uttered or written, when, to whom, in the presence of which objects, in which community; (3) other features of the world, which I shall call the 'remaining truth-relevant conditions'. Facet (1) determines which proposition is uttered, (1) and (2) together determine which statement is uttered, and the other

---

[2] I do of course assume, contrary to Quine, that the notion of synonymy is sufficiently clear to be used in such a definition. On this see my 'Analytic/Synthetic', *American Philosophical Quarterly*, 21 (1984), 31–42, esp. 39 f.

features (i.e. (2) and (3) for a proposition, (3) for a statement) determine whether that proposition or statement is true. The linguistic conventions determine the meaning of general terms, connectives, etc. They lay down how, in the circumstances of utterance or inscription, to determine the referent of indexical expressions, for example, they state that 'you' refers to the person to whom the speaker is talking. It is then those circumstances (i.e. the referential context) that determine what the referent (e.g. 'you') is. The conventions of language, however, contain no rules for determining the reference of proper names; that is not a matter of language, but of community practice (i.e. the referential context). If a name (e.g. John) occurs in a sentence, the sentence expresses a proposition about whoever, given the community practice, is the referent of John. (When a sentence *s* expresses in virtue of the linguistic conventions a proposition *p*, and also in virtue of the referential context a statement *w*, I shall say that *p* in that referential context determines the statement *w*.)

It follows that the truth-value of a statement is invariant—if true, it is true always and everywhere, by whom and to whom it is uttered. This will be because it is true if and only if certain individuals have certain properties at certain places and times, independently of how those individuals, places, and times are picked out. The truth-value of a proposition varies with who utters it, when, and where. The same proposition is true yesterday, but not today; true in Italy, but not in France; true if uttered by you but not if uttered by me. The proposition expressed by a token sentence has a content independent of the who, where, and when of utterance; but these latter come in to determine its truth. So the proposition expressed by 'I am cold' may be true today, false tomorrow, true when uttered by me but false when uttered by you, just as it may be funny, or irrelevant, or contradict what has been said before, today but not tomorrow, when uttered by you but not when uttered by me. Propositions are, as it were, meaning-involved expressions waiting to be pinned down to who, where, and when, before their truth can be determined. Statements are meaning-involved expressions already so pinned down. The truth of statements is absolute, of propositions relative.

The next step taken by those who adopt such vocabulary is to note that 'propositions' are logically related to each other. Often one proposition or several propositions together entail another one,

or entail the negation of another one. One proposition entails another, if the latter being true is involved in the former being true,
and so a speaker who asserts the former in a given context is committed to the latter in that context. The negation of a proposition
p is the proposition that says that things are not as p says. The propositions that all men are mortal and Socrates is a man together
entail that Socrates is mortal. We must construe such claims as
concerned with propositions rather than statements in my sense.
For logic is concerned with relations that hold independently of
what the world is like. What is expressed by 'Tom is old,' may be
true if and only if what is expressed by 'It is not the case that
Robert is not old,' is true—given that in the context of utterance of
the token sentences, 'Tom' and 'Robert' refer to the same individual
—and thus the two statements must both be true, or both be false,
together—but logic is not concerned with that. Logic is concerned
only with the connections of involvement that hold in virtue of the
meaning of what is said—in that sense of 'meaning' in which you
need to know the language alone in order to know the meaning of
a sentence; and so with relations between propositions.

We then note that such logical relations between particular propositions often hold in virtue of general features of these propositions. That enables us to discover a set of rules that state which
kinds of proposition have which logical relations to which other
kinds of proposition, and these we call the laws of logic. The example
of entailment given in the last paragraph holds because it is a law
of logic that any propositions of the form 'all As are B' and 'x is an
A' entails one of the form 'x is a B'. The laws of logic codify general
relations of entailment; and also they rule out various propositions
from ever being true, namely those that entail a self-contradiction.
(A self-contradiction is a proposition that says that both it and its
negation are true.)

The next step is to claim that some 'propositions' are necessary
(i.e. necessarily true) in the 'broadly logical sense'. Now this claim
may concern both 'propositions' and 'statements' in my sense but
because some of the more interesting examples concern the necessity
of statements, I shall discuss mainly the necessity of statements,
and then apply my results briefly to the necessity of propositions.
All statements have an invariant truth-value; if true, they are true
always. But in some sense some of them are not merely always
true, but necessarily true; they could not but be true in some way

for logical reasons. Obvious examples are the statements expressed by the English sentences, 'If one man is taller than a second man, and the second man is taller than a third man, then the first man is taller than the third man,' and 'If anything is a square, it has four sides.' In these cases linguistic conventions alone suffice to determine which statement is made; same proposition determines same statement, whatever the referential context. But we can see that the same kind of necessity belongs to statements, even where the context of a sentence's utterance makes a difference to which statement is expressed. 'Hesperus is Phosphorus' expresses a necessarily true statement, if uttered in a context where 'Hesperus' and 'Phosphorus' pick out the same individual, for example, the context of seventeenth-century astronomy where they both pick out the planet Venus. For in that context the cited sentence expresses the same statement as does 'Hesperus is Hesperus'; and so the logical necessity which guarantees the latter, and is clearly of the same kind as that involved in the two previously cited sentences, must also guarantee the former. But what the example of 'Hesperus is Phosphorus' brings out is that a sentence may express a necessarily true statement without a competent speaker of the language knowing that it does. For someone who used 'Hesperus' to refer to the planet which appears in the western sky somewhat after sunset, and 'Phosphorus' to refer to the planet which appears in the eastern sky somewhat before sunrise need not know that these planets are the same planet.[3] Although there could be a world in which whatever

[3] It is often contended, by a tradition of writing deriving from Kripke and Putnam, that the 'propositions'—and by that must be meant, in my sense, the statements—expressed by such sentences as 'Hesperus is Phosphorus' in a context where 'Hesperus' and 'Phosphorus' pick out the same individual, are, though necessary, only knowable a posteriori; mere a priori considerations will not show their truth. See S. Kripke, 'Identity and Necessity', in M. K. Munitz (ed.), *Identity and Individuation* (New York University Press, 1971), and 'Naming and Necessity', first published in D. Davidson and G. Harman (eds.), *Semantics of Natural Languages* (D. Reidel, 1972); and Hilary Putnam, 'The Meaning of "Meaning"', republished in his *Mind, Language and Reality: Philosophical Papers*, ii (Cambridge University Press, 1975), and subsequent writings. I do not endorse that view, because I hold that a speaker who does not know enough about the context to know that 'Hesperus' and 'Phosphorus' pick out the same individual, does not know which statement 'Hesperus is Phosphorus' expresses. When he does know the former and so knows which statement is expressed, he knows a priori that it is true. More generally, I wish to contend that all truths necessary 'in the broadly logical sense' can be known a priori. See my 'Necessary A Posteriori Truth', *American Philosophical Quarterly*, 28 (1991), 113–23. Nothing much turns on this issue for present purposes.

planet appeared in the western sky was not in fact Hesperus (the planet that appears in our world in the western sky), the planet which is in fact picked by 'Hesperus' could not but be identical with Phosphorus—in any world.

What more precisely is this necessity 'in the broadly logical sense' which I have illustrated so far only by citing statements which it characterizes? It is sometimes said to be truth in 'all possible worlds'; a statement that is logically necessary is one true 'in all possible worlds'. A possible world is a way things could have been. One such is uniquely identified by a set of statements giving a complete history of 'the universe' (in its widest sense of all that there is) through time. A history of a way things could have been that differs in the slightest respect from another such picks out a different possible world. But such attempts to elucidate are only helpful if we first understand what kind of possibility is involved when a world is said to be 'possible', what counts as a history of a way things 'could' have been as opposed to a way things could not have been. In some senses of 'could' there could have been a world in which pigs flew, and in other senses of 'could' there could not have been such a world. The obvious elucidation is to say that the 'could' is the logical 'could'; a 'possible world' is a logically possible world, that is, a world 'possible' 'in the broadly logical sense'. But then in effect, asked what a 'logically necessary' statement is, we have answered that it is one that is true under all logically possible conditions, that is, one that it is not 'logically possible' should not hold; and that does not get us very far.

One can get a bit further by saying that a world is a possible world if no proposition which correctly describes any aspect of that world entails a self-contradiction. The statement expressed by 'All squares have four sides,' is true in all possible worlds, in that it is true in every world of which it is the case that every true proposition that describes it entails no self-contradiction. It could only be false if there was a square which did not have four sides; and since 'square' means 'figure with four equal sides and four equal angles', a world having a square without four sides would be a world in which a proposition which described that world would entail the proposition expressed by the sentence 'There is a figure which has four sides and does not have four sides.' However, given the way in which the notion of possible worlds was introduced, one can dispense with that notion and give a simpler account of the necessity of a statement. One can just say that—subject to a qualification below—a statement is necessary if some sentence that expresses the negation of that statement expresses a proposition which entails a self-contradiction. The statement expressed by the token sentence 'Hesperus is Phosphorus' in a context where 'Hesperus' and 'Phosphorus' refer to the same individual, is necessary because the sentence 'Hesperus is Hesperus' which expresses the same statement has as its negation 'it is not the case that Hesperus is Hesperus', which expresses (and so entails) a self-contradictory proposition.[4]

The qualification on this simple account of the necessity of a statement is as follows. For a statement to be necessary, the sentence that expresses a negation of that statement and that expresses a proposition that entails a self-contradiction, must pick out the individuals, times, and places involved by rigid designators. By a rigid designator I understand an expression that picks out the individual it does quite independently of whether it gains or loses non-essential properties. Without this qualification all sentences would turn out to express necessary statements! 'This lectern is red,' clearly does not express a necessary statement. But it expresses the same statement as 'This red lectern is red,' and the negation of that sentence expresses a proposition that entails a self-contradiction. However, 'This red lectern', is not a rigid designator; it picks out a lectern only while it has the non-essential property of being red. Rigid designators include proper names (e.g. 'Hesperus') and descriptions of individuals in terms of their essential properties. The essential properties of material objects, we saw in Chapter 2, include the essential kinds to which they belong and the matter of which they are made. So 'lectern made of chunk of wood W' (where 'W' is the name of a chunk of wood) is a rigid designator. My restriction arises from the consideration that the notion of a statement whose necessity we are seeking to define is that of a claim concerning particular individuals who are the individuals they are in virtue only of their essential features; accidental features may help us to pick out individuals, but they are no more than devices helping us to locate the individuals, not part of the content of the resulting statement.

[4] I assume that the statement expressed (in this world) by 'Hesperus is Phosphorus' is true in a world in which Hesperus does not exist. If that is denied, then a slightly more complicated account of 'necessary in the broadly logical sense' must be provided, if we are to explain it via the notion of possible worlds; but the reader can see that the same kind of points can again be made.

With this qualification on board, we can see how my definition shows the necessity of another well-used example of a necessary statement, one again for which mere linguistic considerations do not ensure that a sentence which expresses it expresses a necessary truth. Consider the statement expressed on a certain occasion by Kripke saying of a lectern, 'This lectern was not from the beginning of its existence made entirely of ice.'[5] Given that the lectern in question is in fact made of wood, no lectern would be that lectern if from the beginning of its existence it had been made entirely of ice. So the cited sentence expresses a necessarily true statement (even if a competent speaker may not know that it does). It does so in virtue of the linguistic conventions for the use of words (e.g. 'lectern' and 'ice') and the referential context in which it is uttered (which particular lectern is present). A sentence which expresses the negation of the cited statement is, 'The lectern made of chunk of wood W was from the beginning of its existence made entirely of ice' (where the lectern picked out by Kripke's words is in fact made of chunk of wood W). The second sentence (in which the lectern is picked out by a rigid designator) expresses a proposition that entails a self-contradiction, and hence my definition has the desired consequence that Kripke's sentence expresses a necessary statement.

The necessity 'in the broadly logical sense' of a proposition is naturally and more simply explained along similar lines as follows. A proposition is necessary if it is true in all possible worlds—which boils down simply to: if its negation entails a self-contradiction. Any sentence which expresses a necessary proposition will also express a necessary statement[6]—though which necessary statement it expresses may vary with context. 'If John is older than George, and George is older than Harry, then John is older than Harry,' expresses a necessarily true proposition and a necessarily true statement, but

---

[5] 'Identity and Necessity', 152.

[6] In 'Necessary A Posteriori Truth', I defined a necessarily true proposition as 'one true in all possible worlds (i.e. true whatever the referential context in which it is expressed, and whatever the remaining truth-relevant conditions)'. From that definition it followed that there are sentences which express necessarily true propositions without expressing necessarily true statements—e.g. 'I am here.' Such a sentence necessarily expresses a true statement, but the statement which it expresses is not one necessarily true, being for example, if uttered by me in Oxford, the same statement as that expressed by 'Swinburne is in Oxford.' On the narrower definition of necessarily true propositions used here that possibility is excluded.

which necessarily true statement it expresses depends on the referential context—that is, to which 'John', 'George', and 'Harry'
reference is being made. However, clearly a sentence may express
a necessarily true statement without expressing a necessarily true
proposition, as does 'Hesperus is Phosphorus' when uttered in a
context in which the two names refer to the same individual.

Platonism versus Nominalism

All this apparatus, the development of which I have just outlined,
is very useful for the philosopher. Logic, like mathematics, is a
useful tool; it gets us from one sentence that we accept to another
sentence that initially we do not accept but that in some sense we
are committed to. And logic can be articulated more smoothly if
we regard it as holding between timeless entities rather than between
human sentences of somewhat unclear meaning. There is, however,
a view that all this is no mere convenient fiction. There really are
timeless entities such as statements and propositions, having
different logical natures (e.g. necessary or contingent) and logical
relations to each other, and maybe possible worlds as well. These
things exist in as real a way as do tables and chairs. I shall call this
view about statements, propositions, and logic, logical Platonism,
since Plato held that there is a world of timeless forms that governs
the nature and behaviour of ordinary mundane things.

The Platonist holds that these entities exist and are related to
each other, whether or not humans know about them; and would
have existed even if there never were any humans or other rational
beings, and so any human sentences which could express statements and propositions. We might never have known that the
statement expressed by 'Hesperus is Phosphorus' is necessarily
true, or that the proposition that there are 4 men in the room entails the proposition that the number of men in the room is one less
than $\sqrt[3]{125}$, or that various axioms of the predicate calculus are laws
of logic, but they would have been all the same. And, claims the
Platonist, the logical necessities and relations existing in the realm
of forms have consequences for how things must be in the physical
universe. The cited necessary truth and entailment carry consequences for the actual Hesperus and men in an actual room. Logical

necessities, claims the Platonist, make it inevitable that the world is one sort of place rather than another—by a hard, inexorable necessity than which there is none harder.

The Platonist's opponent is the logical nominalist, who believes that the only truths at stake concern *nomina*, words. There is, claims the nominalist, no timeless realm of statements and logical necessity, just facts about how humans use language. There is no need to postulate a timeless realm, he claims, since everything that the Platonist adduces as grounds for adopting his way of talking can be redescribed without the need for it. I shall argue that the nominalist is basically correct. I have already in effect shown that the Platonist does not need to postulate possible worlds, and I shall confine myself to considering his other postulates. The Platonist postulates propositions as the common content of synonymous sentences. But we can just say that there are sentences that are synonymous, mean the same, are inter-translatable; we do not have to say their 'common content' is something that exists apart from them. Two token sentences are synonymous if (almost all) speakers of the language recognize them to be such that if one correctly describes what a believer believes in some context, so does the other, and conversely. The Platonist postulates statements as the common content of sentences which predicate the same properties of the same individuals. But we can just say that there are sentences which predicate the same properties of the same individuals. And the test for whether they do is whether (almost all) speakers of the language recognize the predicates as inter-translatable; and, if suitably positioned, would judge that the referring expressions pick out the same individuals.

Perhaps the major reason why the Platonist wishes to deny this reduction is what he calls the facts of logical relations and necessary truth independent of what humans might ever recognize, to which I have been drawing attention. But, I shall claim, the only logical relations and necessary truths that we have any reason to believe to exist are put forward on the basis of facts of language that can be described without this apparatus—in terms of how speakers of a language treat its sentences, together with facts about the referential context in which those sentences are used. By bringing in facts of the latter kind I advocate only a modified form of nominalism.

Let us begin with logical relations, and illustrate the point with the central logical relation of entailment. That the proposition expressed by a token sentence s_1 entails the proposition expressed by a token sentence s_2 will be true if and only if the sentence s_1 entails the sentence s_2 in a certain sense—which can be spelled out by introducing the notions of negation, self-contradiction, and minimal entailment as belonging to token sentences. By the negation of a token sentence s I mean any sentence synonymous with 'it is not the case that s', any sentence which says simply that things are not as s says. By a self-contradictory sentence I mean a sentence which says that things both are and are not a certain way. A sentence is thus self-contradictory if it is a conjunction of two sentences, such that (almost all) speakers of the language recognize one sentence as doing no more and no less than ruling out the other, in consequence of which speakers cannot see the conjunction as making any claim which they can understand.

By a sentence s_1 entailing a sentence s_2, I mean that s_1 and s_2 are linked by a chain of 'minimally entailed' sentences r_1, r_2, r_3, and so on, such that s_1 minimally entails r_1, r_1 minimally entails r_2, and so on, until we reach s_2. A sentence r_1 minimally entails a sentence r_2 if the rules of the public language are recognized by most speakers of the language to be such (when it is suggested to them) that a speaker of r_1 in the given context is 'committed' to r_2 in that context—in this sense that the speaker of r_1 is thereby also taken to have affirmed r_2; r_1 is seen as 'involving' r_2, and r_2 is seen as part of r_1. Hearers would be at a loss to understand what claim was being made by r_1 if the speaker at the same time affirmed the negation of r_2. If you say, 'There are 3 apples in the box,' you are committed to, 'There are more than 2 apples in the box.' If you say, 'John is taller than George, and George is taller than Robert,' you are committed to, 'John is taller than Robert,' and so on. Two or more sentences $p_1, p_2 \ldots$ entail another one q, if there is a chain of minimal entailments beginning from one of the initial sentences or conjunctions thereof, such that we are allowed to conjoin any of the sentences of the chain to any of the initial sentences at any stage and proceed further by minimal entailments, which eventually reaches q. If there is such an entailment then there is a valid deductive inference from the initial sentences as premises to q as conclusion. Although most speakers of a language will immediately recognize the minimal entailments of its sentences, they will not immediately recognize all their entailments—in some cases that may need a long and difficult proof. Hence the possibility of doubt about entailment—but the doubt concerns whether there is a chain of connecting sentences that speakers of the language would recognize as minimal entailments.

But are there not 'laws of logic' which determine which sentences entail which other sentences, and are these not independent of language? There are laws of logic all right, says the nominalist, but they are simply generalizations about language. The logician notices general patterns of entailment which he codifies. He notices that any sentences of the form, 'A is taller than B,' and 'B is taller than C,' entail 'A is taller than C.' And he notices yet more general patterns, such as that 'all As are B', and 'all Bs are C' entail 'all As are C', which hold whatever the As, Bs, and Cs. He then notices similar general patterns of entailment in other languages to the general patterns which he notices in his own language, and so he devises a formal system with a language of its own, and provides guidance for translating its sentences into and out of the sentences of various natural languages—so that 'all As are B' becomes '(x) $(Ax \supset Bx)$' and so on. This formalization proceeds from ordinary English, Latin, or whatever to formal logic; and generalizes patterns of entailment in ordinary language so as to obtain laws of formal logic. These in turn may be used to provide guidance about which other sentences of ordinary languages entail which other sentences. But the 'guidance' is not infallible. There is an understanding acquired by practice about how to interpret the theorems of formal logic so as to devise consequences for the sentences of a natural language, for instance, that '(x) $(Ax \supset Bx)$' and '(x) $(Bx \supset Cx)$' entail '(x) $(Ax \supset Cx)$' has the consequence for English that 'all humans are animals' and 'all animals are mortal' entail 'all humans are mortal'. But there are always cases where the natural interpretations of the theorems of formal logic yield conclusions at variance with our intuitive judgements about entailments of sentences of natural language in particular contexts—that is, about which sentences can be joined by chains of minimal entailment. Someone may allow that 'All good warriors are dead,' and 'The dead fight no battles,' while denying that 'All good warriors fight no battles,' even though this would seem a natural interpretation of the schema of formal logic. All the time the logician becomes more adept at recognizing which ordinary language sentences are and which are not correctly captured by formulas of formal logic. And his main ground for saying that these sentences just quoted are not a correct interpretation of the logic schema are that the first two sentences do not entail the latter, as judged by a prior understanding of what entails what, that is what can and cannot be joined by chains of minimal entailment.

I conclude that talk of logical relations between propositions which we can pick out by means of sentences will have application if and only if speakers of the language treat its sentences in certain ways. The laws of logic, that is, can be expounded as mere generalizations of logical relations between sentences recognizable in many particular cases.

Why is it that human language users agree in recognizing sentences as having the minimal entailments they do? A major part of the explanation is that the agreement derives from linguistic training. Human language users have the same neurophysiology and linguistic equipment as each other; and training that certain sentences have certain minimal entailments (e.g., training that 'S can defeat any other player at chess' and 'R is a chess player distinct from S' entail 'S can defeat R') leads to agreement about the minimal entailments of recognizably similar sentences (e.g. that 'S can run 100 metres faster than any other runner' and 'R is a runner distinct from S' entail 'S can run 100 metres faster than R'). Yet that cannot be the full explanation, for we regard our recognition of many of the entailments which we recognize not as deriving solely from linguistic training but from seeing what claim is being made by a sentence and seeing what is involved in that.

Our understanding of what a given sentence claims about the world is provided in part, and, in the case of some sentences, wholly, by our understanding of what it minimally entails and what minimally entails it. But our language latches us to the world, and our understanding of many of the words of our language derives from our being taught under what observable conditions sentences which contain them are true or false. That provides us with some understanding of words and sentence forms, which provides further understanding of other sentences in which those words occur, beyond the understanding provided by knowledge of logical entailments. We learn what 'red', and 'desk', and 'game' mean, by being told on various occasions when sentences such as 'This is red,' 'That is a desk,' 'They are playing a game,' are true or false. That provides an understanding of what is being said when claims are made about distant objects being 'red', or ancient peoples playing 'games'; and this understanding is supplemented by training in inference—for example, that 'This is a desk,' entails 'This is a material object.'

But the supplementation is not arbitrary nor always necessary. For we derive from our training about the observable circumstances under which sentences are true an understanding of what those sentences are claiming, and what other sentences formed in part of those words are claiming, which constrains what we can see them as minimally entailing.[7] We could be taught the meaning of 'red' under various circumstances, and of 'coloured' under various different circumstances, so that without having been trained that 'this is red' minimally entails 'this is coloured', we would see it as doing so in virtue of our grasp of which properties the predicates 'red' and 'coloured' designate.

No doubt because of the similarity of the neurophysiology of each of us, when we come to learn that some predicate designates an observable property, what we grasp through the training process is an understanding of the property so designated as one which includes other properties. The understanding of redness which we derive from the training process is an understanding of redness as involving being coloured, a property that we have also been taught to recognize in part by being shown examples of coloured things, including things of colours other than red. What we derive from being shown an example of a 3-membered group is an understanding of the property of 3-memberedness as including the property of having-more-than-2-members, and as excluding the property of having-no-members. Our understanding of the properties which we cannot observe (e.g. 'being exactly 3.06 billion billion miles long') is given by our knowledge of the minimal entailments of the sentences in which predicates designating those properties occur. But some of these minimal entailments are sentences containing predicates designating observable properties (e.g. 'being more than 1 yard long'); and our understanding of those properties is derived

---

[7] Thus Michael Dummett argues that 'it is not enough, in order to understand sentences in a given language, to be master of a practice'. Merely uttering sentences appropriate in a given context would not guarantee that one understood what one was saying. One needs some 'inchoate conception of what gives them significance and determines their content', which seems to be a matter of inner thought. Some practices of using sentences would have the consequence that we could not understand them, and so they could not have a meaning—however uniform a community's practice in using them. See *The Logical Basis of Metaphysics* (Duckworth, 1991), 207–8 and 106.

in part from observation, and this gives content to our understanding of other non-observable properties. The nominalist's claim that truths of logic are truths about human language is thus to be understood as the claim that they are truths not just about our intra-linguistic practices of minimal entailment, but also of our practices of using words to designate properties (and by means thereof substances) in the world in certain ways. We use them to designate properties which are constituted as the properties they are in part by which other properties they recognizably include (or exclude). If we have a name for those other properties, then it is the fact of which observable properties we designate by our words which leads us without further linguistic training to our agreements about minimal entailments.

Our language comes to us with a web of interconnections and practices of use so that we can fit it on to the world in such a way that use of one sentence to describe one aspect of experience will license use of others to describe other aspects; but that does not arise because of logically necessary connections that exist outside language, but because the logical connections within language ensure that the sentence would not be correctly applied unless the other sentences were also applicable.

A proposition is necessary if the negation of a sentence which expresses that proposition entails a self-contradiction. Since entailment between sentences is a notion that I have analysed in terms of the linguistic behaviour of humans, the logical necessity of a proposition is similarly reducible. We may utter a sentence which seems to describe a way things might be—'There is a greatest prime number,' 'There is an event which occurred earlier than its cause.' But a true logic will reveal all the consequences of these sentences; and someone who knew that logic and drew all those consequences would, I believe, reach an explicit self-contradiction (in the way for which, for the second sentence, I sketched the outline in the previous chapter). We may describe this situation by saying that although it is prima facie conceivable that these sentences be true, it is not ultimately conceivable; they only make initial sense. They do not make *ultimate sense*. The only facts which lead to our ascribing necessity to the proposition expressed by the sentence, 'All causes precede their effects,' are facts about language—the words of the cited English language sentence and words of sentences translated into it from other languages—in consequence of which the negation of the cited sentence has no ultimate sense. Hence the cited sentence is compatible with everything non-linguistic.

What, finally, of the logical necessity of statements? Here I bring in my earlier qualification to the claim that necessary truth is mere linguistic truth—some facts about the referential context in which the sentence is uttered may also play a role in determining whether a token sentence expresses a necessary truth. But these facts, I must add, are perfectly ordinary facts in the sense that a world can be described in which any or all of them do not hold by propositions which entail no self-contradiction. A statement is necessary 'in the broadly logical sense', it will be recalled, if it is true in every world of which it is the case that every true proposition which describes that world entails no self-contradiction—or, more simply if we dispense with the notion of possible worlds, if some sentence which expresses the negation of that statement expresses a proposition which entails a self-contradiction. Thus whether 'Hesperus is Phosphorus' expresses a necessary statement is a matter of whether it expresses the same statement as 'Hesperus is Hesperus'. That depends on the conventions of the English language—that 'Hesperus' and 'Phosphorus' are names and 'is' has the linguistic role (among other roles) of asserting identity—and secondly on facts about the referential context. The relevant facts about referential context are of two kinds—first, conventions about the use of names, which are linguistic conventions in a wide sense (not conventions which one needs to know to know a language, but local conventions for using the language); and secondly, non-linguistic facts about which individuals there are in the context. The facts about referential context which determine that 'Hesperus is Phosphorus', uttered by a seventeenth-century astronomer, express a necessarily true statement are that 'Hesperus' is the name of the planet that appears in the western sky somewhat after sunset, and 'Phosphorus' is the name of the planet that appears in the eastern sky somewhat before sunrise; and that whatever planet does appear in the western sky after sunset is the same planet as appears in the eastern sky before sunrise. The latter fact, as also the linguistic facts (in the narrow and wide senses), are perfectly ordinary facts in the sense that a world can be described in which any or all of them do not hold by propositions which entail no self-contradiction. 'Hesperus' could be used in quite different ways from the ways in which it is used, and there is no necessity that whatever planet appears in the evening sky should also appear in the morning sky. Yet these facts together ensure that a token sentence, 'Hesperus is not Phosphorus,' can only be true if a self-contradictory sentence, 'Hesperus is not Hesperus,' is true. It follows that the conceivability of 'Hesperus is not Phosphorus,' is only prima facie. It is not conceivable by someone who begins to fill out (via understanding of linguistic conventions and the referential context) what a world would be like in which it was true, and so I shall say that it does not make ultimate sense. 'Hesperus is Phosphorus' is true because its negation does not make ultimate sense.

What goes for 'Hesperus is Phosphorus' goes generally. All that determines whether a sentence expresses a necessary statement are ordinary facts about linguistic use and referential context. Suppose —to take a new example—that one uses 'Bloggs' as the name of whatever (animate being or material object) is causing the noise upstairs. As a matter of fact Bloggs is a cement mixer, and since a cement mixer could not ever be anything but a material object, 'Bloggs is a material object' expresses a necessary truth. Mere knowledge of the language, and even of the local conventions of reference, will not determine this. But a further ordinary fact will do so—that the one and only object making a noise upstairs is a cement mixer.[8] But someone ignorant of this latter fact might not know whether 'Bloggs is a material object' expresses a necessary truth.

Which logical relations hold between propositions and which propositions and statements are necessary—when those propositions and statements are picked out as whatever is expressed by some sentence of human language—is a matter of human linguistic behaviour, as well as, sometimes, ordinary facts about the referential context. If we understand logical nominalism in the wider sense that logical relations and necessary truths are matters of *nomina* (words) together with the context in which they are used, it looks as if nominalism can describe all the facts of public language for which Platonism seeks to introduce the notions of proposition,

---

[8] The necessity of a statement, in my terminology, is more or less the same as what many philosophers call necessity *de re*—since it arises in part from the particular objects (*res*) which are picked out by referring expressions in the particular referential context; and the necessity of a proposition, in my terminology is more or less the same as what many philosophers call necessity *de dicto*, since it arises solely from linguistic considerations (*dictum* = what is said).

statement, and timeless logical necessity governing their relations. So why postulate the latter? The empirical scientist postulates unobservables to explain observable data by giving their causes; but that is not what is going on here. What explains human linguistic behaviour is facts about humans and their minds or brains—it is not propositions that cause sentences to be uttered, in the way that photons cause spots on photographic plates. It is hard to resist the conclusion that propositions etc. are convenient fictions, covenient for summarizing the relations of token sentences to each other—to say that there is a proposition which two sentences express is just to say that it is *as if* there is a common thing which each express, and so on. Logic, on this view, does not govern the relations of timeless entities to each other, but concerns only the relations of public sentences to each other. It codifies the rules for which sentences commit their utterer to which other sentences, it binds together a packet of sentences to which a speaker is committed by a given sentence. Logic is thus concerned with human behaviour— a matter of psychology; not of how we reason casually, but of which minimal entailments we would publicly recognize if pushed.

'It is logically necessary that', like 'it is true that', or 'it is a fact that', is an operator that governs sentences. Putting such an operator in front of the sentence tells us something about the sentence—for example, that it is true (or corresponds to the facts). From that something we can deduce a conclusion about the world. From 'It is true that my desk is brown,' we can deduce 'My desk is brown.' From 'It is logically necessary that if a stone is red it is coloured,' we can conclude 'If a stone is red, it is coloured.' And we can also conclude something about another sentence, 'There is a red stone which is not coloured,' not merely that it is false but that it cannot be true, because it does not make ultimate sense. But logic puts no limit on nature, only on which descriptions of it make ultimate sense.[9]

Once we think in this way, we are deprived of a misleading picture—of the truths of logic as existing independently of speakers and thinkers and somehow constraining what they can do (as opposed to what they can coherently say). Alas, we feel, if only it were not for the hard rules of logic by which we are bound, we

---

[9] See Additional Note 7.

could be monogamously married to two wives at once, change the past, and discover or perhaps create the greatest prime number. The true state of affairs is that there are sentences that seem to us to describe a way things might be, but do not really. Even though we may not appreciate their ultimate incoherence, an omniscient being who saw all the entailments of sentences, and the properties of objects to which referring expressions referred, would appreciate that ultimate incoherence, and not be tempted to suppose that 'a lack of ability to change the past' designated a weakness in an agent, any more than does 'a lack of ability to open and shut a door at the same time', with respect to which neither he nor we can make sense of what it would be like for an agent to have a property designated by it.

The arguments which I have given in earlier chapters to show that certain states of affairs (or statements or propositions) are logically necessary or possible or impossible are really arguments to show that certain sentences are such that they or their negations do or do not make ultimate sense. I have used the Platonist fiction of statements and propositions, and attributed logical categories to nature rather than to talk about it, simply for convenience of exposition; and I shall continue to do so again for the rest of this chapter and in subsequent chapters. But I would ask the reader to bear in mind the true character of such talk. However, it will not always have been clear in earlier chapters whether in talking about logical necessity etc. I was talking in effect about the necessity etc. of a statement or of a proposition, since I did not then have those distinctions available. Most of the necessities etc. to which I argued were ones to which I argued on the basis of mere conceptual considerations, and thus concerned the necessities etc. of propositions and so of the states of affairs which they described. But in two cases the issue involved the nature of the particular individuals picked out by referring expressions, and so the necessities of statements. The first of these concerned whether two material objects (e.g. iron spheres) of our universe could (it is logically possible for them to) have all the same properties as each other; and so whether the material objects of our universe have thisness (see pp. 37–39 and Additional Note 2). The second concerned whether two human persons of our universe (including the one picked out by 'I') could have all the same properties as each other (see pp. 39–40) and could

exist without bodies (see pp. 21–2 and p. 41) In each case the argument alluded to the natures of those individuals in so far as we
could grasp them. I pointed out (p. 41) that we had a mere external
awareness of the nature of material objects, and so could have misunderstood that; but that our awareness of ourselves as continuing
objects of mental properties was involved in every experience that
we had, and that we had of ourselves as intimate an awareness as
we could have of anything. Hence the case for the logical necessities
etc. claimed was very strong indeed.

Other Kinds of Necessity

Necessity of the logical kind is not, however, the only kind of
necessity which there is. Distinguishing between the different kinds
of necessity was a slow process in the history of thought; and there
only developed a clear concept of the logically necessary distinct
from necessity of other kinds in the eighteenth century.

The necessary is that which must be, but the different reasons
why things must be give rise to different kinds of necessity; and I
shall now distinguish the others from logical necessity in my own
way. I shall initially speak of 'statements' as being necessary for
different reasons, in order to make the comparison to the logical
necessity which I initially attributed to statements, but I shall then
proceed to point out that (as with logical necessity) the necessity in
question belongs more ultimately to something else—only in most
of these cases, no longer sentences but extra-linguistic entities.

First, there is accidental necessity. A statement p is accidentally
necessary at a time t if and only if p is true and it is not coherent to
suppose that any agent by his action at t can make p false, although
it is coherent to suppose that at some other time an agent could
make p false. Given the logical impossibility of backward causation
for which I argued in the previous chapter, all and only true statements about the past have this kind of necessity because it is not
coherent to suppose that they can be made false by present action
(whereas it is coherent to suppose that they could at some earlier
time have been made false by action then); statements about the
future are not thus necessary.

Accidental necessity reduces quickly to logical necessity. Consider some statement accidentally necessary in AD 1995—for instance, that expressed by the sentence, 'John was born two years after the end of the First World War.' There is some proposition which determines that statement—for example, the proposition that John was born in AD 1920, such that what it describes is of logical necessity earlier than AD 1995. Hence the accidental necessity in AD 1995 of the statement in question is a matter of the logical impossibility of an agent making false some proposition which determines that statement. And that logical impossibility is a matter of there being no ultimate sense in a sentence of the form 'S in AD 1995 makes it the case that John was not born in AD 1920.' And that is because 'earlier' and 'later' are what they are in virtue of the direction of causation.[10]

Different, however, from any kind of logical necessity is natural necessity. A statement is naturally necessary if there is a full cause of that which it states to be the case. The statement expressed by 'There was a bomb explosion yesterday in Belfast,' is naturally necessary because the bomb explosion did not just happen by chance, but was caused to happen by physical causes. But natural necessity belongs more basically, not to sentences—for mere reflection on language and knowledge of which individuals are picked out by referring expressions will not reveal it—but to events which they report, and the events being naturally necessary is a matter of their being caused to occur. The naturally necessary is the fully caused. Natural necessity constrains the possibilities within the range of those which make ultimate sense. 'Physically necessary' is sometimes used synonymously with 'naturally necessary'.

---

[10] There is a very careful formal account of 'accidental necessity' by Alfred J. Freddoso, 'Accidental Necessity and Logical Determinism', *Journal of Philosophy*, 80 (1983), 257–78. Very roughly, this defines the accidentally necessary at a time t as anything logically contingent before t. On the assumption of the logical impossibility of backward causation and the logical possibility of affecting any future state of affairs by present action, such a definition will coincide in its classification with mine. I prefer my definition, however, because it makes clear why the accidentally necessary is 'necessary', without relying on the above assumption, which is philosophically contestable. Since, along with most philosophers, I believe the assumption is true—and I argued for it in Ch. 4—the two definitions are equivalent. But if the assumption were false, there would be nothing necessary about Freddoso's accidental necessity as such.

Then there is what I may call temporal necessity. For many scholastics, including Aquinas in many of his writings, angels, human souls, and stars were all necessary beings in the sense that once they exist, they will continue to exist forever in virtue of their essential powers, that is, powers that are among their essential properties (unless those powers depend on God conserving them, and he were to cease to do so). Let us therefore say that a statement *p* is temporally necessary if *p* is true and is a claim about which substances exist at some time, such that those substances will continue to exist in virtue of their essential powers for ever after the time referred to unless God were to cease to conserve those powers. Plausibly, the statement expressed by 'There is a physical universe,' is temporally necessary—whether or not there is God. Clearly this necessity also belongs primarily to something other than statements; in this case substances. Substances have it if they will go on existing unless God were to cease to cause them to continue to possess their essential powers.

And finally there are two kinds of necessity which I shall call ontological necessity and metaphysical necessity. In attributing necessity to God, many writers of the past have been attributing ultimate inevitable existence. But this can be understood in either of two ways, which I shall spell out as ontological and metaphysical necessity. I shall say that a statement is ontologically necessary if it is true and reports the occurrence of some everlasting event E, and there is no cause (active or permissive) of E. A statement is metaphysically necessary if it is true and it reports the occurrence of some everlasting event E, and there is no cause (active or permissive) of E, apart from any cause whose backwardly everlasting existence with certain properties has no cause and whose properties are such as to entail it actively or permissively causing E (either directly or through a chain of causes). The necessity in question clearly belongs in both cases primarily to the event E and only derivatively to the statement which reports it. It is basically the events reported by ontologically or metaphysically necessary statements—namely, substances always existing and having certain properties which are ontologically or metaphysically necessary.

I shall say that a substance is ontologically or metaphysically necessary if its everlasting existence is ontologically or metaphysically necessary. So a substance S is ontologically necessary if there is not at any time any cause, either active or permissive, of its everlasting existence. A substance S_1 is metaphysically necessary if either it is ontologically necessary, or it is everlasting and—if it does have a cause of its existence at least throughout some first (beginningless) period of time—then it is caused actively or permissively (directly or indirectly) by a cause S_2 whose backwardly everlasting existence has no cause, inevitably so in virtue of its properties. An everlasting substance S_1 is metaphysically necessary if—at least for some first beginningless period—it is inevitably caused by an ontologically necessary substance S_2. S_1 is also metaphysically necessary if—at least for some first beginningless period—it is inevitably caused by a substance S_2 which, like an ontologically necessary substance is uncaused and backwardly everlasting but which may cease to exist (e.g. through committing suicide).[11] S_1 is also metaphysically necessary if it exists both everlastingly 'under its own steam' and also because it is permitted—at least for some first beginningless period—to do so by another substance S_2 inevitably in virtue of S_2's properties; that is, S_1 would exist everlastingly if there were no S_2, but although S_2's concurrence is in fact necessary for S_1's existence—at least for some first beginningless period—that is inevitably given. (S_2 is then an inevitable permissive cause of S_1's everlasting existence. If permission is inevitable, that will be because reason dictates the action as the only action, not because the substance is fully caused to permit. By my definition a permissive cause is not fully caused to permit.) The caused substance exists just as inevitably at each period of everlasting time in the latter two cases as in the former, and hence is counted also as 'metaphysically necessary'.

If there were no God, and the physical universe had always existed and would always go on existing, then that universe would be ontologically necessary. For there would be no cause of its existing

---

[11]   The suggestion that an everlasting substance could have, throughout a first beginningless period of its existence, a cause of its existence might seem to fall foul of the principle of Ch. 4, which we might describe loosely as the principle that effects must be later than their causes. For something which has no beginning cannot be later than anything. But all that was and could have been proved in Ch. 4 was that any effect which *has a beginning* must begin at an instant later than its cause begins. That is quite compatible with a backwardly everlasting effect being caused. It will remain the case that for every period of the existence of any effect, and so of the existence of a caused backwardly everlasting substance, picked out by a first instant, that a cause will have acted earlier to bring that about.

at any time, neither active cause nor permissive cause. But it could still be that no part of the universe—for instance, a constituent fundamental particle—was ontologically necessary. For maybe each particle has a finite life, being caused at some time to exist by some other particle. A different possible scenario, however, is that while the whole universe is ontologically necessary, so too are some or all of its constituent particles; it might be that each of them is everlasting and not dependent for its existence on any other one. Another possible scenario is that while some particles are in this way ontologically necessary, they inevitably (because of their causal powers and liabilities) cause certain other particles to exist—the former everlastingly causing the latter everlastingly to exist. The latter would not exist unless the former caused them to exist; but the former have no choice about causing them to exist and, at each period of everlasting time, they must so cause them. In that case the latter particles would be metaphysically necessary, but only the former ones would be ontologically necessary. Particles would be metaphysically necessary even if their inevitable causation by ontologically necessary particles was indirect, i.e. they were caused to exist everlastingly by other particles which were caused to exist (with their relevant causal properties) everlastingly . . . until we get back to ontologically necessary particles. The caused particles would also be metaphysically necessary if they were caused to exist (inevitably by the ontologically necessary particles) only throughout some first (beginningless) period of time, after which they exist everlastingly 'under their own steam'. Everything ontologically necessary is of course metaphysically necessary as well.

Similarly, if there were no God, the possession by the universe of many of its properties over all time might be ontologically or metaphysically necessary. If the universe has a finite amount of energy and it is a law of nature that energy is always conserved (i.e. the constituent particles of the universe have powers and liabilities such that any energy one particle loses must be gained by another and any energy one particle gains must be lost by another), the universe having just the amount of energy it does throughout its existence would be ontologically necessary.

Why call ultimacy of either of these kinds a species of necessity? Partly for historical reasons. I think that most theistic writers have wished to attribute ontological necessity to God and have done so by the use of the word 'necessary'; others, for reasons I will come to in Chapter 8, have wished to attribute only 'metaphysical necessity' to what is in some sense God and again have used the word 'necessary' for this purpose. And partly because if something is ultimate in either of these ways, then it is, as it were, the unalterable nature of reality to be everlastingly thus; nothing could make it ever any other way.

These two kinds of necessity seem to me rival candidates for ultimate necessity. One might think that the ontologically necessary was the most ultimate kind of necessity. For it is as it is, uncaused. But if the ontologically necessary (or anything else backwardly everlasting and uncaused) inevitably (because of its own nature) causes something else everlasting, the something else occurs just as inevitably as the ontologically necessary; and so seems equally necessary. Hence anything metaphysically necessary may seem equally ultimate.

Neither the naturally necessary nor the temporally necessary are, as such, as inevitable as the ontologically necessary. What is naturally necessary depends on the cause which naturally necessitates it, and that cause may not have to act; it may act without reason or natural liability constraining it to act. And what is temporally necessary may be so only because God chooses that it shall be (and his nature does not require him so to choose).

The central metaphysical question is which, if any, substances and their properties are ontologically or metaphysically necessary. Which, if any, is the substance or collection of substances that exist everlastingly and have no cause of their existence but which cause all other things; and which are the properties that they possess everlastingly without being caused to do so? And which substances exist everlastingly, and are inevitably caused to exist by something which has no cause, and which are the properties that they are caused to possess everlastingly? For example—is the universe itself with all its essential and many of its other properties ontologically necessary, or does it depend on God or gods for its existence, and if so, do they depend on yet other things? If the universe exists everlastingly, but is caused to do so by a God who depends on nothing else and who has no option but to cause it, then the universe would be a metaphysically necessary substance; God would be ontologically necessary and so too would the substance consisting of God plus the universe. But if the universe is caused to exist by a God acting by a choice which is not inevitable, then whether or not it exists everlastingly, it is neither ontologically nor metaphysically necessary.

I have argued elsewhere[12] that the principles of rational explanation implicit in science, history, and other branches of empirical inquiry suggest that complex things probably have simple things as their causes, and simple things probably have no causes. These principles suggest (to use my present terminology) that our complex physical universe is probably caused, and that a God, being the simplest possible cause of the universe, probably does intentionally cause the existence of the universe (at every period of its existence) by a choice which is not inevitable. I am not going to argue all these points again here. What, rather, I shall seek to do in Part II is to describe what the hypothesis that there is a God (of roughly the kind postulated by Western religion—Christianity, Judaism, and Islam) amounts to, when set out in the metaphysical categories of Part I. I shall inquire what is the simplest such God there could be—in particular would he be ontologically or only metaphysically necessary? And I shall go on to consider what follows for the Christian doctrines of the Trinity and the Incarnation.

[12] *The Existence of God* (Clarendon Press, 1979).

PART II

Theology

6

Divine Properties

How is the claim that there is a God to be understood? I suggest—
provisionally—in this way: there exists necessarily and eternally a
person essentially bodiless, omnipresent, creator and sustainer of
any universe there may be, perfectly free, omnipotent, omniscient,
perfectly good, and a source of moral obligation. The claim that
the person 'necessarily' has the properties of being essentially bodiless, omnipresent, etc., is to be read as the claim that these properties
are inseparable from him; if he were to cease to be omniscient or
whatever, he would cease to exist. The nature of the 'inseparability'
will be considered in Chapter 7. An individual of the kind defined
I shall call a divine individual or a God.[1] The claim that there is a
God is to be read as the claim that there is at least one divine individual; whether there could be more than one such individual is an
issue to be resolved in Chapter 8. On the provisional assumption
that there is only one such individual, I shall however refer to him
as 'God'; 'God' will be used in the next two chapters as the name
of the individual who is a God (except in those places where I touch
on the question of whether there is more than one divine individual).
The English language, unfortunately, does not today possess a

[1] There is one difference between the list of predicates designating divine properties which I give here and that in *The Coherence of Theism* (Clarendon Press, 1977),
where I wrote of God being 'without a body'. I did not there wish to rule out God's
temporary acquisition of a body in a certain sense which I shall elucidate shortly;
and hence I write here instead of God's being 'essentially bodiless'. In *The Coherence
of Theism* I called an individual who has the listed divine properties eternally (whether
necessarily or not) a 'personal ground of being' and I contrasted such an individual
with a 'divine individual' who could have the properties at one time without having
them eternally. However, as I say briefly in one or two places in this book and said
at somewhat greater length in *The Existence of God* (Clarendon Press, 1979), ch. 5,
the hypothesis of the existence of a being who has the listed properties eternally and
in some sense necessarily is simpler than rival hypotheses and for that reason more
likely to be true. So I am not exploring in this book in any great detail the consequences of a hypothesis of the existence of an individual who has the divine properties
at one time and only contingently. Hence I do not make a contrast between a 'divine
individual' and a 'personal ground of being'; and so my definition here of 'divine
individual' differs from that of *The Coherence of Theism*.

pronoun suitable for referring to persons without seeming to beg questions about their gender. As the pronoun 'he' has been used in the past for making reference to a person without seeming to beg questions about their gender, and 'she' has never been used in this way, I shall use the pronoun 'he' to refer to any divine individual, with the implication that that individual is a person but without the implication that the individual is male.

Why my list of essential divine properties rather than any other? For two reasons. First, because although there have been different ways of spelling out what each of these properties amounts to, that these are the essential properties of God has, with minor exceptions, been a central view of Western religion—Christianity, Judaism, and Islam. Christianity has for two thousand years taught that God is something like this; any evidence that Christianity (or Judaism or Islam) is a revealed religion[2] is evidence in favour of this teaching about God. Secondly, as I shall be arguing in the next chapter, on certain understandings of the divine predicates (i.e. the predicates such as 'omnipotent', 'omniscient', etc.), they fit together so as together to designate one simple property of having (necessarily) pure, limitless, intentional power. Simplicity is evidence of truth. If the divine predicates all fit together, the claim that there is a God becomes a very simple claim and for that reason much more likely to be true;[3] it is not the claim of the coinstantiation of an *ad hoc* jumble of predicates.

In this chapter I give a brief account of the divine predicates,[4] and where there is considerable controversy over how they are to be understood, I give my reason for a preferred understanding. The reason will normally be that—given the arguments of Part I— only if they are so understood, will the claim that there is a God be coherent.

A Person

That God is personal in the sense of having beliefs (of a certain complexity) and being able to perform intentional actions (of a

[2] For discussion of this evidence, see my *Revelation* (Clarendon Press, 1992).
[3] The arguments to the existence of God which I examined in *The Existence of God* are all arguments to the existence of a being having pure limitless intentional power in the sense that I shall analyse in Ch. 7.
[4] For a far fuller discussion of how the divine predicates are to be understood, with historical references to how they have been understood, see *The Coherence of Theism*, esp. pt. 2.

certain complexity) is the common understanding of Western religion. Theologians have, however, often objected to the suggestion that God is *a* person. The objections are of two different kinds. First there is the objection of Christian Trinitarianism that God is 'three persons in one substance'. I will come to this issue in Chapter 8; meanwhile, I re-emphasize that my assumption that there is only one divine individual is merely a provisional one. The other kind of objection is that God is too ultimate and different from us to be regarded as a person when each of us humans is also a person. But if the objector is prepared to allow that there is enough similarity between God and human persons for both to be called 'personal', it is hard to see how that could be unless God, like human persons, is a person; after all he is both personal and different from us. What I think the objector is suggesting is that God is not individuated, that is, constituted this person rather than that, in the same kind of way as human persons are, that is, God does not have thisness. Whether God has thisness is a crucial issue to which I shall come in Chapter 7. Merely by speaking of God as a person, I do not presuppose that God has thisness.

Essentially Bodiless and Omnipresent

By saying that God is essentially bodiless, I mean that, although he may sometimes have a body, he is not dependent on his body in any way. We need our bodies in order to exist—barring divine intervention to keep us in being after the destruction of our bodies—and we need them in order to learn about the world and to make a difference to it. Only by stimuli landing on our sense organs do we learn what is happening elsewhere in the world; and only by moving our limbs and other organs can we causally affect the world. God, Western religion universally holds, does not need a body for these or any other purposes. God is thus (in my terminology) a soul, for whose existence and operation no body is even causally necessary. He is omnipresent in the sense of being able to act intentionally anywhere without intermediary (he can act directly on the world in the way that we can act directly on our brains) and knowing what is happening everywhere without intermediary (he just knows what is happening at any place in the way we know the contents of our visual field).

Creator and Sustainer

God is the creator and sustainer of any universe there may be in the sense that any substance that exists apart from himself exists because God causes it to exist as long as it exists or permits some other being to do so; and if it began to exist at a time, it did so because God caused it to begin to exist or permitted some other being so to do. If the universe (of substances other than God) had a beginning, God caused that beginning; and if it has always existed, God continually sustains it in being.[5] Likewise substances have the properties, including their causal powers and liabilities, that they do because God keeps them in being having those properties, or allows some other being to do so. Laws of nature, that is, mundane substances having the causal powers and liabilities that they do, operate because God causes them to operate (or allows some other being to do so). Henceforward I abbreviate 'creator and sustainer of any universe there may be' to 'creator of all'.

Perfectly Free

God is perfectly free in that nothing—and that again, given the results of Chapter 3, means no substance—acts from without on him to determine or in any way influence how he will act; nor does he act at one period of time so as causally to influence how he himself will act at another. For, if he did so act, he would not be perfectly free at the next period, and given that, as I shall be arguing shortly, the divine properties belong essentially to God, that would involve depriving himself of a property essential to him—and that is logically impossible. He chooses there and then how he will act at each moment, that is, over each period of time. God is guided by rational considerations alone. But such guidance, as we saw in Chapter 3, may leave available to an agent a multitude of different possible acts—and nothing determines which of them God will do.

---

[5] God's 'continual sustaining' of the universe is to be read in the way indicated in Ch. 4 n. 19. God is performing an action all the time the universe exists, such that if you were to make any arbitrary cut in his action, any segment of the action ending at the cut causes every segment of the event of the existence of the universe beginning later than the beginning of the segment and ending at the instant of the cut.

Omnipotent

God is omnipotent in that whatever he chooses to do, he succeeds in doing. This has sometimes[6] been understood as involving a claim that God can do the logically impossible. However, given the results of Chapter 5, that is a senseless claim. God can do anything, that is, any action. The only actions that we can coherently describe him doing are those that we can describe by descriptions which make ultimate sense. We may rightly say of God that there are certain things which, for reasons of logic, he cannot do—for instance, change the past, or make something red and green all over. But, despite appearances, we are not describing a limit to God's power; we are saying that certain sentences—for example, 'God changes the past,' —do not make ultimate sense; or that certain thoughts—for example, that God changes the past—contain implicit contradictions. We cannot coherently describe publicly or think privately some action which the rules of logic prevent God from doing—for our sentences and our thoughts which purport to do so prove incoherent and we fail to describe or think anything; there is nothing which would count as changing the past. Some of us may, however, be subject to confusion on this point. We may suppose that 'God changes the past' does make ultimate sense; yet, not seeing how it could be that God changes the past, suppose that there is something more ultimate than God—for instance, the laws of logic—which prevent God from so acting. God, however, being omniscient, will not be subject to confusion on these matters. He sees the consequences of all sentences; and thus sees which do and which do not make ultimate sense (and which thoughts do and which do not involve contradictions).

---

[6] For example, by Descartes. See Descartes, letter to Mersenne, section trans. in E. Anscombe and P. T. Geach (eds.), *Descartes: Philosophical Writings* (Nelson's University Paperbacks, 1954), 263: 'Not even the so-called eternal truths, like *a whole is greater than its part* would be truths, if God had not established things so.' And: 'Again, you ask what made it necessary for God to create these truths. What I say is that God was just as much free to make it untrue that all straight lines drawn from the centre to circumference are equal, as he was not to create the world. And certainly these truths are not necessarily conjoined with God's essence any more than other creatures are' (p. 262). Sometimes Descartes does talk about the truths of logic and mathematics as 'necessary', but it must be 'necessity' in a weak sense which they have if God could freely have made them not to hold. For a defence of Descartes's view see D. Goldstick, 'Could God Make a Contradiction True?', *Religious Studies*, 26 (1990), 377–87. A. Plantinga calls Descartes's view 'universal possibilism', in *Does God have a Nature?* (Marquette University Press, 1980), 92–126.

Hence if a sentence does make ultimate sense, he will be able to bring about what it describes, and if it does not it will not describe any action God cannot do, because there is nothing which would count as such an action. Similarly with respect to God's thoughts. In thinking each thought, he sees its consequences. In this way all God's thoughts are explicit; he does not have partial thoughts, but thinks his thoughts and all their consequences together.[7] Hence he cannot conceive as a possible action one which involves a self-contradiction, for, as I argued in Additional Note 7, it is not possible to suppose true an explicit contradiction. So, whatever God can conceive, he can bring about.

Omniscient

God's omniscience has usually been understood as his knowledge of all true 'propositions'. Given my distinction between proposition and statement, how is that to be understood? Not merely as knowledge of all true statements. God could know all true statements if he knew of each period of time picked out non-indexically, namely, by its date or its temporal relation to a named event, what happens (i.e. happened, is happening, or will happen) then. He could know that Jerusalem falls in 587 BC, that Charlemagne is crowned in AD 800, and that Japan surrenders three months after Germany surrenders at the end of the Second World War. Such knowledge would be knowledge of what McTaggart famously called the B-series of events.[8] But God could know all true statements without knowing whether the events they report are past or future. To know that, he needs to know what is happening or what is the date now. To know that, he needs to know at least one true proposition which says that—for example, that expressed by the sentence 'It is now AD 1994' (and not merely some proposition which determines the same statement—for example, that expressed by the sentence 'In AD 1994 it is AD 1994').

So should we not construe divine omniscience as knowledge of all true propositions? But then, as we saw in Chapter 5, there are

---

[7] 'He sees everything at once and not successively', Aquinas, *Summa theologiae*, 1a. 14. 7.

[8] J. M. E. McTaggart, *The Nature of Existence* (Cambridge University Press, 1927), ii. ch. 33.

propositions which are only true at certain times, or if entertained by certain persons. The proposition expressed by 'It is raining,' is only true at certain times; and the proposition expressed by 'I am a mere human person,' is only true if entertained by certain persons; and the proposition, 'I am now in hospital,' is only true if entertained by certain persons at certain times. Since one can only know what is true, God's omniscience must be construed at most as: he knows at each period of time all those propositions which it is logically possible that he entertain then and which if entertained by him then are true.

A further restriction on divine omniscience is suggested by the difficulty otherwise of reconciling divine omniscience and human freedom. For if humans are sometimes free in the sense that sometimes their choice at a time as to how they will act is not determined by any prior cause (nor does reason make it inevitable how they will act), then they are sometimes in a position to make false any belief that some person has about how they will act. Whatever proposition I believe in advance about what you will do, if you act freely in this sense, you have it in your power to make my belief false. Hence no one can be guaranteed to have true beliefs in advance about the actions of free agents. So, even if someone does always have true beliefs that are justified in such a way as to amount to knowledge[9] about what such agents will do, that can be no more than a lucky accident. So there cannot be a necessarily omniscient being existing at the same time as some free agent, if 'omniscient' is construed as 'knowing all true propositions'. And the same applies if it is construed in the more limited way proposed at the end of the last paragraph.

There are various ways of attempting to avoid this difficulty. The most usual one is to claim that God does not exist before free agents, because God does not exist in time. I shall come shortly to

[9] Knowledge is generally, and surely, correctly thought to involve true belief. If S knows that p, then p and S believes that p. Philosophers differ about what else is necessary for true belief to amount to knowledge—some think that either the belief has to be justified by other beliefs or it has to be a belief of a special kind, a 'properly basic belief' (such as a belief about the contents of one's present experiences); other philosophers think that it has to be caused in a certain kind of way. Nothing for our purposes turns on which of such views is correct. The argument in the text to the incompatibility of divine omniscience and human freedom, construed in the stated ways, is due classically to Nelson Pike, 'Divine Omniscience and Voluntary Action', *Philosophical Review*, 74 (1964), 27–46.

discuss and reject the view that God does not exist in time.[10] Another
way out is to deny that humans are ever free in the stated sense. I
think that this way out would make a nonsense of human responsibility for our actions, and so of those Christian doctrines which
involve the view that humans are responsible for their actions.[11]
Anyway, it would not resolve the similar problem of the compat-
ibility of God's omniscience with his own future free actions (in
those cases where reason does not make it inevitable how he will
act). Another way out is to claim that there is backward causation
—the agent's actions cause God's earlier beliefs; so, just as God
seeing what we do after we act does not make our actions less free,
no more does God seeing what we do before we act—in each case
we act freely and God's beliefs are as they are because of how
we have acted. The argument of the last paragraph assumed that
human actions had no effect on earlier divine beliefs, and so could
vary without the divine belief varying. I have, however, already
argued against the possibility of backward causation in Chapter 4.
Somewhat similar to the 'backward causation' defence is the defence
that God's beliefs today about what I will do tomorrow are not
'hard facts' about today. A 'hard fact' about a certain time is a fact,
all of whose truth-conditions, the states of affairs which make it a
fact, are states of affairs at that time. A 'soft fact' about a certain
time, by contrast, is a fact whose truth-conditions are (at least in
part) states of affairs at some other time. It being my birthday
today is not a hard fact about today, because what makes it true is
what happened many years ago, my being born then on a certain
day. *The Times* having the correct prediction today about who
will win tomorrow's Derby is not a hard fact about today, because
whether it has a correct prediction today depends on (i.e. is constituted by) what happens tomorrow. Similarly, the suggestion
goes,[12] while my having a certain belief today about what will
happen tomorrow is a hard fact about today, God's having a certain
belief today about what will happen tomorrow is not—it is a soft
fact, because God's beliefs about tomorrow are the beliefs they are
in virtue of what happens tomorrow. That, however, seems to me
to empty of all content the notion that God has a 'belief' today

---

[10] Even if God were outside time, there would still be a difficulty in reconciling his
omniscience with human freedom. See David Widerker, 'A Problem for the Eternity
Solution', *International Journal for Philosophy of Religion*, 29 (1991), 87–95.

[11] On this see my *Responsibility and Atonement* (Clarendon Press, 1989), *passim.*

[12] For a modern defence of this view, which was that of William of Ockham, see
A. Plantinga, 'On Ockham's Way Out', *Faith and Philosophy*, 3 (1986), 235–69.

about what will happen tomorrow. Of course whether the belief is true depends on what happens tomorrow, but what the belief is does not. Finally, there is the defence of denying that there is such a thing as a truth about what a free agent will do before he does it; all propositions about what a free agent will do—or perhaps all propositions about any future state of affairs—are only true or false after the future date in question. Our ordinary understanding, however, of what it is for a sentence, and so whatever proposition it expresses, to be true, does not have that consequence. Ordinarily we think that if I say today that you will cut the lawn tomorrow, and tomorrow you cut the lawn, then what I said today was true; was true then, not became true tomorrow—although what made it true today is what was going to happen tomorrow. 'Proposition' is, however, a philosopher's technical term, and we could put a restriction on the definition given in Chapter 5, such that a proposition is never true until after the occurrence of the event it reports (at any rate if that event is a free action). In that case God's omniscience would be so construed as not to conflict with human freedom; God does not know infallibly what we will do until we do it, when our actions are free.

Yet, although 'proposition' is a philosopher's technical term, 'sentence' is not; and it does seem to be a distortion of ordinary language to deny that my sentence uttered today, 'You will cut the lawn tomorrow,' could be true when uttered. And if we define 'proposition' in the way suggested in the last paragraph, it becomes a technical term that is far from capturing what a sentence, as ordinarily understood, expresses. However, that solution seems to be on the right lines in its basic intuition that God does not have essential knowledge of future human free actions. But it seems to me more satisfactory to say that explicitly and so to define God's omniscience accordingly, not as knowledge at each period of time, of all true propositions, but as knowledge of all propositions that it is logically possible that he entertain then and that, if entertained by God then, are true, and that it is logically possible for God to know then without the possibility of error. Of course, given God's omnipotence, that there are free agents other than God arises only from God's free choice; and so therefore do the limits to God's knowledge that the existence of these agents involves.[13]

---

[13] The extent to which humans having free will in the stated sense limits the predictability of their actions, even by other humans, is fairly small. On this see my *The Evolution of the Soul* (Clarendon Press, 1986), 259–61.

However, God being necessarily and eternally perfectly free does place a much larger limit on God's omniscience than the limit concerned with future human free actions on which I have concentrated so far. God, if he is necessarily and eternally perfectly free, must be ignorant of his own future actions—except in so far as his perfect goodness (see below) constrains him to act in certain ways. And since he is omnipotent, and thus able to make any difference he chooses to the future, he must in general be ignorant of that future. With the exception noted, God's omniscience concerns the past (the causally unaffectible), his omnipotence the future (the causally affectible).

The alternative to understanding divine omniscience in a restricted way so as to maintain God's perfect freedom over the future, is to understand his perfect freedom over the future in a restricted way so as to maintain God's omniscience. But if God's omniscience is to include foreknowledge of his future actions, there would seem no reason to confine that foreknowledge merely to foreknowledge of some such actions; and if it included all God's future actions, he would have no freedom left. If at any time God does have perfect freedom, then always prior to that God will have been ignorant of how he will act. To leave God with any freedom at any time, God's omniscience must be understood in a restricted way. The obvious natural restriction that God is ever ignorant of how he will act, except when rational considerations, that is, his perfect goodness, require him to act in a certain way, has the consequence that, since in virtue of God's omnipotence the whole future of everything depends on God (including whether there are any free human beings after the present instant), his ignorance of the future must be vast—confined only to what his perfect goodness requires him to bring about. That ignorance does not diminish his greatness, since it arises from the greatness of his power over the future.

Perfectly Good

God is perfectly good. Taking each conjunction of actions which an agent can do simultaneously as one action, then—I claimed in Chapter 3—a perfectly good being will do (among the actions that he can do) no action which is overall a bad action (any bad aspects will have to be counterbalanced by good aspects); if there is a best action, he will do it; or, if there are alternative equal best actions, he will do one of them. But often the range of actions open to God is an infinite range of actions, each of which is inferior to some other action. Thus for any world of conscious agents which God could create *ex nihilo*, there is, plausibly, a better one—for instance, one obtained by adding one more conscious agent (sufficiently distant from the others not to crowd them). And so among the actions of creating conscious agents *ex nihilo* there is no best. What goes for conscious agents goes also for creating inanimate things *ex nihilo*. And no doubt, though I do not need to argue this here, for much else too, for the kinds of knowledge and powers he gives to things and for the length of days he keeps them in being. But where there is a best kind of action even if no best action of that kind, God's perfect goodness will lead to his doing some action of that best kind; for here is a maximum that can be attained, and so, as I argued in Chapter 3, a perfectly good being will attain it. Thus, suppose that the only actions open to God are actions of creating inanimate things, and actions of creating conscious agents (with or without inanimate things as well). There are an infinite number of possible actions in each category, but, plausibly, any action in the latter category is better than any action in the former category and better for a kind of reason—for instance, that it is not merely an act of creating but an act of creating an agent who himself can intentionally make a difference to things—which applies to all actions in the latter category and none in the former. And suppose that the difference among actions in the latter category is a purely quantitative one—the number of agents created. In that case, I suggest, there is overriding reason to do an action in the latter category; and so a perfectly good being will do one. In so far, then, as there is a best act, or an equal best act, or a best kind of act, God by his very nature will do it or one of them (as applicable), and his so doing we may call an act of essence; it follows from his nature. In so far as he acts within that framework, his perfect goodness does not dictate what he will do; and any acts within the framework we may call acts of will. In the example cited, God's perfect goodness does not dictate how many conscious agents he will create. God's perfect goodness is a matter of his doing all acts of essence and no overall bad act. Because God's goodness thus limits his capacity for choice, there will be many things which God can do, in the sense that he will do them if he chooses; but which he cannot choose to do. I shall say that he can do such things in the compatibilist sense of power, but not in the absolute sense of power.

It is obligatory to keep one's promises, and unless one has been foolish enough to make incompatible promises or to promise to do something one is obliged not to do (or unlucky enough to have made a promise incompatible with doing some very important act which one had not foreseen that one might have the opportunity to do), it will always be the best act in some situation to keep one's promises. God, being perfectly good and omniscient (and knowing which acts he might have the opportunity to do), will not make promises of these types, and for him therefore it will always be the best act to keep his promises. God can restrict his future freedom of action and extend his knowledge of the future by promising that he will act in a certain way in the future. This restriction is not a causal restriction; but by a past act God makes available to himself in future the possible actions of keeping or breaking a promise, and reason then dictates how he will act. However, since, as I shall argue more fully in Chapter 8, it is a best kind of act to create other persons, God will create other persons. It would be bad if having done so he had little spontaneous interaction with them. To the extent to which God has bound himself by promise, he has limited the possibility of spontaneous interaction. Hence he will not make any promises substantially limiting his future freedom.

A Source of Moral Obligation

God is a source of moral obligation in that his commands to do actions make those actions obligatory and his forbidding actions makes it wrong to do them. There have been philosophers who have claimed that all actions which are obligatory or wrong are obligatory or wrong, as the case may be, quite independently of divine command. But that is obviously way out of line with the tradition of Western religion. It is also implausible—beneficiaries have some obligation to please their benefactors; and thus for example children have some obligation to please their parents in the ways which they have made clear by giving orders, when that obligation did not exist before the orders were given, at any rate if those parents are not mere biological parents but ones who nurture and educate them. *A fortiori*, if God has created us and sustains us in existence at every moment and so all the good things of life come to us through his agency or permission, we have some obligation to please him and so conform to his commands and forbidding. What is not too clear is the extent of that obligation. Clearly God, being perfectly good, will not command or forbid what he has no right to command or forbid (i.e. anything in respect of which we would have no duty to obey him). But what does he have a right to command? Could he command anything—for instance, rape and lying—or are there limits to his right? I suggest that the moral intuitions of most of us teach us that some actions are obligatory, such as feeding one's children, and others are wrong, for example, rape, quite independently of God's commands and God could not change their moral status. And since he could not, he would not purport to do so. He might well, however, command us to do many actions, which but for his command would not be obligatory and which his command— in virtue of his status as our supreme benefactor—would make obligatory. Similarly he might forbid actions, which but for his command would not be wrong. And also he might command us to do what was obligatory anyway, and that would make it doubly our duty to do it; and forbid what was wrong anyway, and that would make it doubly wrong to do it.[14]

Eternal

The claim that there is a God involves the claim that there exists a person of the above kind, eternally. But there are two different ways of understanding that—that he is everlasting (i.e. exists at each period of time past and time future) or that he is timeless (he exists outside time).

The simple, naïve, initial view is that God is everlasting. He determines what happens at all periods of time 'as it happens' because he exists at all periods of time. He exists now, he has existed at each period of past time, he will exist at each period of future time.

---

[14] On the extent of God's moral authority, see my *Responsibility and Atonement*, ch. 8.

This is, I believe, the view explicit or implicit in Old and New Testaments and in virtually all the writings of the Fathers of the first three centuries.

Why should any theist find that view unsatisfactory? Because it seems to make God less than sovereign over the universe. It seems to imply that time stands outside God, who is caught in its stream. The cosmic clock ticks inexorably away, and God can do nothing about it. More and more of history is becoming past, accessible to God only by remote memory, and unaffectible by any action of his. The future, however, God does not yet enjoy, but more and more of it is unavoidably looming up on God; and, as it keeps on appearing, if creatures have free will, it may contain some surprises for him. God can only act at the present period of time, and his lordship of the universe is ever confined to the time of his action.

Let us call the view of God's relation to time stated in the last paragraph, the view of 'God as time's prisoner'. That it implies these unwelcome consequences was the burden of a major neo-Platonist criticism of the view that God was everlasting—it involved too low a view of God.[15] Hence later theologians took over from neo-Platonism the view that God is outside time; he is timeless. Origen[16] had expressed that view at the beginning of the third century, but it became the normal view only with Augustine at the end of the fourth century, and was then universally taken for granted for the next millennium, and in general also assumed by most Catholic theologians for the past 500 years.

The view of God as timeless was given its classical exposition by Boethius: 'eternity is the complete possession all at once of illimitable life'.[17] Everything God knows or does is done all-at-once in a

---

[15] These criticisms are contained in Boethius, *De Consolatione philosophiae*, 5. 6. 'Whatsoever liveth in time . . . has not yet attained tomorrow, but has already lost yesterday', he wrote. He went on to claim also that divine timelessness leaves 'unrestrained the free will of mortals', and hence reward and punishment and prayer to God have a point, which, he implies, they would not if God were within time and always knew all our actions in advance. I suggested earlier that God's omniscience is to be understood in a restricted sense so as to avoid this problem.

[16] 'The phrase which we use . . . That there never was a time when [The Son] did not exist, must be accepted with a reservation. For the very words, when, or never, have a temporal significance, whereas the statements we make about The Father and The Son and The Holy Spirit must be understood as transcending all time and all ages and all eternity', Origen, *De principiis*, 4.4.1 (Latin version), trans. G. W. Butterworth (Harper & Row, 1966). For the Greek origins of the understanding of eternity as timelessness, see R. Sorabji, *Time, Creation and the Continuum* (Duckworth, 1983), ch. 8.   [17] *De Consolatione philosophiae*, 5. 6.

moment of time which has no beginning or end. Hence there are no limits to God's knowledge or action. He knows 'at once', in his eternal present, everything; but since that present is not 'before' the time of any human action he *fore*knows no human action. Hence his knowledge of that action is no more incompatible with the action being free than our observation of someone else's present action is incompatible with its being free. Likewise God can 'at once' in his eternal present choose to bring about at any moment of time any (consistently describable) state of affairs. If backward causation is impossible, that imposes no limit on God—for his 'eternal present' is later than no time of any state of affairs. We are like travellers moving along a road at the bottom of a mountain. The stages on the road are the periods of time through which we pass. We cannot see or act except at the stage at which we are. But God is like an observer standing on the mountain who can see the road (all of time) in one glance, and can cast a rock from above on to whatever stage of the road he chooses.

The results of Chapter 4 do, however, have the consequence that the 'timeless' view is incoherent, and also that to the extent that the 'everlasting' view does have the consequence that God is time's prisoner, this only arises from God's voluntary choice.

I spelled out, above, the doctrine of God's timelessness loosely in terms of his existing at a single 'moment'. The most natural reading of the tradition seems to me to read 'moment' as 'instant',[18] and in that case the doctrine is in conflict with the first principle of Chapter 4. A state of affairs must last for a period of time; it cannot occur at an instant. God cannot be omnipotent or omniscient just at an instant. However, if the 'moment' is a period, the doctrine is not open to this objection.[19] It remains open, however, to a conclusive objection from the third principle of Chapter 4: if God causes the

[18] In 'Eternity', *Journal of Philosophy*, 78 (1981), 429–56, E. Stump and N. Kretzmann claim that the 'timeless' tradition is most naturally read as holding that the divine 'moment' has duration and thus is a period (pp. 432 f.). Paul Fitzgerald, in 'Stump and Kretzmann on Time and Eternity', *Journal of Philosophy*, 82 (1985), 260–9, denies that this view can be held consistently with the rest of what Stump and Kretzmann wish to claim.

[19] Some theological accounts of God's eternity can be read as defending an even stronger view of timelessness than that of Boethius. Boethius holds that there is a moment, an eternal 'all at once' moment, at which all the divine predicates are true of God. An even stronger view holds that there is no moment at which the divine predicates are true of God—he knows, acts, etc. but there is no moment at which he knows, acts, etc. This view is also ruled out by the third principle of Ch. 4.

beginning or continuing existence of the world, and perhaps inter-feres in its operation from time to time, his acting must be prior to the effects which his action causes. Similarly, his perception of events in the world must be later than those events.[20]

So we must revert to the doctrine that God is everlasting, which we must read as claiming that God exists throughout all periods of time. I now seek to show that that doctrine does not have the con-sequence that God is time's prisoner, for the reason that although God and time exist together—God is a temporal being—those aspects of time which seem so threatening to his sovereignty only occur through his own voluntary choice. To the extent to which he is time's prisoner, he has chosen to be so. It is God, not time, who calls the shots. To show this, I ask the reader first to think of God, the temporal being, existing by himself, not having created a universe in which there are laws of nature. There would then, by the second principle of Chapter 4, be no 'cosmic clock' which ticked unstoppably away—that is, there would be no temporal intervals of any definite length. There would just be an event or sequence of events in the divine consciousness. Think of him too as the subject of just one mental event, a conscious act which does not have qualitatively distinguishable temporal parts (e.g. it does not consist of one thought followed by a different thought). Now by the first principle of Chapter 4 any event has to take some time, but there would not be a truth that this event (this act) had lasted any particular length of time rather than any other. There would be no difference between a divine act of self-awareness which lasted a millisecond and one which lasted a million years. That is hard for us to grasp, for two reasons. The first is that our conscious acts are distinguished by the different intervals of public clocks which tick away while the acts occur (and we can usually recognize roughly how long that interval is for a given act). But that difference would not be there with this divine act. The second is that any acts of ours that are qualitatively identical throughout are usually immediately followed and preceded by acts of different kinds. But that too is a contingent matter, and I am supposing otherwise with respect to this divine act.

Would there be a difference between a divine conscious act that was God's only conscious act and was qualitatively identical

[20] See Additional Note 8.

throughout, that was of finite length, and one that was of infinite length? No—so long as the former really is qualitatively identical throughout, and so contains no experience of a beginning or end. For consider a supposedly finite act—call it the SF act, which has the instants A and B as its exterior bounding instants. Compare the SF act with an act of supposedly infinite duration—call it the SID act—which will of course have no boundaries. If the SID act was of infinite duration, it would still, like the SF act, consist of an infinite number of segments, each of finite duration as can be seen if we represent the two acts geometrically by lines. We impose upon the lines some arbitrary metric (i.e. arbitrary way of measuring the lengths of segments of the lines). Take the midpoint Z of the SF line, AB, under that metric. Take any point Q on the SID-line. Divide AZ by a midpoint Y. Mark on the SID-line an interval equal in length to YZ—call it PQ. Then divide AY by a midpoint W; mark on the other line an interval KP, of the same length as PQ.

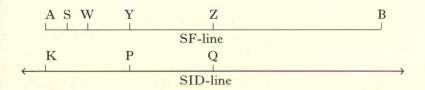

Divide the interval AW by a midpoint S. Mark on the SID-line another interval of the length of PQ corresponding to SW. Continue this process *ad infinitum*, so that for each yet smaller interval of AB, you mark on the SID-line an interval of the same length as each other length. Perform the corresponding process for the other half of the two lines. Then the two lines will have been divided in such a way that all intervals of the SF line will have been put into one–one correspondence with intervals of the SID-line. By previous arguments, there can be no difference between a segment of a divine act qualitatively identical throughout and such a segment of twice or any other finite number of times the temporal length of the former. Hence there will be no difference between a divine act qualitatively identical throughout of 'finite duration' and one of 'infinite duration'—for each consists of an infinite number of segments of indistinguishable duration.

So if God does not choose to disturb his one act of self-awareness, or whatever the one act qualitatively identical throughout is, any 'duration' for it will be the same as any other. Although such an act does not in a literal sense have its 'duration' 'all at once' in the sense of 'at a single instant', it does have the feature for which I believe timelessness-theorists were groping—that it is not qualitatively distinguishable from an act which lasted a millisecond or any period at all however small.

If God had left himself like that, the aspects of time that seem to threaten his sovereignty would not hold. There would be no cosmic clock ticking away—for there would be no laws of nature. The past would not be getting lengthier by any period of time that could be picked out, let alone measured. God would be aware of every period of the past as directly as we are of events that we have just that millisecond experienced; for in God there would be no distinction between perception and memory. God cannot affect the past—but all there would ever be to the past is his having his one divine act, that is, what he is always aware of in his own experience. Anything else could be brought about and made past in the twinkling of an eye. The future however remains under God's total control; he need not make free creatures—in which case nothing will surprise him; or anything at all—in which case nothing will loom upon him.

However, does not the fourth principle of Chapter 4 have the consequence that, even in the universe where God is the subject of just one mental event, he would ever be losing items of knowledge? For that mental event lasts for a period of time, and all periods of time contain smaller periods within them. Then, surely, at each smaller period of time God knows that he is 'now' in some state S, and although his experiential state remains experientially indistinguishable from any other state, the knowledge which it contains is different, for its 'now' refers to a different 'now'; as time moves on God no longer knows what he knew in the previous small period (i.e. in the terminology of Chapter 5, the proposition, 'I am now in state S,' determines a different statement). So would there not be more to the past than God's one present divine act, and some of it lost for ever? That might be so if knowledge occurred at instants and was about instants; but by the first principle of Chapter 4, it occurs over periods and concerns periods. But how, in the universe described, are these periods to be picked out and distinguished from other periods? The answer is, of course, that they cannot be.

In the universe described the only period to which reference can be made is the whole of time in which God is in state S, and the only period at which reference can be made is the same period. The 'now' refers to a period, of which there is no way of marking a beginning or an end—so long as change does not occur in God's experiential state or he brings about something outside himself. So time is not ever depriving God of knowledge.[21]

But God need not leave things like that, and if there is a God, he has not done so. God may choose to have a succession of qualitatively distinct mental acts, and in that case temporal order (though not a temporal metric) will have been introduced into the divine life. By bringing about some effect A, God divides time into the realm where it is not logically possible that anyone (even God) could make any difference to whether or not A occurs, and the realm where that is logically possible; and by bringing about many such effects, he creates a rich assembly of the unalterable, ever present to God by perception.

God may choose to create a universe distinct from himself, governed by laws of nature. In that case the universe will have a temporal metric. And we can date God's acts by the time at which they occur on the universe's clock. And we can even say that they last as long as those events in the universe with which they coincide. To say the latter would be a little misleading, for it would suggest that they seem as long to God as they do to us—and there is no reason to suppose that. And God may choose to create creatures with free will (as I have understood that), and in that case the universe may indeed contain the occasional surprise for God; for as I have argued earlier, no one can have essential foreknowledge of such free actions.

The unwelcome features of time—the increase of events that cannot be changed, the cosmic clock ticking away as they happen, the possibility of surprise in the future—may indeed invade God's time; but they come by invitation, not by force—and they continue for such periods of time as God chooses that they shall. So there is

---

[21] In 'Omniscience and Immutability', *Journal of Philosophy*, 63 (1966), 409–21, Norman Kretzmann argued that if God was to be omniscient at any time, he would need to know what was happening at that time; and so, as the world changed, he would need to change with it. (For Islamic thinkers who also made this point, see Sorabji, *Time, Creation and the Continuum*, 260). But Kretzmann added that 'if as a matter of fact nothing else [i.e. apart from God] ever did change, an omniscient being could of course remain immutable'. That is what I am arguing here.

no reason for the theist to object to the view that God is everlasting on the grounds that it makes God time's prisoner; and since the rival view is incoherent, he should adopt the view that God is everlasting.[22]

A Necessary Being

Finally, the claim that there is a God involves the claim that a person of the above kind exists 'necessarily'; God is a necessary being. But in what sense 'necessary'? Some philosophers have interpreted this as 'logically necessary'. In that case the claim that God is a necessary being must be read as the claim that the statement or proposition expressed by the sentence 'God exists' is logically necessary. The difference between the claim about the statement and the claim about the proposition could be quite important. The claim that the proposition is logically necessary is the claim that it is logically necessary that there be some divine individual or other (in the sense of 'divine individual' described at the beginning of the chapter), whether the one who exists or some other one. The claim that the statement is logically necessary is the claim that it is logically necessary that there exist one particular divine individual, the one who actually exists. It may be that there is no difference between these two claims—that any divine individual would be the same as any other one. We shall discuss this issue in the next chapter. But if there could be a different sole divine individual in charge of the world then the two claims differ very substantially.

However, neither claim seems to me in the least plausible, for the reason that a world without a particular substance or a particular kind of substance seems always to be a coherent supposition and to involve no contradiction; no set of propositions which describe such a world seem to entail a self-contradiction.[23] The supposition

---

[22] The view that 'God created time' (see Augustine, *Confessions*, 11. 3 and *De Civitate Dei*, 1. 6, can be intelligibly construed either in the sense that he created a temporal order of qualitatively distinct events or in the sense that he created a temporal metric.

[23] As Hume put it: 'Whatever *is* may *not be*. No negation of a fact can involve a contradiction. The non-existence of any being, without exception, is as clear and distinct an idea as its existence. The proposition, which affirms it not be, is no less conceivable and intelligible, than that which affirms it to be,' D. Hume, *An Enquiry*

of the existence of a Godless universe (either one without any divine being or one without the particular one that, I suppose, there is) seems evidently coherent, and so should be taken to be so in the absence of positive counter-argument. All ontological arguments known to me that purport to show the logical necessity of God's existence seem to me unsound.[24]

There seems to me in any case an important reason arising from within theism why—even if God were to be a logically necessary being—there could not be an ontological argument of anything like the traditional kind to show this. For such an argument proceeds from some general purported logically necessary principle and endeavours to show that it is a consequence of that principle that there is a God. It thus claims that it is because of something about God that—in virtue of that principle—he has to exist. The premises of such an ontological argument do not merely entail the existence of God, but provide a reason why he exists. The traditional version of the ontological argument is of this kind—it is, it claims, because the existent is more perfect than the non-existent that there must be a God. But God would seem less than totally supreme if he depended for his existence on something quite other than God—for instance, on such a general logically necessary principle. Such dependence would not be formally inconsistent with possession of any of the divine properties that I have discussed so far. Thus even if God depended for his existence on a logically necessary principle, he could still be omnipotent; for omnipotence is only the power to do the logically possible, and so an omnipotent being cannot be required to have the power to change or abolish general logical principles. Still, the claim that there is logically sufficient reason why God exists would seem to make God in some way less ultimate than he would otherwise be. That there are no sound ontological arguments of the traditional kind for the existence of God does not merely follow from general philosophical considerations but seems

Concerning Human Understanding, xii. pt. 3. Hume's claim, to be immediately plausible, must be regarded as concerned only with substances. The supposition of the non-existence of abstract things, such as logical relations or prime numbers, may involve contradiction—unless we suppose these to be mere fictional entities, as I have done.

[24] For discussion of ontological arguments, and grounds for their rejection see (e.g.) the extracts from Anselm, Gaunilo, Kant, Plantinga, Rowe and Haight, in L. P. Pojman (ed.), *Philosophy of Religion: An Anthology* (Wadsworth, 1987); and J. Hick, *Arguments for the Existence of God* (Macmillan, 1970), chs. 5 and 6.

better consonant with theism itself.[25] Other arguments for the existence of God do not seek to provide a reason that explains why there must be a God, but seek to provide the best explanation of other things (the universe, its orderliness, etc.) in terms of the action of God. They do not claim that there has to be a God, only that the (logically contingent) evidence shows that there is. They, unlike the ontological argument, are therefore to be welcomed by a theist.

The above argument, against the claim that 'God exists' expresses a logically necessary statement or proposition, holds whether we adopt a Platonist or a nominalist account of logical necessity.[26] However, in Chapter 5 I argued in favour of a modified nominalist account—that the necessity of the 'broadly logical kind' that is attributed to statements and propositions is ultimately a matter of human sentences and thoughts, the context in which they are had, and which other sentences and thoughts humans see them as involving. If 'God exists' were to express in some sense a logically necessary truth, this would be a matter of which human sentences and thoughts make ultimate sense. It follows that the fact that 'God exists' does not express a logically necessary truth is a fact about what can coherently be said and thought, not a deep fact about God's status in a real realm of possible worlds.

I argued, however, at the end of Chapter 5, that there were two kinds of necessity with equal claims to be the most fundamental kind of necessity—what I called there ontological necessity and what I called metaphysical necessity—and that these kinds of necessity belonged primarily to events, that is, substances existing or having certain properties everlastingly. I defined a substance as ontologically necessary if there is no cause, either active or permissive, of its everlasting existence. I defined a substance as metaphysically necessary if either it is ontologically necessary or its everlasting existence is caused (at least for some beginningless period) actively or permissively (directly or indirectly) inevitably in virtue of its properties by an uncaused and backwardly everlasting substance.

All the arguments from the physical universe to the existence of a God are arguments to the existence of one simple substance who is the terminus of explanation and forms the starting point of causal

---

[25] See Additional Note 9.   [26] See Additional Note 10.

chains, and who has the divine properties which I have discussed so far.[27] Such an individual might indeed be ontologically necessary. But it does not follow from his possession of the other divine properties that he will be. For he—let us call him G_1—may owe his everlasting existence to another individual G_2 who inevitably in virtue of his perfect goodness has to permit G_1 to exist (i.e. is permissive cause of G_1). In that case G_1 would be metaphysically necessary (he exists inevitably in virtue of the ultimate principles governing things—i.e. in virtue of G_1 and G_2) but not ontologically necessary. If there were such a G_2 as well as G_1, the simplest supposition about him would be (if this were logically possible) that he too possessed the other divine properties, and so too was metaphysically necessary. G_2 in turn could only exist because G_1 everlastingly actively caused or permitted that existence—that is, was at least the permissive cause of it, inevitably, in virtue of G_1's perfect goodness. But if we are to follow the arguments to the existence of God and suppose as simple as possible a terminus to explanation, we must suppose the G_1 to which they lead to be the active cause (at least for some first beginningless period) of all else, including G_2, who would be only the permissive cause of G_1's existence.

This mutual sustenance of G_1 and G_2 would not be causation in a circle, but a continuous act (in the sense of n. 5) whereby (to speak loosely) one keeps in being the other for the next period of time. If you were to take any arbitrary period in G_2's life; it would be actively caused or permitted by an act of G_1, beginning before that period and ending at the end of that period; and similarly for any period of G_1's life, it would be permitted by an act of G_2, beginning before that period and ending at the end of that period. To say this is not to imply that there are any distinguishable periods in G_1's or G_2's life (any more than there need be in the existence of anything sustained by the continuous act of some other substance). It is simply to elucidate the meaning of continuous creation in terms of its consequence for distinguishable periods. Because any period of causing is always earlier than any effect caused, there is no simultaneous causation and no causation in a circle.

So in this scenario there would be two metaphysically necessary substances, each with all the other divine properties, each omnipotent and so having the (compatibilist) power to annihilate the

---

[27] See my *Existence of God, passim.*

other but prevented by his goodness from choosing to do so. One would be the active cause of the other, and yet would only exist because the other everlastingly refrained from annihilating him, which he inevitably would refrain from doing. The everlasting existence of G_2 would nevertheless belong to the essence of G_2, because although it was dependent on the goodness of G_1, G_1's goodness would itself be everlastingly dependent on G_2. Although the essence of G_2 involves ceding powers, they are powers which cannot be used against him. And the same holds for G_1, *mutatis mutandis*. So—barring further problems to be explored in Chapter 8—possession of the divine properties discussed so far might not ensure ontological necessity. Hence in view of the point which I argued in the last chapter, that the metaphysically necessary is just as necessary as the ontologically necessary, I shall for the moment include as a divine property merely the property of being metaphysically necessary. I shall argue in Chapter 7 that the property of being ontologically necessary would not fit well with the other essential divine properties, unless its possession followed from those properties. In Chapter 8 we shall see whether it does follow from those properties. We shall then reach there a final conclusion about whether there can be more than one divine individual; but until then I shall continue to assume for purposes of simple exposition (unless I state otherwise), that there is just one such divine individual whom I will call God.

I suggest that in claiming that there is a God theism is claiming metaphysical necessity for the existence of the individual who is God, not just for the existence of a God. Whether there is any difference between these two claims is an issue that we shall explore in the next chapter, and it may be that any individual with the divine properties would be the same as any other. But if there is a difference, the uncaused ultimate substance who is the active cause of all else is such that nothing else can have caused there to be this divine individual rather than that one. If there is more than one divine individual, any such must exist as inevitably as does any other one, and that involves it being metaphysically necessary that that divine individual exist, not merely that a further divine individual exist.

In either case the supposition that there is a divine individual is the supposition that the divine properties are necessarily tied together in the individual who has them.[28] Without them he would not exist. How is this second 'necessary' to be read? I shall suggest in the next chapter that it is to be read as 'logically necessary'. Being omnipotent, omniscient, etc. are logically necessary for being God; they are essential properties of the individual who is God.

[28] See (e.g.) St Thomas Aquinas, *Summa theologiae*, 1a. 6. 3, 'Power, wisdom and the like which belong to other things accidentally belong [to God] essentially.' Almost every theologian who has considered the issue explicitly has held this view.

7

The Divine Nature

Pure Limitless Intentional Power

I claimed that all the essential divine properties described in the previous chapter fit neatly together. It is time to show that.

That some of the properties include others will be fairly evident. To be a person is to have beliefs (of a certain complexity) and to be able to perform intentional actions (of a certain complexity). God's being a person is therefore included in his being omniscient—knowing everything (or everything logically possible to know) includes having beliefs about everything (similarly qualified)—and omnipotent—to be omnipotent is to be able to do everything in the sense of succeeding in doing it if you choose to, and that involves intentionality. To be essentially bodiless is not to be tied down to acquiring knowledge of the world and making a difference to it through one particular chunk of matter. An omnipotent and omniscient being will not be tied down to such a mode of causality and knowledge acquisition. Being omnipotent, he can act on the world without doing so through a body and can acquire his knowledge directly. He could have a body in that if he chose he could acquire, as an additional mode of operation on the world and acquisition of knowledge about it, a body which was subject only to his will (and not to the will of a created individual) and provided beliefs only for him. But his body would give him no extra knowledge and power, and he would be able to slough it off at will. An omnipotent and omniscient being will therefore be essentially bodiless. I understand by an essentially bodiless being being omnipresent that he is able to exercise his power without intermediary at every place and that he has knowledge of what is happening at every place that does not depend on any intermediary. An omnipotent and omniscient being will have that sort of power and knowledge.

Given that the universe and we who inhabit it depend so totally on God, he will have the right to tell us to use the world that he has given us in certain ways, and his telling us will create for us the corresponding obligation. If he is perfectly good, he will not tell us to do what he does not have the right to tell us to do; and hence all that he tells us to do will be obligatory for us to do. His being a source of moral obligation thus follows his perfect goodness.

God's perfect goodness follows from his perfect freedom and his omniscience. We saw in Chapter 3 that agents always pursue the good, that is, do no actions which they believe to be overall bad, and do what they believe to be a best action (or a best kind of action) if there is one—unless they are subject to non-rational influences, desires which influence them and which they need to resist if they are to pursue the good. A perfectly free being will not be subject to such influences, and so will always pursue what he believes to be the good. An omniscient being has true beliefs about what is good. Hence an omniscient and perfectly free being will necessarily be perfectly good.

God being creator of all follows from his omnipotence. God being omnipotent, everything else that exists at some time exists because he permits it to exist at that time; and so in the sense defined, he is creator of all. And finally, a metaphysically necessary being is an eternal being in the sense of an everlasting being.

So the supposition that there is a God boils down to the supposition that there exists of metaphysical necessity a necessarily perfectly free omniscient and omnipotent individual, that is, substance. I do not think that any further reduction of one property to another is possible, on my definitions of the properties.

However, the remaining divine properties do, I now suggest, fit together in that they all follow from a very simple property which I shall call having pure, limitless, intentional power. I understand by an individual having such power, first, that all his causing is intentional; everything which he brings about he means to bring about, and hence he acts only on reason. I understand by the power being limitless that all events other than that individual existing that occur can only do so because of the current exercise of that power, either bringing them about or allowing some other substance to bring them about (i.e. as at least permissive cause of them; and all events that do not occur do not occur for that same reason). I stress in the last sentence the word 'current';[1] it belongs to such an

---

[1] In the sense defined in Ch. 6 n. 5.

individual to cause such other events so inseparably that their occurrence depends on his currently (active or permissive) sustaining power; they cannot have the independence that would be involved in their occurring now because of an earlier act of his (separated from them by an interval of time). The intentional power being limitless involves its possessor knowing which actions are logically possible and being able to choose between them; his exercise of power is not limited in consequence of any ignorance of what he can do with it. Nor is it restricted by any substance from without causally influencing how he acts. Intuitively, I suggest, this notion of limitless, intentional power of which I have spelled out various aspects is a very simple one, the maximum degree of a kind of causality (known intimately to ourselves when we perform intentional actions). It is a causality of that kind so pure, so great, and tied so essentially to one individual that no other thing can be except as dependent on it.

It follows from a substance having pure, limitless, intentional power that he is perfectly free—his power is so pure and great that nothing exerts causal influence on him to act as he does. He will be omnipotent because he can do any action, that is, any action the description of which makes ultimate sense. He will also be omniscient, for the following reason. All actions described in a way that makes ultimate sense are knowingly available to him; he knows and can do all possible actions. Since backward causation is logically impossible, that means all future-related actions. But among actions are actions picked out as the actions they are in virtue of a past-related description, that is, one which picks out the action as the action it is in virtue of what happened in the past. Thus an action of causing a major earthquake in London may be also an action of causing the first major earthquake in London; whether it is will depend on what has happened in the past. For God to know which actions described under past-related descriptions are available to him, he must know what has happened in the past. If he is to know whether the action of causing the first major earthquake in London is available to him, he must know whether there have previously been any major earthquakes in London. What goes for this example goes generally. For anything that might have happened in the past can be used in the description of a present action. There can be an action of causing the 8-trillionth collision of an electron with another electron—whether such an action is now available to God depends on whether there have already occurred 8 trillion collisions. And so on. An individual with pure limitless intentional power must know all that has happened (and for similar reasons everything else except what he will subsequently freely bring about or permit some other being to bring about). Hence he will be omniscient in the sense defined in the previous chapter.

An individual with pure, limitless, intentional power would also exist of metaphysical necessity. To start with, he would exist ever-lastingly. For suppose such an individual began to exist; then by the argument of Chapter 4 there would be a period of time before the existence of that individual. In that case how things were then, for instance, that there were no substances or that there were sub-stances, would not, given the impossibility of backward causation, be caused by that individual. In that case it would not be that all events that occur other than his existing occur, and all events that do not occur do not occur, because of the exercise of his causal power. Similarly suppose that the individual ceased to exist. Then there would be a period of time after his existence during which events would occur or not occur other than because of his currently sustaining power. Now if this individual—call him G_2—were caused to exist (at some first beginningless period of time or everlastingly) by another substance, G_1, it must be that that causation is inevitable (i.e. G_1, in virtue of its nature, cannot but cause G_2)—for otherwise the dependence of things on G_2 would be contingent on G_1 non-inevitably choosing to cause G_2; and then it would not be essen-tially tied to G_2 that no other thing could be except as dependent on him, for the universe could have continued to exist without G_2. Hence G_2 will exist of metaphysical necessity.

Just as an individual who has pure, limitless, intentional power would be a perfectly free, omnipotent, and omniscient individual existing of metaphysical necessity, so conversely any individual of the latter type would be an individual having pure, limitless, inten-tional power. There is mutual entailment, which I now demon-strate. An omniscient individual will know all the effects of his causing; hence everything that he brings about he means to bring about. As the creator of all, every substance existing or other event occurring occurs because of his currently sustaining action or per-mission. An omniscient individual knows which actions are logically possible; being perfectly free, he can (within the limits of reason) choose between them, and being omnipotent, his choices will be efficacious. If the individual exists of metaphysical necessity, he will be everlasting and so this will always be so. It follows too from the individual existing of metaphysical necessity that there is nothing more ultimate on whose act of will he depends for his existence and properties, and so other things could not exist except as dependent on him.

It is because God's essential properties all follow from the very simple property of having pure, limitless, intentional power, that I claim that God is an individual of a very simple kind; certainly the simplest kind of person there can be. Would not the kind be even simpler if we supposed that the necessity of existence which it involved was ontological necessity rather than just metaphysical necessity? No, it would not; that would be to make a very much more complicated supposition. The divine essence, as defined so far, of necessarily having pure, limitless, intentional power, makes God the kind of being he is in virtue of his power, of what he can do, of his control over things. This essence is a monadic property; it belongs to its possessor in virtue of what he is, not in virtue of any relation he might have to any other actual things. Ontological necessity is, however, a relational property. It adds to metaphysical necessity a relational element—the element of being related to every other actual substance there may be by the relation of not being caused by it.

Now it might *follow from* the monadic properties of an individual that it would have a certain relational property, and others have tried to argue that God has no cause on the grounds that he is so powerful that he could not have; I have shown in the previous chapter (barring further problems to be explored in Chapter 8) that such attempts fail—having necessarily pure, limitless, intentional power does not guarantee that he is uncaused. On the whole we think of individuals as the kinds of individual they are in virtue of their monadic properties. Electrons are electrons, and souls are souls, in virtue of what is internal to them, not in virtue of how they are related to other things. True, we may need to distinguish between individuals of some kind by their relational properties— for example, if material objects do not have thisness, we distinguish between different material objects by their spatial relations. But we can distinguish kinds of individuals by their monadic properties alone; and a system of (minimum) essential kinds or natures that does this is the simpler for doing so. A thing's causal powers may be involved in its being an individual of some kind, and so may its liabilities to exercise those powers in certain ways. But whether or not it is uncaused is not involved in what it is to be an individual of that kind but derives from other things—for instance, it may be so great that it cannot be caused, or there may be nothing else great enough to cause it. It is much simpler and so much more likely to be true that the divine nature involves metaphysical necessity but not (unless derivative from its other elements) ontological necessity.[2]

God is said to have the divine properties necessarily. Why should we suppose that in any sense they are tied to him necessarily? Why not suppose that God is a person who just happens to be omnipotent etc., who could, if he chose, abandon his divine nature, and revert to a humbler role in the scheme of things? Certainly, God's perfect goodness might prevent him from committing suicide or leaving any universe he creates without putting a good person in control of it. But why should he not, like earthly monarchs, abdicate, and hand his powers over to another?

The view that the divine properties are not tied necessarily to God is already ruled out by the account that I have given of those properties. For if the tie was not a necessary one, God would not have pure, limitless, intentional power. For a being with pure, limitless, intentional power is one to whom his causality is tied so essentially that no other things can be except as dependent on his currently sustaining power. I see no reason to amend my account. For any arguments for theism, any grounds we might have for believing that there is a God are arguments to the simplest causal source of everything else there could be. If divinity were tied to the individual who is a God merely accidentally, and he could continue to exist without the divine properties, then that divinity is so tied would have no explanation, and how things would go if it came untied would have no explanation. In that case God would not be as simple a being as on the traditional view (because his properties were separable from him), nor (although he might be the cause—active or permissive—of everything actual) would he be the source

---

[2] In the original edn. of *The Coherence of Theism* (Clarendon Press, 1977), 225, I argued, unsoundly, that there could only be one being with the divine properties, i.e. in the terminology of that book, one 'personal ground of being'; and I therefore went on to suppose that being to have an essential nature of a kind which could not be duplicated. That—to use my present terminology—involved attributing to that being ontological rather than metaphysical necessity. I now argue that these moves were mistaken.

of everything else there could be. For there would be possible events, compatible with the structure of reality, of which he would not be the cause—namely, how things would go if God lost or abandoned some of his divine properties.

Given that the tie is a necessary one, it must be a logically necessary one—for otherwise there would be some state of affairs that it is logically possible that God bring about—God not having some property (e.g. his omniscience)—that it is not in fact possible that God bring about. And in that case he would not be omnipotent. It follows that the divine properties are essential to his being the individual he is. God is a person of a different kind from ourselves such that he has continuity of experience with a later individual only if that individual has the divine nature. The referring expression 'God' in the sentence 'God is divine,' picks out an individual of that kind; and so 'God is divine' has logical necessity for the same kind of reason as does (see p. 113) 'Bloggs is a material object' when 'Bloggs' picks out a cement mixer. 'God' picks out an individual of a kind which, being divine, exists of metaphysical necessity and so exists everlastingly.

I think that God can be a person only in an analogical sense if being divine is essential to being God.[3] For, given my arguments in Chapter 2, in saying of a human or a Martian that he is a person, we thereby say that he is an individual with beliefs and the capacity for intentional action (of a certain complexity). He could lose or

---

[3] I call a sense of a word analogical with its normal sense if it has only some of the same synonyms, antonyms, etc., with normal uses of the word—see my account of analogy in *Revelation* (Clarendon Press, 1992), ch. 3; and the account expressed somewhat differently but in essence the same in *Coherence of Theism*, ch. 4. Normally, to say that someone is a person is to say that he is a 'subject of (possibly changing) powers of intentional action and knowledge acquisition'. Since to say God is a 'person' does not have this as a synonym the sense of 'person' in the latter is analogical; but of course not equivocal, as normal uses of 'person' and the use in 'God is a person' have much in common, and especially many of the same synonyms, e.g. 'subject of powers of intentional action and knowledge acquisition'. I argued in *Coherence of Theism* that we would be expected to need to use words in senses analogical with their normal senses in order to talk of supra-mundane things, and above all in order to talk of God; but that the more stretched were our analogical uses of words, the less clear would it be what we were saying by means of them. If theology is to be informative, it must use analogy very sparingly. I also argued in *Coherence of Theism* that the place at which we could not help bringing analogy into our talk about God was where we sought to talk of God as a 'person'. In the passage cited at the end of that chapter Aquinas stresses that talk of divine individuals as 'persons' is analogical, but he holds that analogy pervades all talk about God and I do not wish to hold that.

gain power or knowledge and yet remain the same person (i.e. preserve continuity of experience). If that is not so of God, then the
sense in which God is a person is a stretched one. However, as we
saw in Chapters 1 and 2, different properties are essential for different kinds of being. And supposing different properties to be essential
for divine individuals from those that are essential for non-divine
persons (i.e. since God is the subject of mental properties and so a
soul, for divine as opposed to human and similar souls) does not
involve such a stretch beyond the readily conceivable as we would
need, for example, if we supposed God to have logically necessary
existence—since substances of all kinds seem to be such that their
non-existence is conceivable.

I conclude that the existence of a substance who has necessarily
pure, intentional, limitless power entails and is entailed by the existence of a substance who has necessarily the divine properties described in Chapter 6. I understand by a divine individual one who
has necessarily pure, intentional, limitless power. To have that is
his nature. The claim that there is a God is therefore to be read as
the claim that there is such an individual. If follows not merely
that no individual who is not divine could become divine, but also
that no individual who is not divine could ever (even everlastingly)
have been divine. For being divine is essential to the individuals
that are divine, and is part of what makes them the individuals
they are.

To divide the property of being divine up into constituent properties such as being omnipotent, being omniscient, etc., analysed
in Chapter 6, is to divide it into constituents that with our conceptual
scheme we humans find the property of being divine easiest to grasp.
But the division can be misleading in that it can suggest, may suggest subsequently, and may have already suggested in Chapter 6,
that the constituent properties are in some way in competition. I
write of God's omnipotence making it possible for him to do various
acts that his perfect goodness prevents him from doing. But I do
not intend such talk to suggest a competition within God, only to
suggest (e.g.) the limits of application to God of the human word
'omnipotent' and so the humanly drawn property of omnipotence
that it designates.

It has been the unanimous theistic tradition that we do not know
fully in what the divine nature consists. In saying that the properties
described in Chapter 6, and now found to be bound together in the

property of having pure, limitless, intentional power, are essential to God, I do not seek to deny that. In writing of properties as 'the' essential properties, I meant only that among properties of which humans can form an understanding, those are the essential ones. 'Pure, limitless, intentional power', spelled out in the way I have spelled it out, is the best understanding humans can achieve of the divine nature, and in our reasoning in these and all matters we must operate with the best understanding we can get. But there is no doubt far, far more to being God than I have been able to understand—so that the divine nature is far simpler than my human words have been able to picture, and far more is involved in pure, limitless, intentional power than I have been able to draw out from it.

Other Accounts of the Divine Unity

Other thinkers have seen the divine properties as bound together by other bonds, as following from different unifying principles.

For Anselm[4] and for Plantinga,[5] God is the greatest conceivable being, he has all the great-making characteristics. (I shall assume, for the moment, that there can only be one such being; and similarly with respect to other characterizations of God to be considered.) On my characterization of God, he does indeed seem to be the greatest conceivable being; and I suspect that having necessarily pure, limitless, intentional power and being the greatest conceivable are logically equivalent properties, in the sense that of logical necessity a being which has one has the other. But 'greatest conceivable', like all evaluative properties (good, right, ought to be done, etc.), is supervenient on natural (i.e. non-evaluative) properties. That is, God is the greatest conceivable being because he has necessarily pure, limitless, intentional power, and not vice versa. Just as, to

---

[4] At least that is the obvious way to read Anselm. For he claims that God 'can be conceived to exist in reality' (Proslogion 2), and that 'nothing greater can be conceived' (Proslogion 5), and that that is why God is 'just, truthful, blessed, and whatever it is better to be than not to be. For it is better to be just than not just; better to be blessed than not blessed' (Proslogion 5, trans. S. N. Deane (Open Court Publishing Co., 1903)).

[5] In his *God, Freedom and Evil* (George Allen & Unwin, 1975), 106–12, Plantinga understands God as 'a being that has maximal greatness'.

take a slightly different example, God is not our creator because he is worthy of worship: he is worthy of worship because he is our creator. Hence if God is the greatest conceivable being, that must be because he has some natural property on which the former supervenes. Having necessarily pure, limitless, intentional power is, I suggest, that natural property.

Leibniz attempted to ground his notion of the most perfect being in a different kind of simplicity from that with which I have been concerned, the simplicity of a being who is the subject of all 'perfections' in a different sense from the more natural sense of all the 'great-making qualities'. For by a perfection, Leibniz wrote, 'I mean every simple quality which is positive and absolute or which expresses whatever it expresses without any limits.'[6] To put his point more carefully—a perfection in his sense is a maximum degree of a positive, simple (i.e. unanalysable) quality. All simple qualities, being unanalysable, are, he held, compatible with each other. Thus, being hot or long are not perfections, because they do not exemplify qualities to maximum degrees, and there is no quality of being maximally hot or long (for, however hot something is, it could be hotter). However, Leibniz claimed, knowledge and power can be exemplified to a maximum degree,[7] and, holding these qualities to be simple, he therefore claimed that omnipotence and omniscience are perfections.

Now, it needs more argument than Leibniz gives to show that the divine properties are 'perfections' in his sense, and that they are the *only* properties which are. But even if Leibniz is right about the divine properties, he needs to explain what brings all the properties together; what makes the property of having all the perfections a simple, unifying property. Why should there be more unity to a being which had maximal degrees of all simple properties rather than to one which had just some of these which fitted better together?

Aquinas derives the divine properties from God being 'the primary efficient cause of things'[8] which seems to come to somewhat the same as my notion of having (necessarily) pure, limitless, intentional power. It does not have intentionality explicitly built into

[6] G. W. Leibniz, *Philosophical Papers and Letters*, trans. and ed. L. E. Loemker (D. Reidel, 1956), 167.

[7] G. W. Leibniz, *Discourse on Metaphysics*, trans. P. G. Lucas and L. Grint (Manchester University Press, 1953), ch. 1—'The greatest knowledge and omnipotence contain no impossibility.'   [8] *Summa theologiae*, 1a. 4. 2.

it, but Aquinas thought of all causation as involving final causation
(the cause acting to realize its own chosen end, or one chosen by
another agent, who was making it operate—but the latter would
not be a possibility for the first cause). It is because God is the first
cause that he cannot but exist—hence 'his very nature is to exist'.[9]
God being the first cause, this can be true of nothing else; so 'He
who is' is the most appropriate name for God.[10] God's perfection
and supreme goodness and then the other properties are held by
Aquinas to derive from this; although there is a necessary equival-
ence between the existing and the good, and between the first cause
and the supremely good, 'existing is a more fundamental idea than
being good'.[11]

I do not find Aquinas's derivation of the divine properties always
very satisfactory. For example, he argues for God having 'knowledge
in the highest degree' from his being 'immaterial in the highest
degree',[12] which does not seem to follow in any very obvious way.
However, Aquinas finds the unity of the divine properties in a
similar place to the place in which I find it, and there is so much in
many of his predecessors along similar lines. John Damascene,
frequently quoted by Aquinas, claimed that the uncreated creator
for which he had argued[13] was best described as 'He who is' because
'he keeps all being in his own embrace'.[14]

Divine Simplicity

All these writers held that there was a natural unity to the divine
nature and hence they wished to maintain that he was a very simple
being. This is a claim that I wish strongly to endorse. But it
has recently got a bad name for itself by being equated with the
very paradoxical way in which it was expounded in late patristic
and subsequent medieval philosophy. The Fathers, beginning with
Irenaeus,[15] developed an account of divine simplicity which became
more explicit in Augustine[16] and attained its fullness of paradoxical
explicitness in Anselm: 'Life, wisdom and the rest are not parts of

---

[9] Ibid. 3. 4.   [10] Ibid. 13. 11.   [11] Ibid. 5. 2.   [12] Ibid. 14. 1.
[13] *De fide orthodoxa*, 1. 3.   [14] Ibid. 1. 9.
[15] On the sources of this doctrine, see C. Stead, *Divine Substance* (Clarendon Press,
1977), 163, 187–9.   [16] e.g. *De Trinitate*, 6. ch. 7.

thee, but all are one; and each of these is the whole, which thou art and all the rest are.'[17] That is, all the divine properties are identical with each other and with God. But how can God, who is a substance, an entity who possesses properties, be the same as those properties? And how can they be identical with each other? How can omnipotence be the same property as omniscience?

Aquinas expresses the doctrine in a slightly different but initially more plausible way. The claim, as he expresses it, is not that the divine properties are the same as each other and as God, but that the instances of the divine properties in God are the same as each other and as God—for example, God's omnipotence, not omnipotence as such, is the same as God's omniscience and this is the same as God.[18] In my terminology, property-instances are events (namely, God being omnipotent always, or God being omniscient always).

Now, as we saw in Part 1, the ordinary understanding of properties, which we need in order to describe the world, contains clear enough criteria for saying that omnipotence is not the same property as omniscience, and power not the same property as wisdom. Our ordinary understanding does not, however, it seems to me, provide clear criteria of what it is for property instances (alias events) to be the same as each other, and perhaps a philosopher can develop that ordinary understanding in a natural way to yield criteria on which instances of the divine properties turn out to be identical with each other. William Mann[19] attempted to do this. He needed first to deny that what are on my account accidental properties of God are properties at all (e.g. 'creating John Smith' is not a property of God, because God would still be God if he had not created John

---

[17] Proslogion, 18.

[18] For an assembly of relevant quotations from Aquinas, see William E. Mann, 'Divine Simplicity', *Religious Studies*, 18 (1982), 451–71, 454 f. It is because, according to Aquinas, subject and predicate cannot be distinguished in God, that our normal 'modes of signification', which distinguish sharply between subject and predicate, cannot be applied in a straightforward way to our talk about God; and so all talk about divine properties, God being good, wise, etc., is analogical. This is well brought out in William P. Alston, 'Aquinas on Theological Predication: A Look Backward and a Look Forward' in E. Stump (ed.), *Reasoned Faith* (Cornell University Press, 1993).

[19] Mann also seeks to defend the view that God is identical with his property instances ('Divine Simplicity', ibid.). For criticism of Mann's project and some of its details, see Thomas V. Morris, 'On God and Mann: A View of Divine Simplicity', *Religious Studies*, 21 (1985), 299–318.

Smith). He then suggests that x being P is identical with y being Q, if $x = y$ and of logical necessity whenever P is instantiated, Q is instantiated (and conversely). Something along these lines might eventually give Mann Aquinas's claim about the identity of instances of divine properties, but I think that Mann's account would need to be made a lot more complicated before that claim would follow. My earlier discussion suggests that even the properties peculiar to God, such as omnipotence and omniscience, would need to be understood in rather special ways before it would follow that whenever one was instantiated, necessarily the other was also. And also it follows from the definition as stated that the instances of most divine properties that are not peculiar to God, such as being knowledgeable or being powerful, are not identical with each other. One could deal with that problem by adding to the definition that x being P is the same as x being P^1, if x is P^1 and x being P^1 is the maximum degree of a property P. So God's omnipotence would be the same as God being powerful, and God's omniscience would be the same as God being knowledgeable, and hence by the previous result God's being wise would be the same as his being knowledgeable.

All of this seems quite unnecessary. The unity of the divine properties follow from their being included in a simple property, which I have called having pure, limitless, intentional power.[20]

What moved Aquinas, who saw this, to talk of instances of the divine properties as being identical with each other was, I think, a residual Platonism which so hypostatized abstract entities such as properties that it had to say that unless they were part of God, they would be entities independent of God—which would be a view which did not fit well with theism. And since God cannot have distinct parts, they must be identical with each other. All of this becomes quite unnecessary once we abandon Platonism and acknowledge that abstract entities are not constituents of the universe but mere convenient fictions. Wisdom and suchlike are properties and not substances; they have no existence apart from their existence in substances; and when they exist in substances, they are not parts of those substances.

[20] For a very thorough exposition of Aquinas's account of the identity of the divine properties or their instances, and a proposal for modifying it to make it coherent, along lines similar to mine, see Christopher Hughes, *On a Complex Theory of a Simple God* (Cornell University Press, 1989), chs. 1 and 2.

Platonism was also the motivating force behind the other patristic-medieval claim that the divine properties or property-instances, being the same as each other, were also the same as God himself. And superficially this is an even less plausible claim. How can God, who is a substance, be identical with properties or events?[21] However, those who claimed that God is identical with his properties were, I think, trying to say something very important and quite probably true, even if they did not express it very well and it is time now to bring out what that is.

Individuating Divine Individuals

The doctrine that all the divine properties or property-instances are the same as each other may be seen as trying to articulate the doctrine that there is no less to God than the traditional properties discussed in Chapter 6. They are all essential and belong together. I have tried to show how they all fit together. The doctrine that God is identical with his properties or their instances may be seen as trying to say that there is no more to God than his essential properties.

As we saw in Chapter 2, we distinguish what is essential to being an individual of some kind from what is essential to being a particular individual of that kind—for instance, what is essential to being a soul from what is essential to being a certain individual soul. We shall come in Chapter 8 to the question of whether there could be more than one divine individual. If there could be, and is, the question then arises of what makes each the particular individual he is, and there are two possible answers. The first is that further properties suffice to individuate, in the way that what makes some magnetic field the particular one it is is its shape and strength (monadic properties) and location (relational property). The second answer is that while further properties might be necessary for individuating divine individuals they are not sufficient—which is to say that divine individuals have thisness. If there exists more than

---

[21] For powerful articulation of this objection as well as the objection that not all the divine properties or even all the divine property-instances are the same as each other, see A. Plantinga, *Does God Have a Nature?* (Marquette University Press, 1980), 37–61.

one divine individual, they could have all their properties in common, and yet be different.

Even if there is not (and so—since divine individuals are everlasting—never has been and never will be) more than one divine individual, the question still arises as to what makes a single divine individual the one he is. The two answers given in the last paragraph are also available here: that a single divine individual is constituted as the one he is by further properties than those essential to divinity as such; and that such properties would not suffice for individuation and the sole divine individual has an underlying thisness. There is also here a third possible answer—that the divine nature itself suffices to individuate, and so that any sole divine individual would be the same as any other. The first and second answers allow that things could have been different (for all time) in the sole respect that a different God was in charge of the universe.

If divine individuals are individuated by further properties alone, the individuating properties (or conjunction thereof)—P_1 which makes G_1 who he is, P_2 which makes G_2 who he is, etc., must have the following two characteristics. First, the properties must be incompatible—otherwise they would not suffice to distinguish individuals (an individual could have both). Secondly, the properties must be such that if there was a divine individual with such a property, there would always be and have been a divine individual with that property. This is because since divine individuals exist forever, that which individuates them must exist in them forever. Now it does not look as if monadic properties will suffice for this individuating role. A monadic property of a divine individual G_1 would be one which belonged to him, quite apart from his relations to anything else. Certainly the divine properties, which we analysed in Chapter 6, are monadic properties, but it does not look as if any other monadic properties not essential to divinity as such would suffice permanently to distinguish one divine individual from another. For just because the possession of a monadic property does not consist in any relation to other individuals, and so does not carry any consequences for other individuals, it would seem that any other individual of the same kind could have it. If for example the monadic property suggested for individuating a divine individual was having a certain thought, why should not all divine individuals have that thought? The examples of Chapter 2 of other substances which may be individuated by their properties alone bring out that while monadic properties may determine that a substance belongs to a kind, it is relational properties that individuate substances of a kind. If iron spheres lack thisness, they are constituted as the ones they are in part by their location, that is, their spatial relations to other material objects.

Yet a divine individual could not be individuated by his relations to anything other than another divine individual. For as tradition teaches, and as I shall argue in Chapter 8, no divine individual needs to bring about anything else than a divine individual (and nothing else would exist unless one does bring it about). The only possible individuating properties would seem to be relations to other divine individuals. The relational properties would have to be general relational properties, since the other divine individuals would be constituted the individuals they are by their relational properties. It would be principle [D] of Chapter 2 that was the strongest principle that could be affirmed for the identity of divine individuals.

I shall come to consider in more detail in the next chapter what these properties would be, but for the present I seek only to make the point that there could be general properties of relation to other divine individuals that satisfied the two requirements on properties individuating divine individuals. Let P_1 be the property of having continuity of experience with no individual who was throughout any initial (beginningless) period of his existence actively caused to exist by a divine individual, and P_2 the property of having continuity of experience with an individual who was throughout a (beginningless) period of his existence actively caused to exist by a divine individual. These properties are incompatible. If a divine individual at one time has P_2 he cannot cease to have P_2—he always has continuity of experience with himself and so will always have continuity of experience with an individual who had his earlier state. And—given the impossibility of fusion of souls (see Ch. 1)—if a divine individual does not have continuity of experience with an individual who had a certain initial state, he cannot acquire such continuity. So if a divine individual has P_1 at one time, he has it always. Hence there could always be two divine individuals whom properties would suffice to distinguish.

So if divine individuals are individuated by their properties, these properties will be properties of relation to other divine individuals. It follows that—if properties suffice to individuate—any sole divine individual would be the same as any other. The possibility initially allowed above that a sole divine individual might be individuated by further properties is ruled out. It also follows—if properties suffice to individuate—that there would be no difference between a world in which two divine individuals have certain distinct relations to each other, and any other world in which two divine individuals have just those relations—the same individuals would be involved in each case.

If properties do not suffice to individuate divine individuals, they will have thisness (which is just to say that no form of the identity of indiscernibles applies to them). Divine individuals would be, in this respect, like human persons. There would be a thisness underlying their properties, those forming the divine nature and perhaps other individuating properties as well, which made a divine individual the individual he is. For each divine individual would be an individual essence, a particular way of being divine, whose existence was not simply the instantiation of properties. So there would be a difference between the existence of one sole individual God, G_1, who was essentially omnipotent, omniscient, etc., and the existence of another such sole God, G_2, who had all the same properties (essential and non-essential) as G_1. G_1 may be the divine individual who actually exists, but there is a logically possible universe in which instead some other individual G_2 is in charge and does exactly what G_1 does in our universe. Similarly, if there was more than one divine individual, what made them different from each other would not be their properties alone, but what underlay their properties. This 'thisness-view' of divinity, that a divine individual is something underlying his properties, is to be contrasted with the alternative view sketched earlier which I shall call the 'essence-view', that a divine individual just is the instantiation of his properties—both those essential to divinity as such and any which individuate him. It is this latter essence-view which I think that those who claimed that God is identical with his properties were getting at.

Which view is to be preferred? If, as on the thisness-view, one thinks of a divine individual as one who has his essential properties such as power and knowledge which are distinct from him, the question arises as to why it is that he retains that power, and what guarantees the efficacy of his actions. And if one thinks of a divine individual as a person who has knowledge, the question arises as to why it is that he never makes a mistake, what guarantees that knowledge always comes to him. And above all, the question arises as to why it is this individual who is in charge of the universe rather than some other possible individual. Of course one may answer these questions by saying that a divine individual just is a being of the required sort, and it is a metaphysically necessary truth that that particular one is in charge of the universe. These are ultimate facts. And indeed there have to be some ultimate facts. But the fewer ultimate facts we postulate, the simpler our account of the underlying nature of the world; and simplicity, I have urged elsewhere[22] and repeated several times in this book, is evidence of truth—indeed the only criterion we ever have for choosing among theories equally compatible with the data of observation. If however, as on the essence-view, one supposes that all there is to being a divine individual is just having properties (both those essential to divinity and perhaps also individuating properties), then these questions do not arise. Any sole divine individual would be the same as any other; and any divine individual having the same individuating properties would be the same as any other. And why a divine individual could not lose his power and knowledge and yet continue to exist, is because there is nothing more to him than his properties; and there is really only one property—pure, limitless, intentional power—that constitutes his divinity, of which any individuating properties are specializations (relations between different exemplifications of it). He is the pure, intentional power that knowledgeably guides things. There is no gap to be opened up between a divine individual and his power and knowledge, about which one can ask why it is not opened up. He is so close to the universe as the power which knowledgeably sustains it and moves it; but of course not tied to the universe, which he could abolish at a stroke.

On the other hand the essence-view seems a bit difficult to make sense of, and so its simplicity may be merely superficial; the simplicity of a formula, the cashing out of which is unintelligible. How can there be divinity without the divinity belonging to an *underlying* substance? So maybe the thisness view is the best solution. We still do not have to say that there is anything metaphysically necessary beyond the existence of one (or more) divine individuals, who—because of the kind of being they are—could not but be divine. Yet

---

[22] See, among other places, my *The Existence of God* (Clarendon Press, 1979), 52–69 and 102–6.

the kind of divinity which it postulates is, at any rate superficially, less simple than that postulated by the essence-view because it postulates a kind of divinity distinct from the substance in which it inheres. I do think that we have sufficient analogies in kinds of substance other than persons for a substance lacking thisness (see Chapter 2), for me to judge that there is enough intelligibility in the apparently simpler supposition that God lacks thisness—that he is his essential properties—to make it marginally simpler and so a priori more probable. However, the issue is by no means clear and I shall continue to pursue the consequences of both views.

The later patristic and medieval traditions advocated the view that 'God' does not have thisness. His nature is all there is to God. Thus Augustine denies that God is properly called a substance that has properties; he is more properly called an essence because he is properties.[23] And I quoted earlier Aquinas's remark: 'God himself is his own nature . . . It is therefore in virtue of one and the same fact that he is God and this God.'[24] This remark continues: 'And thus it is impossible for there to be many Gods.' But Aquinas does not in this passage distinguish the properties essential to an individual being divine, and the properties essential to an individual being the particular divine individual he is; and because he has forgotten about the latter possibility, his conclusion is ill-justified. But when he comes to discuss the Trinity, he does see that divine individuals not having thisness does not preclude there being properties which individuate one as against another.

In the section of the *Summa theologiae* on the Trinity, Aquinas claims that relations in creatures are accidental to them; what makes me me is not a matter of who my father is, let alone who my maternal uncle is. That is indeed so, I have urged, for creatures which have thisness; though Aquinas may have been mistaken in suggesting that all creatures have thisness. However, with God, Aquinas claims, it is different. 'Real relations', that is, ones which are really there and not produced by some arbitrary way of description, belong to the divine essence. He writes: 'In divine beings a relation is not as an accident inhering in a subject but is the divine essence itself; hence it is something subsisting just as the divine essence subsists.'[25]

[23] *De Trinitate*, 7 ch. 5.

[24] *Summa theologiae*, 1a. 11. 3. For discussion of Aquinas's less than satisfactory arguments on this issue, see Hughes, *Complex Theory*, ch. 3.

[25] *Summa theologiae*, 1a. 29. 4. For discussion of Aquinas's contorted attempts to reconcile his account of divine simplicity with the doctrine of the Trinity, see Hughes, *Complex Theory*, ch. 6.

How are we to read 'the relation is the essence'? My obvious suggestion is that it is saying that what makes a divine individual the
one he is is his relational properties. 'The notion of a relation is
involved in the meaning of a "divine person", though not in the
meaning of "angelic person" or "human person". It is true that the
meaning [of "person"] is not univocal, for nothing can be said uni-
vocally of God and creatures.'[26] I shall consider in the next chapter
whether there can be more than one divine individual and what in
that case Aquinas's claim and the normal Christian claim that 'there
is only one God' amounts to.

[26] *Summa theologiae*, 1a. 29. 4–4.

8
The Trinity

Given the doctrine of God developed in the last two chapters, what follows concerning the two affirmations about God's nature—that he is 'three persons in one substance', the doctrine of the Holy Trinity; and that he became incarnate in Jesus Christ, 'true God and true man'? In this chapter I shall explore the meaning and coherence of the doctrine of the Trinity, and in the process develop an a priori argument for the necessity of that doctrine, to back up the argument from revelation for its truth. In Chapter 9 I shall consider the meaning and coherence of the doctrine of the Incarnation, and in Chapter 10 I shall consider grounds for believing it to be true.

Could There be More than One Divine Individual?

I considered in the last chapter two issues about the divine nature which turned on the issue of which of two rival hypotheses was the simpler, and so had greater prior probability—whether the necessity of a divine individual is metaphysical or ontological; and whether such an individual has thisness. I came down firmly in favour of the view that the divine necessity was metaphysical rather than ontological, and marginally in favour of the view that a divine individual does not have thisness.

Which view one takes on these issues is crucially relevant to the question to which we come at last, of whether there can be more than one divine individual. A divine individual who exists of ontological necessity would be such that there is no cause active or permissive of his existence at any time. But, if he is the creator and sustainer of any universe there may be, any other substance can only exist if he is, at least in part, the cause of its existence. Hence there cannot be, beside an ontologically necessary divine being, another such.

But what if the necessity of a divine individual is understood as metaphysical necessity? We suggested in Chapter 7 that being divine should be understood as entailing and being entailed by being necessarily perfectly free, omniscient, omnipotent, and existing of metaphysical necessity. Now there certainly could be two or more individuals who were necessarily perfectly free, and omniscient. The latter property, it will be recalled from Chapter 6, is construed as knowledge of all that is logically possible for the individual to know and so does not include knowledge of the future actions of free agents.

The problem arises with omnipotence. Could there be two omnipotent individuals who existed of metaphysical necessity (i.e. everlastingly, and uncaused or inevitably caused by a backwardly everlasting uncaused substance)?

As I argued in Chapter 6, an omniscient and perfectly free individual will always be perfectly good. I spelled this out as follows. I understand all the acts which an individual can do simultaneously as one possible act available to such an individual. Then a perfectly good individual will act as follows. He will do no bad act, and where there is a unique best act, he will do it. Where there are equal best acts he will do one of them; and where there is a best kind of act, but no best of the kind but rather an infinite number of acts each less good than another act, he will do one act of that kind. Otherwise his perfect goodness does not restrict how he will act. I called the acts that such an individual does and has to do in virtue of his perfect goodness—for instance, the best act in the circumstances if there is one—acts of essence; and the acts which he does but does not have to do, despite his perfect goodness, acts of will. These latter are acts between which he chooses, and between which no balance of reason dictates how he will choose. A divine individual's compatibilist power is his omnipotence, the power to do anything logically possible, if he so chooses; his absolute power is the power to choose and do, and that is limited not merely by logical possibility but by perfect goodness.

So could there be two omnipotent individuals having also the previously cited divine properties? An initial gut reaction is 'No'. Would not the omnipotence of one such individual be subject to frustration by the other individual and so not be omnipotence? Not in general—for the omnipotence of such an individual, being also perfectly good, is only the power to do good actions within ranges of the kind available to a perfectly good being. Each individual would be bringing about many good states, within himself, in relation to the other individual, and creating and sustaining without. Since each would recognize the other as having the divine properties, including perfect goodness, it is plausible to suppose that each would recognize a duty not to prevent or frustrate the acts of the other, to use his omnipotence to forward them rather than frustrate them. If the second individual creates a universe which the first individual by himself would not have chosen to create, there would be wrong in the first individual attempting to prevent or frustrate this creative work; on the contrary, it would be good that he should give it his backing.

The only possibility of conflict between the acts of individuals with the above properties would arise where each tried to do an act compatible with his perfect goodness but incompatible with the act which the other was trying simultaneously to do. Thus, it might be an equally good event that Abraham be called by a divine individual to settle in Iraq as that he be called to settle in Iran, and thus there might be before both divine individuals two equally good possible acts. One might try to perform the one, and the other the other. Or (if we call the present direction of revolution of the Earth round the Sun clockwise) it might be equally good that the Earth revolve anticlockwise as that it revolve clockwise, and thus again there might be before both divine individuals two equally good possible acts of bringing about these states of affairs. One might choose the one and the other the other. There could not be two divine individuals unless there was some mechanism to prevent interference and the mechanism could not limit their power in the compatibilist sense, only in the absolute sense (by making it no longer good to do acts of a certain sort). It could do that only by there being something which made it a bad thing for each to act in an area where the other was operative, for instance, an agreement between them not to do so. But how are the lines of distribution of the proper exercise of power to be drawn up? By one divine individual? But there is nothing to guarantee that at the moment at which he draws up a proposal for distributing power, the other divine individual might not draw up a different proposal; and even with the best will in the world, only luck could prevent an actual collision of wills. (Compare the situation where two people are approaching each other along a pavement, and each tries to move to that side of the pavement where he guesses the other will not go; they may or may not collide.) Only if one lays down what the rules are, and his decision is accepted because he has the authority to lay down the rules, will the collision necessarily be avoided. But a difference in authority would have to arise from some other difference of status between the divine individuals; in some way one would have to be the source of being of the other. And for other reasons it surely must be that if there are two divine individuals, one is the ultimate source of being. As I suggested in Chapter 6, arguments to the existence of God derive their force from their ability to explain the orderly complexity of our world as deriving from a single source of being. To suppose that there were two or more ultimate sources of being, neither of which was dependent on the other, would be to make a suggestion contrary to what is indicated by arguments for the existence of God.

As I showed in Chapter 6—if there can be more than one divine individual, one divine individual can derive his existence from another divine individual, so long as the derivation is inevitable. For each of two divine individuals G_1 and G_2, it can be the case that there is no cause of it existing at any time while it exists, neither active cause nor permissive cause, except (directly or indirectly) an uncaused and backwardly everlasting substance, namely a divine individual, who causes his existence inevitably in virtue of his properties. If G_1, inevitably in virtue of his properties throughout some first (beginningless) period of time actively causes G_2 to exist, and thereafter permissively causes (i.e. permits) the continued existence of G_2; while G_2 is such that G_1 only exists at each period of time which has a beginning because G_2 permits G_1 to exist, then both would be metaphysically necessary—once existent, they inevitably always exist, and there is no time at which they do not exist. The eternal (active and then permissive) bringing about of G_2 by G_1 would be an act of essence by G_1, just as the (permissive) bringing about of G_1 by G_2 would be an act of essence by G_2; and the former would provide a mechanism by which to ensure that there was no conflict of action between them. For G_1 would prescribe what the mechanism was. The same will hold in the simpler case with which I will work henceforward, that G_1 is everlastingly (inevitably in virtue of his properties) the active cause of G_2; while G_2 is for every period of time which has a beginning (inevitably in virtue of his properties) the permissive cause of G_1.

There are many different ways in which unity of action can be secured among individuals who might otherwise impede each other's efforts. One of them could take all the decisions and the others simply execute those decisions. Another way is to have a vote on every issue and for each then to carry out the result of the vote. A third way is to have a division of functions. One individual takes decisions on certain kinds of issues, and the others support him in these. Another individual takes decisions on other issues, and the others support him in those, and so on. Which would be the best way for divine individuals to secure unity of action, to determine a choice between alternatives equally available to a perfectly good individual? The first way would seem an imperfect way of sharing power between divine individuals, and so one which G_1 would not adopt. The second way, taken strictly, is not a possible way when there are only two individuals, for, unless chance produces a prior coincidence of their views, votes will always be tied. (Marriage cannot be a democracy.) And even where there are more than two individuals, but many alternative actions (such that there is no overriding reason for doing one rather than another), is there any reason to suppose that there will often be a majority in favour of one course of action? Only the third way would seem a viable way of securing unity of action in shared power among divine individuals.

Such unity of action could be secured if the first individual solemnly vows to the second individual in causing his existence that he will not initiate any act (of will) in a certain sphere of activity that he allocates to him, while at the same time the first individual requests the second individual not to initiate any such act outside that sphere. The vow of the first individual would create an obligation on him not to initiate any act (of will) within the second individual's allocated sphere of activity. So, although the first divine individual retains his omnipotence, it is, as before, limited by his inability to do other than what is perfectly good, and in virtue of his promise this limitation will ensure that he does not frustrate the actions of the second divine individual. Conversely, although all power is given to the second individual, it comes with a request that it should not be exercised in a certain way. The overall goodness of conformity to that request (not to conform would be not to conform to a reasonable request from the source of his being and power) will ensure that, although omnipotent, the second individual cannot frustrate any action of the first individual. The sharing of divinity could (logically) only occur subject to some restriction preventing mutual impediment of action. I have presented a highly fallible human judgement as to what the best such mechanism (and so the one which would be adopted) would be.

Each of the postulated divine individuals would be omnipotent in the sense that each could at any period of time do anything logically possible—for example, bring it about that the Earth moves round the Sun in a clockwise direction. But the omnipotence of each individual is limited by his perfect goodness, and if one individual has promised the other individual that he will not perform actions (when there is not a unique best action) in this area (e.g. the area of movements of heavenly bodies), then his perfect goodness limits his omnipotence so that he does not do such an act. Thus each of two individuals with the earlier divine properties can be omnipotent.[1] (I repeat my warning from the last chapter with respect to such phrases as that 'perfect goodness limits omnipotence'. Talk of one property 'limiting' another only arises when we divide the property of being divine into such constituent properties as we humans can best grasp. The 'limit' is a limit on the application of a human word to God; it is not to be understood as a constraint within a divine individual.)

So there can be more than one divine individual if it is necessary that the first divine individual brings about the existence of a second divine individual. It is possible that there be more than one divine individual only if it is necessary that there be more than one divine individual. But since nothing affects how a divine individual acts except reason, this can only be if the first divine individual has an overriding reason to bring about the existence of a second individual, that is, he brings this about as an act of essence.

I have talked only of a second divine individual. But similar arguments will obviously show that there can be a third divine individual only if it is necessary that there be a third divine individual, and that will be only if the first divine individual, or the second individual, or both together, have overriding reason for bringing about (everlastingly, or for an initial beginningless period) the third individual. If there is such overriding reason, then one way in which this could come about is if the first divine individual in bringing about the second individual requests him to confine his

---

[1] See Additional Note 11.

acts of will to a narrower field of activity, and one or the other or both together then bring about the existence of the third divine individual, with both divine individuals undertaking not to initiate acts of will in a certain sphere and requesting the third individual to confine his acts of will to that sphere. Such requests and undertakings would again limit the absolute power of each individual, but not the compatibilist power.

But now there is a problem which arises if divine individuals have thisness. I shall consider shortly how it can be that there is overriding reason to bring about another divine individual. But if there is such a reason, and if divine individuals have thisness, then there has to be overriding reason to bring about *this* second divine individual rather than any other one. For only if there was, would the individual brought about be a metaphysically necessary being. If it was equally good for the first divine individual to bring about this second individual or that, then bringing about this one rather than that one would be an act of will rather than an act of essence, and so the individual brought about would not have the metaphysical necessity of the first individual. But a reason for bringing about this individual rather than that one would consist in one having an essential property that the other lacked. Yet if divine individuals have thisness, there will always be possible divine individuals which have the same essential properties (those essential to divinity and any further individuating properties), and so no reason for bringing about one rather than another. Nor could there be reason for bringing about all possible divine individuals (even all ones having the same individuating properties). For there could be no set of such individuals; there would be no 'all'—however many divine individuals were caused to exist (even an infinite continuum of such), there would still be infinitely more which could be caused to exist. If divine individuals have thisness, there cannot be reason to bring about one rather than another. Hence if divine individuals have thisness, there can only be one of them.

If, however, divine individuals do not have thisness, and are individuated solely by further properties beyond those essential to divinity, there is no problem. We saw in Chapter 7 that these properties would have to be properties of relation between the divine individuals, and the argument of this chapter suggests that they will have to be properties of causal relation. Divine individuals will have to differ in the way in which they are mutually dependent on each other. And so any sole divine individual brought about by the first divine individual would be the same as any other such. For the property of being so brought about is a property necessarily possessed by that divine individual (i.e. the one who has continuity of experience with such a caused individual)—he could not exist otherwise. Contrariwise, the first divine individual would be uniquely identified as the uncaused one in the sense of the one who had no active cause of his existence. Since the mere act of bringing about a divine individual would necessarily bring about the same divine individual, there is no issue of a need for reason to bring about this divine individual rather than that one. A third divine individual could only be different from the second if he had different relational properties, and so if the active cause of his existence was different from that of the second individual. The only way in which this could happen would be if he were actively co-caused by the first and second individuals.[2] The preceding argument makes the distinction between divine individuals in terms of how they are caused. But this distinction entails a corresponding distinction in terms of what they cause. The first divine individual is one who actively causes another divine individual and, in co-operation with him, a third divine individual. The second divine individual is the one who actively causes the only one further divine individual and that in co-operation with another divine individual. The third divine individual is he who is the active cause of existence (either by himself or in co-operation) of no other individual.

So is there overriding reason for a first divine individual to bring about a second or third or fourth such? I believe that there is overriding reason for a first divine individual to bring about a second divine individual and with him to bring about a third divine individual, but no reason to go further. If the Christian religion has helped us, Christians and non-Christians, to see anything about what is worthwhile, it has helped us to see that love is a supreme good. Love involves sharing, giving to the other what of one's own is good for him and receiving from the other what of his is good for one; and love involves co-operating with another to benefit third parties. This latter is crucial for worthwhile love. There would be something deeply unsatisfactory (even if for inadequate humans sometimes unavoidable) about a marriage in which the parties were

[2] See Additional Note 12.

concerned solely with each other and did not use their mutual love to bring forth good to others, for example by begetting, nourishing, and educating children, but possibly in other ways instead. Love must share and love must co-operate in sharing.[3] The best love would share all that it had. A divine individual would see that for him too a best kind of action would be to share and to co-operate in sharing. Now a first divine individual is such that but for his choice there would be none other with whom to share. So the love of a first divine individual G_1 would be manifested first in bringing about another divine individual G_2 with whom to share his life, and the love of G_1 or G_2 would be manifested in bringing about another divine individual G_3 with whom G_1 and G_2 co-operatively could share their lives. G_2 and G_3 would then (i.e. for every period of time which had a beginning) co-operate in allowing G_1 to continue in being, for, but for their action, there would be no G_1[4]. But their action would be an inevitable action, an act of essence; the power not to keep G_1 in being would be only compatibilist power, not absolute power. (The love of the first and second individuals might be manifested in an initial active causing and thereafter permissive causing, or in an everlasting active causing. The same consequences of everlasting mutually sustaining coexistence of divine individuals follow on either supposition.) All three would go on to co-operate further in backing (i.e. putting their causal power behind) the activities of each other in their respective spheres of activity.[5]

[3] On 'non-possessive love' involving more than a 'two-membered relationship' see Robert M. Adams, 'The Problem of Total Devotion', in R. Audi and W. J. Wainwright (eds.), *Rationality, Religious Belief and Moral Commitment* (Cornell University Press, 1986), 175.

[4] Augustine considers but rejects as an analogy for the Trinity the analogy of human father, mother, and child, mainly on the grounds of lack of scriptural support. See his *De Trinitate* 12. chs. 5 and 6. His discussion treats Scripture in this place in a very literal way, and is in any case marred by supposing that since the Father is called 'father' and the Son 'son', the analogy would require him to look in Scripture for a comparison of the Spirit to a mother. But since the Spirit is supposed to be the third member of the Trinity who in some sense depends on the other two, that comparison is obviously not the appropriate one. Gregory Nazianzen makes a comparison of the Trinity to Adam, Eve, and Seth whom he claims also to be 'consubstantial', his main point being that one person can come from another person by means other than begetting—Eve coming from Adam's rib—and that this provides an analogy for the non-begetting means of origin of the Spirit from the Father. See his *Theological Orations*, 5. 11.

[5] Important to medieval thought was the Dionysian Principle that goodness is by its very nature diffusive of itself and so of being. A perfectly good being will cause

If divine individuals can thus multiply, why should not the process continue further? The reason why it was an overall good that
the first divine individual should bring about the second was that
otherwise there would be none with whom to share totally; and the
reason why it was an overall good that the first and second divine
individuals should bring abut a third was that otherwise there would
be no one with whom to co-operate in sharing totally. But that
argument does not provide a reason for any more bringing about.
In allowing the other divine individuals to exercise sovereignty in
a certain area, and thus backing that sovereignty with his own sovereignty, each gives and co-operates in sharing. But if giving and co-
operating in sharing are overriding goods, why not co-operating with
two others in sharing? My ethical intuitions are inevitably highly
fallible here, but it seems to me that co-operating with two others
in sharing is not essential to the manifestation of love so long as
co-operation with one in sharing is going on. There is a qualitative
difference between sharing and co-operating in sharing, and hence
overriding reason for divine acts of both kinds; but, as it seems to
me, no similar qualitative difference between co-operating with
one in sharing and co-operating with two. So one divine individual
(or two or three such together) could not create a fourth as an act
of essence. But no divine individual could create another divine
individual as act of will. For any being created by an act of will
might (metaphysically) not have existed, and so could not be divine.

I conclude (tentatively) that necessarily if there is at least one
divine individual, and if it is logically possible that there be more
than one divine individual, then there are three and only three divine
individuals. The logical possibility seems to exist if there exists one
divine individual with metaphysical but not ontological necessity,
and if divine individuals lack thisness. Otherwise there is no possibility of there being more than one divine individual. I have presented a priori arguments why one might expect a divine individual
to have only metaphysical necessity and to lack thisness, but those

---

more and more existence. A crucial issue was whether the perfect goodness of God
was adequately expressed in the continual mutual sustenance of the Trinity, or
whether perfect goodness needed to express itself further, e.g. in creating a universe.
I am much indebted to lectures by Norman Kretzmann for drawing my attention
to this issue. See his 'Goodness, Knowledge, and Indeterminacy in the Philosophy
of Thomas Aquinas', *Journal of Philosophy*, 80 (1983), 631–49; and two papers in S.
MacDonald (ed.), *Being and Goodness* (Cornell University Press, 1991).

arguments can hardly be regarded as other than balance of probability arguments.

The Traditional Doctrine

If my two conditions on divine individuals—that a divine individual has metaphysical but not ontological necessity, and lacks thisness—are satisfied, and also my moral intuitions about the overriding goodness of different kinds of causing existence are correct, then there follows the traditional Christian doctrine of the Trinity, understood in a certain way. This doctrine was first stated in credal form in the Nicene Creed promulgated by the Council of Constantinople in AD 381, and famously captured in the Athanasian Creed, a late document of perhaps the sixth century AD.

This doctrine involves the claim that there is only one God, but three divine individuals, each of whom is God; and whether that follows from my account depends on how 'there is only one God' and 'each divine individual is God' are to be understood. If 'there is only one God' meant 'there is only one divine individual', then the doctrine of the Trinity would be manifestly self-contradictory. So clearly Church councils in affirming both must have understood 'there is only one God' in a somewhat subtler sense—since no person and no Council affirming something which they intend to be taken with utter seriousness can be read as affirming an *evident* contradiction. What in denying tritheism, the view that there are three Gods, were Councils ruling out? I suggest that they were denying that there were three *independent* divine beings, any of which could exist without the other; or which could act independently of each other.[6]

On the account which I have given, the three divine individuals taken together would form a collective source of the being of all other things; the members would be totally mutually dependent and necessarily jointly behind each other's acts. This collective would be indivisible in its being for logical reasons—that is, the kind of being that it would be is such that each of its members is necessarily

---

[6] In his discussion of how the Fathers understood the unity of God, Stead comments that 'Christian thinking on the unity of God remained largely intuitive'. See G. C. Stead, *Divine Substance* (Clarendon Press, 1977), 180–9, esp. 181.

everlasting, and would not have existed unless it had brought about or been brought about by the others. The collective would also be indivisible in its causal action in the sense that each would back totally the causal action of the others.[7] The collective would be causeless and so (in my sense), unlike its members, ontologically necessary, not dependent for its existence on anything outside itself. It is they, however, rather than it, who, to speak strictly, would have the divine properties of omnipotence, omniscience, etc.; though clearly there is a ready and natural sense in which the collective can be said to have them as well. If all members of a group know something, the group itself, by a very natural extension of use, can be said to know that thing:[8] and so on. Similarly this very strong unity of the collective would make it, as well as its individual members, an appropriate object of worship.[9] The claim that 'there is only one God' is to be read as the claim that the source of being of all other things has to it this kind of indivisible unity.

But then how is the claim that each of the individuals is 'God' to be understood? Simply as the claim that each is divine—omnipotent, perfectly good, etc. Each such being would be an all-perfect source of all things—what more could councils intelligibly mean by that claim that an individual is God? On this reading, unavoidable if we are to make any sense of the creeds, 'there is one God' is to be read in such a way that '*a* is God' and '*b* is God' and 'there is only one God' do not entail '$a = b$'. There is an ambiguity in the Greek and Latin of the creeds, which justifies a different understanding of θεός and *deus* (normally both translated into English as 'God') in different places in the creeds. Both words may function either as a predicate meaning 'a god' (a divine individual, in some sense of 'divine' without any implication of uniqueness) or as a referring expression 'God' (being either the proper name or the definite description of the, in some sense, unique Supreme Being). Latin does not have a definite article and so *deus* may mean either

---

[7] As e.g. the Father and Spirit 'themselves did not become incarnate, but the Father approved and the Spirit cooperated when the Son himself effected his Incarnation', St Maximus the Confessor, *On the Lord's Prayer*, (PG 90: 876).

[8] The claim of Chapter 6 that the features of the passage of time which might seem unwelcome (making God 'time's prisoner') come to God only by his own choice, must now be read as claiming that they come only by the choice of some member of the collective.

[9] For discussion of what makes a being worthy of worship, see my *The Coherence of Theism* (Clarendon Press, 1977), ch. 15.

'a god' or 'the god', and if it means the latter, divinity amounts to a lot more than it does in the former case. And although Greek does have a definite article (ό), it may not always be used when uniqueness is assumed, and θεός by itself may be 'a god', 'God', or even function as an adjective ('divine', often then translated into Latin by *divus*). Given this ambiguity, it is not implausible to read the creeds as asserting that three divine individuals (in my sense) together constitute one God (in my sense). The creeds are less paradoxical in Greek or Latin than their English translation makes them.

On this understanding of what the creeds mean by saying that there is one God (θεός, *deus*) but three individuals who are each 'God' (i.e. divine, θεός, *deus*), the rest of their claims about the Trinity follow straightforwardly from my account. The individuals are said to be *hypostases*, (ὑποστάσεις), that is, individuals, or *personae* (πρόσωπα); a *persona* is simply a rational individual—'person' in the sense described in Chapter 1.[10] As it follows from my argument that there will be, so there is, according to the creeds, a difference between the persons in respect of which depends on which and also in respect of function, and the traditional names bring out both of these aspects of the differences. Traditionally, the first divine individual is called 'Father', the second 'Son' (or 'Word'), the third 'Spirit'. 'Father' seems a name appropriate to the original source. Both 'Son' and 'Word' suggest a second or third divine individual. Biblical tradition apportions both these names to Christ, and if the second person of the Trinity became incarnate, they are then appropriate names for that second person. Apart from insisting that the second person of the Trinity alone became incarnate, the early church had no very clear view about which members of the Trinity did what,[11] although the name of 'Spirit' derived from

[10] David Brown claims that in the patristic period πρόσωπον and *persona* both carried a sense of 'character' as well as of individual. See his 'Trinitarian Personhood and Individuality' in R. J. Feenstra and C. Plantinga (eds.), *Trinity, Incarnation and Atonement* (University of Notre Dame Press, 1989). It would follow that the earliest attempts to formulate the doctrine of the Trinity clearly would be initially susceptible of a variety of interpretations, which would need to be refined in the course of subsequent discussion and doctrine formulation.

[11] M. Wiles, 'Some Reflections on the Origins of the Doctrine of the Trinity', *Journal of Theological Studies*, NS 8 (1957), 92–106, 95–9. For response to Wiles, see Sarah Coakley, 'Why Three? Some Further Reflections on the Doctrine of the Trinity', in S. Coakley and D. A. Pailin (eds.), *The Making and Remaking of Christian Doctrine* (Clarendon Press, 1993).

many biblical sources was often recognized as giving the third individual a primary role in sanctification. Later centuries saw the earlier confusion about who did what as reinforcing a view that all three were at work in each divine act[12]— which does follow from my account in the form that any act of each is backed by the others. My arguments do, however, suggest a different primary role for each (in areas where reason does not dictate a unique action). But I have no arguments beyond any deriving from biblio-ecclesiastical tradition for tying the members of the Trinity defined by their relative dependences with any particular roles.

If the second person of the Trinity is to be called 'Son' an obvious name for the kind of way in which the Father brings him about is 'begets'. Early church theologians and scholastics thought of 'creates' as applicable only to the bringing about of something finite by an act of will, and so they avoided that word for the bringing about within the Trinity. 'Made' for them meant made out of some pre-existing matter. Hence their wish for a new word; but they were careful in all expositions of its meaning to explain that 'begetting' connoted no sexual process, a fact made clear by there being no other 'parent' beside the Father. Since there is a difference in the mode of dependence of Son on Father from that of Spirit on Son and Father, since the dependence is on two rather than on one, and results from the overriding goodness of co-operation in sharing rather than the overriding goodness of sharing itself, Church councils gave a different name to the mode of origin of Spirit from Father and Son—'proceeding'. (Avoiding the word 'begotten' for this process of dependence on two does have the additional advantage of avoiding the obvious analogy for the second divine individual of 'mother', which would make the assumption that some sort of sexual process was involved in the origin of the Spirit almost unavoidable.) Augustine expresses agnosticism about the nature of the difference between 'begetting' and 'proceeding'.[13] Aquinas uses a different terminology so that 'proceeding' is a generic name for what results from both bringings about, 'begetting' is the species of bringing about which applies to the Father/Son case, and he hesitantly suggests a word 'spirating' to cover the bringing about

---

[12] Wiles, 'Reflections', 101–3.
[13] *Contra Maximinum*, 2. 14 (PL 42: 770). See also St John Damascene, *De fide orthodoxa* 1. 8, 'We have learned that there is a difference between generation and procession, but the nature of that difference we in no way understand.'

of the Holy Spirit.[14] He also insists there is a difference between the two bringings about but can tell us little more about it. I have tried to say a little more about wherein it must consist, namely, simply in dependence on two co-causes as opposed to dependence on one cause. That the difference between 'begetting' and 'proceeding' consists simply in this was the teaching of Gregory of Nyssa in the later fourth century:

That is the only way by which we distinguish one Person from the other, by believing, that is, that one is the cause and the other depends on the cause. Again, we recognize another distinction with regard to that which depends on the cause. There is that which depends on the first cause and that which is derived from what immediately depends on the first cause. Thus the attribute of being only-begotten without doubt remains with the Son, and we do not question that the Spirit is derived from the Father. For the mediation of the Son, while it guards his prerogative of being only-begotten, does not exclude the relation which the Spirit has by nature to the Father.[15]

The Western Church's version of the Nicene Creed asserts that the Spirit 'proceeds from the Father and the Son', whereas the original version preserved by the Eastern Church asserts that the Spirit proceeds 'from the Father', though individual Eastern theologians taught that the procession from the Father is 'through the Son'.[16] It seems to me that the Western version brings out the fact, which alone on my argument could account for it, that the generation of the Spirit is a co-operative act.

The three individuals all have the same essence, that is, they are each of the same essential kind, namely, divine. The mutual dependence of the three persons is naturally called περιχώρησις, 'interpenetration' or 'coinherence'. In acting towards the outside world (i.e. in creating or sustaining other substances), although (unless there is a unique best action) one individual initiates any action, the initiating act (whether of active or permissive causation) is backed by the co-causation of the others—hence the slogan *omnia opera Trinitatis ad extra indivisa sunt* ('all the acts of the Trinity towards the outside world are indivisible'). (In consequence of

[14] *Summa theologiae*, 1a. 27. 4 ad 3.
[15] Gregory of Nyssa, 'An Answer to Ablabius: That we Should Not Think of Saying—There Are Three Gods', trans. C. C. Richardson in E. R. Hardy (ed.), *Christology of the Later Fathers* (The Westminster Press, 1954), 266.
[16] See e.g. St Maximus the Confessor, PG 91: 136.

such co-causation, I shall often continue to write of 'God' doing
this or that, except where it is important to bring out which member
of the Trinity initiates such action.) But within the Trinity there
must be, I argued, some asymmetry of dependence—God the Father
is not caused to exist actively by the Son or Spirit. He is in this
sense uncaused, although throughout any period which has a beginning he is permitted to exist by the others. And there is inevitably
a similar asymmetry of dependence for each of the others.[17] But since
the Father had no option but to cause the Son, and Father and Son
had no option but to cause the Spirit, and all exist eternally, the
dependence of Son on Father, and of Spirit on Father and Son,
does not diminish greatness. Each could not exist but as eternally
causing or permitting the other or others to exist. A king who at
some stage in his reign voluntarily shares his kingdom with another
may well be thought to be greater than the other. But a king who
for all his reign has to share his kingdom with another may reasonably be considered no greater than the other.

All of this is what we find in what the Nicene Creed has to say
about the Trinity:

We believe in one God (θεός), the Father Almighty . . . and in one Lord
Jesus Christ, the only-begotten Son of God, begotten of the Father before
all ages, . . . true God of true God, begotten not made, of one substance
(ὁμοουσιός) with the Father . . . And in the Holy Spirit that proceeds from
the Father [and the Son] who with the Father and the Son is worshipped
and glorified together.

The Council of Nicaea declared the Son to be ὁμοουσιός with the
Father. It may well have meant by that only that Father and Son
were both (to use the technical patristic term) 'of the same second
substance', that is, both divine.[18] But a stronger understanding of
ὁμοουσιός soon arose, to the effect that Father, Son, and Spirit
were all 'of the same first substance', namely, in some sense formed
the same individual thing. I have explained the sense in which that
also is true. The words 'and the Son' (filioque) describing the source

---

[17] See Additional Note 13.

[18] St Athanasius, the Council's most famous subsequent advocate, gave four
analogies for the Father/Son relationship, three of which were relations between
distinct individuals (substances in my sense or 'first substances', to use the patristic
term) (including the analogy of the literal father/son relationship) and only one of
which was a relation of things within an individual (the analogy of a mind and a
word spoken by the mind). See Stead, *Divine Substance*, 262 f.

of the Spirit's procession were not originally in the Nicene Creed, but were added later to the Western version;[19] but, as I have noted, even the Eastern version seems to allow a certain asymmetry of dependence.

Likewise the account of the Trinity which I have derived fits in with what the Athanasian Creed has to say about it:

the Catholic Faith is this: that we worship one God in Trinity, and Trinity in Unity; neither confounding the Persons, nor dividing the substance. For there is one Person of the Father, another of the Son, and another of the Holy Spirit. But the Godhead of the Father, of the Son, and the Holy Spirit is all one: the Glory equal, the Majesty coeternal . . . The Father uncreated, the Son uncreated, and the Holy Spirit uncreated . . . the Father eternal, the Son eternal, and the Holy Spirit eternal. And yet there are not three eternals but one eternal . . . So likewise the Father is Almighty, the Son Almighty, and the Holy Spirit Almighty. And yet there are not three Almighties, but one Almighty . . . Like as we are compelled by the Christian verity to acknowledge each Person by himself to be God and Lord; so we are forbidden by the Catholic religion to say that there are three gods or three Lords. The Father is made of none, neither created nor begotten. The Son is of the Father alone, not made, nor created but begotten. The Holy Spirit is of the Father and the Son; neither made, nor created, nor begotten but proceeding . . . In this Trinity none is before or after another, none is greater or less than another . . . He therefore that will be saved must thus think of the Trinity.

I derived the traditional formulas by reading the *deus* (θεός), which the Father, Son, and Spirit are each said to be, differently from the *deus* (θεός) which is used when it is said that there are not three *dei* but one *deus*. Unless we do this, it seems to me that the traditional formulas are self-contradictory. If we read all occurrences of *deus* as occurrences of the same referring expression, the Athanasian Creed then asserts that Father, Son, and Spirit are each of them the same individual thing, and also that they have different properties, for example, the Father begets but is not begotten. But that is not possible; if things are the same, they must have all the same properties. Alternatively, if we read all occurrences as occurrences of the same predicate, attributing the same property, the

---

[19] On the controversy which led up to this insertion and has subsequently been a point of division between Roman Catholicism and Eastern Orthodoxy, see J. N. D. Kelly, *Early Christian Creeds*, 3rd edn. (A. & C. Black, 1972), 358–67.

Athanasian Creed then claims that each of the three persons, which are not the same persons as each other, is divine; but there is only one divine thing which is a substance, God the Holy Trinity.[20] But how can there be three divine things, and yet only one? Contradiction looms. There have been attempts to make sense of there being three divine persons, and yet only one divine substance, by means of the philosophical doctrine of relative identity, especially recently by Peter van Inwagen.[21] The reader will recall from Chapter 1 that a philosophical doctrine of relative identity claims that one thing, a, which is (ϕ and ψ) may be the same ϕ as b but not the same ψ as b; sameness is relative to the sortal (ϕ or ψ). The sort of example the doctrine has in mind is that some statue may be the same statue as an earlier statue but not the same lump of brass as the earlier one (because the lump of brass has been gradually replaced in the interval by new brass formed into the same shape). Van Inwagen then claims analogously that 'substance' (which he equates with 'being'), 'God', and 'person' are sortal terms, such that the Father is the same substance, and so the same God, as the Son; but not the same person as the Son. Likewise the Spirit is the same substance and God as the Son, but not the same person. From this it follows that there are three persons, each of which is God, but only one God. Van Inwagen has developed a very rigorous formal logic of relative identity, which, he claims, prevents us from drawing any contradictions from statements such as these.

However, the philosophical objections to any doctrine of relative identity deployed in Chapter I remain. If 'the Father', 'the Son', and 'the Spirit' are to have clear uses, then each must have associated with it a substance-sortal (or more than one sortal, so long as the sortals carve up the world in the same way); they cannot have sortals associated with them which diverge in their subsequent applications. If 'the Father' is the name of a person who is not the same person as the Son or the Spirit, then it cannot also be the name of a God (or a substance) who is the same God (or substance)

---

[20] Note the difference between this version and mine. Both claim in effect that there is one logically indivisible substance, God; but I am not claiming that it is the only substance—the persons which form it are also substances—nor am I claiming that it is divine in exactly the same sense as the persons are divine.

[21] Peter van Inwagen, 'And yet there are not three Gods, but one God', in T. V. Morris (ed.), *Philosophy and the Christian Faith* (University of Notre Dame Press, 1988).

as the Son and the Spirit.[22] And if we deny that 'the Father' etc. do have clear uses, we deny any clear content to the doctrine of the Trinity at all.[23]

In AD 1215 The Fourth Lateran Council claimed firmly, in purported refutation of the views of Joachim of Fiore, that the unity of the Godhead was not just a collective unity 'in the way that many human beings are said to make one people, and many believers one church'. Rather it is the same 'thing', 'that is divine substance, essence or nature' which 'truly is the Father, and is the Son, and is the Spirit', 'That thing is not begetting, nor begotten, nor proceeding, but is the Father who begets, and the Son who is begotten, and the Holy Spirit who proceeds, so that there may be distinction of persons but unity of nature.'[24] These expressions can certainly be read in such a way as to be claiming that there are three divine individuals and each is the same substance (in my sense), leading to the clear contradiction from which the doctrine of relative identity cannot help us to escape. It is so read if we read the *res*, 'thing', which is said to be 'substance' (*substantia*) as *a* substance in my sense. But if 'substance' just means 'essence' or 'nature', as the Council glosses it, then there is *a* way of reading what it said along the lines which I have developed in this chapter. We saw in the previous chapter that there was a sense in which a divine individual is his essence,

---

[22] Timothy W. Bartel has shown that the Relative Trinitarian (i.e. a theologian who relies on a principle of relative identity to save the doctrine of the Trinity) cannot save his doctrine by modifying the absolute doctrine of identity to a doctrine which brings in '*qua*-ness', i.e. talks of the Son having certain properties only *qua* human or *qua* divine. The modified doctrine would hold not that: 'for any x and any y and any sortal f, if x is the same f as y, then for any property P, x has P if and only if y has P', but only that: 'for any x and any y and any sortal f and any property P, if x is the same f as y, then x has P *qua* f if and only if y has P *qua* f'. He shows that even this principle forces the relative Trinitarian to deny that Father, Son, and Spirit have any distinct properties, e.g. to deny that 'begetting the Son' is a property only of the Father. See Timothy W. Bartel, 'The Plight of the Relative Trinitarian', *Religious Studies*, 24 (1988), 129–55.

[23] As van Inwagen points out, the same might still be said of some sentences purporting to describe the content of such deep physical theories as Quantum Theory. But in physics a scientist simply has to operate with the sentences, he is not required in any sense to believe the propositions which they express. Since belief in the Trinity is commended to Christians by the Church, the Church must be purporting to teach the doctrine as one of which there is some graspable content; and if a certain form of that doctrine has the consequence that there cannot be, the Church cannot coherently commend that form for belief, for there is nothing in which belief in it would consist.

[24] H. Denzinger, *Enchiridion Symbolorum*, 23rd edn. (Freiburg, 1963) (henceforward 'Denzinger'), nos. 803 f.

namely, that he lacks thisness—there is nothing more to a divine individual than the instantiation of the divine essence and any further individuating relational properties (e.g. 'being begotten'). Hence what the Council *may* be saying is this: the Godhead is not just three individuals, each with its thisness, who have common essential properties. Rather, it is exactly the instantiation of the same essence of divinity which makes the Father God, as makes the Son God, as makes the Spirit God. They would be the same individual but for the relational properties which are distinct from the divine essence and which distinguish them.[25]

Articulations in the Christian tradition of the doctrine of the Trinity are often distinguished into forms of social Trinitarianism that stress the separateness of the persons, and forms of relative Trinitarianism that stress the unity of the Godhead. What I have expounded is, I suppose, a moderate form of social Trinitarianism but one which stresses both the logical inseparability of the divine persons in the Trinity, and the absence of anything by which the persons of the Trinity are individuated except their relational properties.[26]

[25] Christopher Hughes, *On a Complex Theory of a Simple God* (Cornell University Press, 1989), chs. 5 and 6 rightly sees (p. 176) that we need to interpret 'of the same substance' (ὁμοουσιός) as a relation 'which links the persons closely while allowing them to be discernible with respect to a certain range of properties', and rightly rejects Aquinas's theory on the grounds that to get a non-Sabellian trinity (i.e. to get the doctrine that there are three distinct persons, not just three modes of operation of one person) we have to allow that in some sense there is composition in God. However, I find Hughes's own positive suggestion as to how to construe the doctrine unappealing. He suggests understanding 'of the same substance' as 'made of the same stuff', and the three persons as, as it were, three different ways in which that stuff is organized. My principal objection is that stuff cannot individuate persons, for the reasons given in Ch. 2.

[26] The most influential modern statement of social Trinitarianism is Jürgen Moltmann, *The Trinity and the Kingdom of God*, trans. M. Kohl (SCM Press, 1981). He opposes the relative Trinitarian views of the early Karl Barth (Church Dogmatics, 1. 1, *The Doctrine of the Word of God*, trans. G. T. Thomson (T. & T. Clark, 1936), ch. 2, pt. 1, 'The Triune God'), and Karl Rahner (see, among other places, the short essay in his *Theological Investigations*, iv, 'Remarks on the Dogmatic Treatise "De Trinitate"', trans. K. Smith (Darton, Longman, & Todd, 1966)). Although it seems to me that Moltmann does not give an adequate account of what binds the members of the Trinity together, my sympathies are more with him than with Barth and Rahner. For Barth, the Trinity is simply three 'modes of existence' of the one God. For Rahner (*Theological Investigations*, iv. 101 f.) the Trinity is simply 'the three-fold quality of God in himself', his triune 'personality'. He denies that there are 'three different consciousnesses'. For a typology of modern theological writing on the Trinity see Coakley, 'Why Three?'.

The reason which I have given for why a divine individual must give rise to another and hence a third, that goodness is essentially diffusive and generous, was, I believe, implicitly or explicitly, at the heart of the thinking of many of those of early centuries who advocated the doctrine of the Holy Trinity. Of course the biblical texts had enormous influence, yet on their own they could have given rise to a hundred different theologies. Certainly emanations and trinities formed part of the common stock of religious ideas current in the Mediterranean of the first centuries AD, but these ideas took many different forms, and there were other ideas around. So why did Christians choose to see in the biblical texts Trinitarianism of the kind which subsequently became the orthodoxy? The answer is, I think, this. They had two basic convictions. One was that our complex and orderly universe derived its being from a single personal source of being, possessed of all perfection. The other was that perfection includes perfect love. There is something profoundly imperfect and therefore inadequately divine in a solitary divine individual. If such an individual is love, he must share, and sharing with finite beings such as humans is not sharing all of one's nature and so is imperfect sharing. A divine individual's love has to be manifested in a sharing with another divine individual, and that (to keep the divine unity) means (in some sense) within the god-head, that is, in mutual dependence and support.

Augustine made the remark with respect to the Father generating an equal, *Si voluit et non potuit, infirmus est; si potuit et non voluit, invidus est*: 'if he wished to and could not, he is weak; if he could but did not wish to, he is envious'.[27] But for explicit a priori argument of the kind which I have given as to why there need to be three and only three divine individuals, we have to wait for Richard of St Victor in the twelfth century. In *De Trinitate* he developed the points both that perfect love involves there being someone else to whom to be generous; and also that perfect loving involves a third individual, the loving of whom could be shared with the second. The Father needs *socium et condilectum* (an ally and one fellow-loved) in his loving.[28] Richard also gives what are in effect two further arguments for the necessary bringing about of a third divine individual—that anyone who really loves will seek the good

---

[27] *De diversis quaestionibus* 83. q. 50 (Migne, PL 40: 31).
[28] *De Trinitate* 3. 14 and 3. 15.

of the beloved both by finding someone else for him to love and (by the same act) finding someone else for him to be loved by. That demand too will be fully satisfied by three persons. Other medievals echoed Richard's views, often quoting him by name.[29]

Aquinas claims that the doctrine of the Trinity cannot be known by natural reason,[30] but only by revelation; and he then goes on to explain (in effect) that while sound deductive arguments from evident data can be given for the existence of God, only somewhat weak inductive arguments can be given for the Trinity.[31] My own view, and that of many, is that Aquinas has overestimated the capacity of human reason with respect to the existence of God. Only fairly strong inductive arguments can be given for the existence of God.[32] Given that, arguments for there being a God and God being 'three persons in one substance' will be of the same kind. My claim is that the data which suggest that there is a God suggest that the most probable kind of God is such that inevitably he becomes tripersonal. It is for this reason that the doctrine of the Trinity is not a more complicated hypothesis than the hypothesis of a sole divine individual; the simplest sort of God to whom arguments lead inevitably tripersonalizes, to coin a word. If some simple hypothesis put forward by a scientist to explain complex data entails some further complex consequences, that makes it no less simple—especially if there can be other evidence for those consequences.

The Christian revelation teaches the doctrine of the Trinity as a central element of its creeds. Any evidence from the circumstances of its origin that that revelation is true[33] confirms the doctrine of the Trinity; just as any a priori grounds for supposing the doctrine of the Trinity to be true is evidence that the Christian revelation (and so any elements it contains) is true. What I have presented as a priori a marginally more probable account of the divine nature than any other, becomes enormously more probable if backed up by revelation.

---

[29] Alexander of Hales (*Summa theologiae* 1. 304) quotes Richard of St Victor. St Bonaventure (*Itinerarium*, 6) writes of the need for an eternal principle having a 'beloved and a cobeloved'.

[30] *Summa theologiae*, 1a. 32. 1.   [31] Ibid. 1a. 32. 1 ad 2.

[32] See my *The Existence of God* (Clarendon Press, 1979), 119 for the negative claim that deductive arguments cannot be given. See *The Existence of God, passim,* for the positive claim that fairly strong inductive arguments can be given.

[33] For the nature of such evidence see my *Revelation* (Clarendon Press, 1992).

9

The Possibility of Incarnation

The Coherence of Chalcedon

The central doctrine of Christianity is that God intervened in human history in the person of Jesus Christ in a unique way; and that quickly became understood as the doctrine that in Jesus Christ the second person of the Trinity became man, that is, human. In AD 451 the Council of Chalcedon formulated that doctrine in a precise way utilizing the then current philosophical terminology, which provided a standard for the orthodoxy of subsequent thought on this issue. It affirmed its belief in 'our Lord Jesus Christ . . . truly divine (θεός) and truly human (ἄνθρωπος) . . . in two natures . . . the distinction of natures being in no way annulled by the union, but rather the characteristics of each nature being preserved and coming together to form one person'.[1] One individual (ὑπόστασις), one thing that is; and being a rational individual, one person. An individual's nature are those general properties that make it the sort of individual it is. The nature of my desk is to be a solid material object of a certain shape; the nature of the oak tree in the wood is to take in water and light, and to grow into a characteristic shape with characteristic leaves and give off oxygen. Chalcedon affirmed that the one individual Jesus Christ had a divine nature, was a divine individual that is; and it assumed that the divine nature was an essential nature. That is, any individual who is divine cannot cease to be divine and become something else instead, and could not ever have been anything else instead. If you lose your essential nature you cease to be (see Ch. 1). The desk's nature, as described above, is an essential property of the desk. If you chop the desk up for firewood or vaporize it, so that there is no longer the material object of a certain shape, then there is no longer the desk. Chalcedon assumed that human nature is not (or not invariably) an essential nature. That is, just occasionally, an individual could become human

---

[1] Denzinger, 302.

or cease to be human while remaining the same individual. It then affirmed that the one individual, the second person of the Trinity, who was eternally divine, became also (at a certain moment of human history, about AD 1) human (i.e. man). He acquired the characteristics of man in addition to those of divinity.

Let us call this claim of the Council of Chalcedon the Chalcedonian definition. My object in this chapter is to investigate first whether the Chalcedonian definition is internally consistent (i.e. coherent), and secondly whether it is consistent with the picture of Christ in the New Testament, utilized in theories of the Atonement, and summarized in another affirmation of the Council of Chalcedon that Christ was 'like us, in all respects, apart from sin'. Is the Chalcedonian definition, that is, consistent with a wider spectrum of Christian teaching? I shall consider in Chapter 10 what grounds there can be for believing it to be true, and I shall there contrast with it other attempts to spell out the doctrine of the Incarnation, rival to Chalcedon.

My analysis of what it is to be divine shares with Chalcedon the view that divine nature (of the kind described in Chapter 7) is an essential nature. The Word of God, the second person of the Trinity could not cease to be divine. I did however argue in Chapter 1 that an individual could become human or cease to be human while remaining the same individual; human nature is not an essential nature—and on this too I am in agreement with Chalcedon's assumption. I suggested there that we have a rather vague understanding of what it is to be human (and my reading does not suggest to me that the Fathers of Chalcedon had any more precise understanding). A human being has as its essential core a human soul, normally connected to a human body. A soul is clearly a human soul if it is capable of having sensations, thoughts (including logical sequences thereof), and purposes (freely chosen); a structure of beliefs and desires (including moral beliefs); all of this caused by an underlying essence, with the right ancestry, with a limitation imposed by the human's body on the extent of his powers and knowledge. But our rather vague ordinary-language understanding of 'human' allows an individual still to count as human even if not all these conditions are satisfied. You get wider and wider understandings of humanity as you drop more and more conditions; and clearly if many of the conditions are not satisfied, it becomes unreasonable to call an individual human.

Given that the soul is the principle of identity of the individual human, nothing can become a human being (while remaining what it is) unless it has, as its principle of identity, the soul which is subsequently the human soul. Becoming a human would involve that soul acquiring the features essential to humanity. In the case of ordinary humans such as ourselves, that individual soul, we found in Chapter 2, was an individual essence, a restriction on a universal such as 'animate being'. But if I am right in what I have suggested in Chapters 7 and 8, that a divine individual, though by analogy a 'personal' being in having like us a mental life, does not have thisness, what individuates it is the divine essence with certain individuating relational properties. In virtue of it being the subject of mental life, such an individual is, on my (Chapter 1) definition, a soul. On which understanding of what are the features essential to humanity, could the soul which is divine, the divine being who is the second person of the Trinity, become also human?

A divine individual could certainly acquire a human body in the sense of a body through which he acts on the world and acquires beliefs about it. Many of the effects he produces through the body will be ones he could (but need not) bring about in other ways. The beliefs which the divine individual would acquire through his body are ones he would have anyway—but now he would acquire them through a new route. He would also, through his sense-organs, acquire some inclinations to hold false beliefs caused by illusion or misinformation striking the ears of his human body. But these inclinations would be overborne by his strongly held true beliefs, which were his through his divine omniscience. A divine individual could also acquire sensations through a human body; and, more generally, a mental life with all the features of a human mental life. For in acting he would have purposes; and being conscious of his beliefs he would have thoughts. And, with two apparent crucial qualifications, he could even have desires. A desire is an inclination to perform an action of some kind, an inclination which causally influences the agent. It does not necessarily determine him to act, but, if there is no countervailing stronger desire, he needs to 'fight against' its influence in order not to act upon it. The first qualification is that, in order to maintain his perfect freedom (that no thing from without causally influences how he acts), a divine individual would himself have continually to cause in himself his desires. And secondly, it would seem that a divine individual can only allow himself to be subject to desires, non-rational inclinations, which, as it were, top up his rational inclinations. A normal agent need not desire to do actions in proportion to his beliefs about the worth of doing them. He may, for example, have no strong desire to do what he believes that he ought to do. For a divine individual, however, desires would have to be aligned with believed worth, and given that in virtue of his omniscience such an individual will have true beliefs about the worth of actions, that means actual worth. A divine individual could desire to do every good action, but he could only have a strongest desire to do what is best to do. Any other desire would be a non-rational influence limiting his perfect freedom of choice. It would do this even if it were to incline him to act in ways compatible with his perfect goodness— for instance, inclining him to do a certain one among a number of equal best actions or a certain one among the infinite number of good actions, each less good than some other good but incompatible action. Above all, a divine individual could not have what we normal humans so often have—a strong desire, not outweighed by a contrary desire, to do an action less good than the best available, let alone a wrong action (i.e. one obligatory not to do). For if the divine individual had such a desire, he might yield to the influence of the desire; and so he could not be necessarily perfectly good.

A divine individual clearly has the four further characteristics listed in Chapter 1, of logical thought, moral awareness, free will, and a structured soul, possessed by humans and not animals. What of the three additional conditions suggested there? Could his body and mental life be caused by the same underlying essence as ours? Yes, an embryo which developed into the divine individual's body could have our genes, and (connected with it) whatever else was necessary to produce human mental life. The natural mechanism which gives rise to souls cannot dictate which soul will arise, for in general souls do not exist before birth, and so there can be no law dictating that a particular bodily process will give rise to this soul as opposed to that one. All the mechanism can do is to ensure that it gives rise to *a* soul, which will then have a certain mental life. That soul, a divine individual could ensure, without violating that mechanism, was his own soul.

Clearly a divine individual would not fulfil the limitation condition. If there is a maximum to abilities (including the ability to acquire true beliefs) if they are to be human abilities, the divine individual would have abilities which exceeded it. On the other hand a divine individual could fulfil the historical condition in that the physical causes which gave rise to his body could be genes derived from the human gene pool.[2] As I wrote earlier, we might reasonably deem the historical condition to be fulfilled sufficiently by genes being derived from one parent rather than two.

I conclude that the only qualifications on the possibility of a divine individual becoming human concern a limit to the kind of desires he can have, and that he cannot satisfy any limitation condition. Clearly the Council of Chalcedon understood 'human' in such a way that it did not involve a limitation condition. For a divine individual could not become human, if to be human an individual has to have limited powers; and this is so obvious that the Fathers of Chalcedon could not have failed to notice it. As we saw in the last chapter, we can readily suppose Councils or individuals to make claims that are internally inconsistent, but only if the inconsistency is not too obvious. If Chalcedon had understood 'human' in such a way that being human involved a limitation condition, the inconsistency in supposing that a divine individual became human (while remaining divine) would have been too obvious to escape notice, and the definition would not have been adopted in its original form.

So if we do not draw the limit of the human too strictly, certainly a divine individual can become human. He would do this by acquiring a human body (joining his soul to an unowned human body), acting, acquiring beliefs, sensations, and desires through it. Remaining divine, he would have become human by acquiring an extension to his normal modes of operation. A divine individual who became incarnate in Christ in this way would, I suggest, have satisfied the Chalcedonian definition of being one individual with both a divine and a human nature, on a not unreasonable interpretation of the latter. Chalcedon also declared that Christ had a 'reasonable soul' ($\psi \upsilon \chi \acute{\eta}$ $\lambda o \gamma \iota \kappa \acute{\eta}$) and by this it seems to have meant an acquired 'human soul'. But the Council could not have meant by this that there were in Christ both a divine and a human soul in my sense of 'soul'. For that would have been to say that Christ was

---

[2] The Fathers did not regard satisfaction of the historical condition as necessary for humanity. 'God could have taken upon himself to be man . . . from some other source, and not from the race of that Adam who bound the human race by his sin.' Augustine, *De Trinitate*, 13. 18.

two individuals, a doctrine to which Chalcedon was greatly opposed. Rather in the affirmation that Christ had a 'reasonable soul', 'soul' is to be understood in an Aristotelian sense; and so the affirmation is to be understood as saying that Christ had a human way of thinking and acting, as well as his divine way.[3]

Although both divine and human properties belonged to the same individual, Christ, it was customary to say that some of them were his *qua* (as) divine, and others were his *qua* human—'Christ as God was omnipotent', 'Christ as man suffered'. What was being said by saying that various actions and properties were his, *qua* human, was that they were his in virtue of his having taken on a human body and a human way of thinking; and what was meant by saying that various actions and properties were his, *qua* divine, was that they were his apart from his having taken on any limitations.

Suffering for example, the Fathers and Church Councils wished to insist, was Christ's only *qua* man. Christ did indeed feel pain, hunger, thirst, and weariness. But *qua* divine, Christ was impassible, unable to suffer. There seems to be one clear correct point here. Suffering is something, pain, happening to you. A divine individual as the cause of all does not have things happen to him, unless he allows them to happen to him. So only if he puts himself in a special position, e.g. by taking on a human nature, can he suffer. But the denial that Christ, *qua* God, suffered cannot be read as a denial that God suffered. For a very clearly advocated patristic doctrine—and one to my mind clearly implied by the Chalcedonian definition—was the doctrine later called *communicatio idiomatum* (ἀντίδοσις ἰδιωμάτων), the doctrine that the human and divine attributes are predicable of the same individual, Christ. In virtue of that, it may be said that God was born of Mary, and so Mary may be called θεότοκος, the Mother of God—as proclaimed by the Council of Ephesus in AD 431. If God can have a mother, he can certainly suffer—although of course he only has either of these properties *qua* man. The Second Council of Constantinople recognized this when it declared it an article of faith that 'one of the Trinity was crucified'.[4]

---

[3] See Additional Note 14.

[4] Denzinger, 432. It follows that if the Father took on, for a split second or permanently, another nature, he could also suffer. But it does not follow from that that the Father did suffer when Christ was crucified.

The controversy resolved by the Council of Chalcedon's declaration that there were two natures in the individual who was Christ, revived two centuries later in an attenuated form in the monothelite controversy—did Christ have only one will (θέλησις or θέλημα) and one source of action (ἐνέργεια) or two? The third Council of Constantinople in AD 681 resolved the controversy by declaring that there were in Christ two natural wills, and two natural sources of action, the human will being 'subject' to the divine.[5]

I do not think that this declaration added very much significant to the Chalcedonian definition. But to see that, we need to understand clearly what it was saying. Both the dyothelites ('two wills') and the monothelites ('one will') firmly held that there was only one individual who willed and acted; and, θέλησις and ἐνέργεια not previously having been given sharp technical senses, the Council could have expressed this point by saying that there was only one will and one source of action. It would thus have construed θέλησις and ἐνέργεια in such a way that their principle of individuation (e.g. what makes a θέλησις the unique one it is) was the individual who had them—for instance, a θέλησις being individuated by whose it is. But in fact the Council chose so to understand these terms that they were individuated by the kind of willing and acting they designated. There was a human kind of willing and acting and a divine kind, and Christ had both, since he acted and willed in both divine and human ways.

The sayings of Christ that, above all, were the source of the two wills doctrine, were the sayings in which Christ contrasts his will with that of the Father to which he submits—for example, the saying in Gethsemane, 'not my will but thine be done' (Luke 22: 42). Now given that the three persons of the Trinity, apart from any incarnation, would have no tendency for their wills to conflict, such sayings must be read, as Gregory of Nyssa urged, as 'Not what I as man will, but what thou and so I as God will.'[6]

By a human kind of willing, I mean a willing of the kind of actions available to humans subject to the kind of desires to which humans are normally subject. By a divine kind of willing I mean a willing to do actions of the kind available to God subject only to desires of the limited kind described earlier. The 'subjection' of the human will to the divine is then naturally interpreted as any

---

[5] Denzinger, 556.   [6] *Antirheticus*, 32.

human desires always being kept in place by stronger divine desires, so that Christ, although subject to human desires, is subject to no balance of human desires which in any way impedes his perfect freedom. Christ could be subject to a desire to avoid pain, but when it was not good to avoid pain, he would also have a stronger desire not to avoid pain. Christ would not, on this account, even be subject on balance to any desire to do just one of two or more equal best actions—for that would impair his perfect freedom to choose between them. He could not be subject on balance to a desire to befriend one disciple more than the others, unless there were a good reason so to do—for that desire would impair his perfect freedom to choose which disciple to befriend most. (Of course it would often be that the mere fact of his incarnation would make certain acts best acts or even obligatory for him when they would not otherwise be so—e.g. to show more love to Mary than to all other humans, because she was his mother.) All of this is a perfectly internally coherent further explication of Chalcedon.

The Limitedness of Christ

As so far expounded, the Chalcedonian definition simply says that God the Son acquired an additional nature to the divine nature; and, as he walked on earth, he continued to have all the divine properties, such as necessary omnipotence, omniscience, perfect freedom, and perfect goodness. In consequence it seems to fit badly with certain things said about Christ in the New Testament, and also to make it so easy for Christ to live a good human life that his doing so would not be the costly sacrifice needed to achieve our salvation.

It seems to fit badly with certain things said about Christ in the New Testament in respect of his ignorance, his weakness, and the extent to which he was open to temptation. St Luke's Gospel asserts that the boy Jesus 'advanced in wisdom' (Luke 2: 52), that is, grew in knowledge, which seems to imply that he was not omniscient all the time. So too does the passage in St Mark's Gospel, to which I referred earlier, in which Jesus is reported as claiming that he, 'the Son', does not know something which the Father does know—'the hour' at which 'Heaven and Earth shall pass away' (Mark 13: 31 f.).

And Christ's cry of dereliction from the Cross, 'My God, my God, why hast thou forsaken me?' (Mark 15: 34) might seem to suggest that Christ at that moment ceased to believe that God was sustaining him. There is a passage in St Mark that casts similar doubt on Christ's omnipotence. It is reported that in a visit to his own country, Jesus 'could do there no mighty work' (Mark 6: 5). The Epistle to the Hebrews claims of our 'High Priest', namely, Jesus, that he is not one who 'cannot be touched with the feeling of our infirmities', and that suggests (though does not entail) that Jesus is weak, and so again not omnipotent. And, finally, although perhaps not formally incompatible with any obvious biblical passage, the view that Christ's being tempted was simply a matter of his being subject to a desire to which he could never yield, does not seem the natural picture suggested by the agony of Gethsemane, nor by two remarks in the Epistle to the Hebrews. Christ is said to have 'learned obedience by the things which he suffered', and to have been 'made perfect' (i.e. over time) (Heb. 5: 8 f.); this might suggest that he was not immune to temptation to begin with, but by not yielding to it became immune. And if Christ was 'in *all* points tempted like as we are' (Heb. 4: 15), more openness to temptation would seem to be suggested.

Some of these passages are susceptible of other interpretations which have some plausibility and I have urged elsewhere that biblical passages should be interpreted in the light of Christian doctrines.[7] Nevertheless the general feeling which many readers of the New Testament surely get is that it pictures a Jesus rather more like ourselves than the Christ of the Chalcedonian definition. Other Christian doctrines also suggest that the traditional exposition of Chalcedon needs improvement. The Chalcedonian definition itself rephrases the Epistle to the Hebrews to assert that Christ was 'like us in all respects, apart from sin'. All Christian theories of the Atonement have claimed that it was effected by Christ doing good when men did ill, although he was no better equipped than they for doing good; if he was as knowledgeable and predetermined to do the best as the traditional exposition affirms, that claim would be hard to justify.[8] As St Gregory Nazianzen famously remarked, 'What

[7] See my *Revelation* (Clarendon Press, 1992), *passim*, esp. ch. 10.

[8] For such theories, and the role of Christ's supererogatory acts, according to my favoured theory of the Atonement, the Sacrifice Theory, see *Responsibility and Atonement* (Clarendon Press, 1989), esp. ch. 10.

Christ has not assumed, he has not healed; but what has been united with God is saved.'[9] The traditional exposition of Chalcedon might not seem adequately to affirm that he has taken on board all of us.

Many of the Fathers, especially the earlier ones and especially those of the Antiochene tradition, held that Christ was more like ourselves in the respects described than the traditional interpretation of Chalcedon later allowed.[10] Can we interpret the Chalcedonian definition in a way that respects their viewpoint? I think that we can with the aid of a modern idea, the divided mind. It was Freud above all who helped us to see how an agent can have two systems of belief to some extent independent of each other. In performing some actions, the agent is acting on one system of belief and not guided by beliefs of the other system; and conversely. Although all his beliefs are accessible—they would not be his beliefs unless he had privileged access to them—he refuses to admit to his consciousness beliefs relevant to his action, on which he is not acting. Thus, to take a well-worn example, a mother may refuse to acknowledge to herself a belief that her son is dead or to allow some of her actions to be guided by it. When asked if she believes that he is dead, she says 'No', and this is an honest reply, for it is guided by those beliefs of which she is conscious. Yet other actions of hers may be guided by the belief that he is dead—for instance, she may throw away some of his possessions—even though she does not admit that belief to consciousness. The refusal to admit a belief to consciousness is of course itself also something that the agent in this example refuses to admit to herself to be happening.

The Freudian account of the divided mind was of course derived from analysis of cases of human self-deception, when the beliefs of one belief system and the belief that the systems have been separated are not consciously acknowledged, and where the self-deception is a pathetic state from which the individual needs to be rescued. But such cases and the Freudian account of them helps us to see the logical possibility of an individual for good reason with conscious intention keeping a lesser belief system separate from his main belief system, and simultaneously doing different actions guided by different sets of beliefs of which he is consciously aware.

[9] *Epistola* 101. 7 (PG 37: 181).
[10] On the ignorance of Christ, see e.g. J. Tixeront, *History of Dogmas*, 2nd edn. (B. Herder Book Co., 1926), ii. 287 f.

Indeed even those of us who do not suffer from bad cases of a Freudian divided mind can sometimes perform at once two quite separate tasks—for example, having a conversation with someone and writing a letter to someone else—in directing which quite distinct beliefs are involved, which we can recognize as 'on the way to' a divided mind in which the beliefs of both parts are consciously acknowledged.

Now a divine individual could not give up his knowledge, and so his beliefs; but he could, in becoming incarnate in Christ and acquiring a human belief-acquisition system, through his choice, keep the inclinations to belief resulting therefrom to some extent separate from his divine knowledge system. Different actions would be done in the light of different systems. The actions done through the human body, the thoughts consciously entertained connected with the human brain, the interpretation of perceptual data acquired through the human eyes, would all be done in the light of the human belief-system. So, too, would any public statement made through his human mouth. However, his divine knowledge-system will inevitably include the knowledge that his human system contains the beliefs that it does; and it will include those among the latter which are true. The separation of the belief-systems would be a voluntary act, knowledge of which was part of the divine knowledge-system but not of the human knowledge-system. We thus get a picture of a divine consciousness and a human consciousness of God Incarnate, the former including the latter, but not conversely.[11]

The beliefs in the two parts of a divided mind may sometimes be explicitly contradictory (e.g. a belief that the son is alive and a belief that the son is dead). In such a case, it is misleading to call both beliefs 'beliefs' without qualification, since at least one does not form part of a general view of the world but merely guides the subject's actions in certain circumstances. The overall constant and ever-present view of the world of a God who became incarnate in the way described would be his divine view; and so the 'beliefs' belonging to that view could be described as 'beliefs', whereas the

---

[11] Models of Christ's knowledge on these lines are developed in David Brown, *The Divine Trinity* (Duckworth, 1985), 260–7; and in Thomas V. Morris, *The Logic of God Incarnate* (Cornell University Press, 1986), 102–7. The Freudian model of the divided mind has been applied to Christology quite a bit in this century, beginning with W. Sanday, *Christologies Ancient and Modern* (Oxford University Press, 1910).

'beliefs' belonging to the human perspective would be mere inclinations to belief or propositions guiding a limited set of actions. But it would be those inclinations belonging to the human perspective which guided Christ's honest public statements (honest, because guided by those beliefs of which he is conscious in his human acting).

Christ's human acts are the public acts done through his human body and the private mental acts correlated with the brain-states of that body; and if it is to be a human body its capacities must not be radically different from those of our bodies. So there is a limit to Christ's power *qua* man. If the human actions of God the Son are done only in the light of his human belief-inclinations, then he will feel the limitations that we have. God, in becoming incarnate, will not have limited his powers, but he will have taken on a way of operating which is limited and feels limited. So using the notion of divided mind we can coherently suppose a divine individual to become incarnate while remaining divine, and yet act and feel much like ourselves.

But could he become like us in our liability to yield to temptation? For if he could, his failure to yield would seem so much more the victory over evil which the New Testament and later theories of the Atonement picture it.

Let us take a few steps backwards in order to sort out what is at stake here, using some results from Chapter 3. Wrong is of two kinds—objective and subjective. Objective wrong is failing in your obligations (or duties) to someone whether you realize it or not: for example, taking money that is not yours, whether or not you reasonably believe it to be yours. Subjective wrong is seeking to do what you believe to be failing in your obligations. In both cases, a wrong is, I suggest, a wrong to someone. If you take what is not yours, you wrong the person from whom you take it. If you take, believing that you are taking what is not yours, that is, stealing, you wrong the person from whom you believe that you are stealing. God has, I suspect, relatively few duties to humans—for example, plausibly, he could kill a human without wronging him, for, as the source of his being, he may keep him in being as long or as short a time as he chooses. But, with majority Christian tradition, I suggest that a divine individual does have some duties to human beings—for instance, to keep promises. God Incarnate must keep his promises to humans. If he failed in any of the duties he has to humans, he would wrong them. He would wrong a human objectively if he failed to fulfil some duty to him, for instance, failed to keep a promise to him, whether or not he realized that he was failing to fulfil the duty. He would wrong a human subjectively if he did (or merely tried to do) what he believed was failing in his duty to him.

The narrow range of duties to which a divine individual is subject does, however, give him vast scope for supererogatory good actions (i.e. good actions beyond the call of duty) benefitting humans. We humans have a limited number of duties to our fellows, and endless scope for good action beyond the call of duty. Exactly where the line is to be drawn is disputed, but there is a line. For example, the act of saving the life of a comrade at the expense of one's own is hardly a duty owed to him, but it is evidently a good action. Doing a supererogatory act is praiseworthy, but failing to do one is not blameworthy.[12] For by so failing you wrong no one. Plausibly, as Christian thinkers have normally maintained, no divine individual had any obligation to create a world (for if he failed to do so, there would not ever have been any creatures who had been wronged), let alone become incarnate.[13] If he did so, it was an act of supererogatory goodness.

As I argued in Chapter 3, an agent will do intentionally what he sees reason for doing, that is, what he believes to be good to do, in so far as he is rational. Hence he will only fail to pursue what he believes to be good if he is subject to desires inclining him to act contrary to reason, and in that case if he is to do the believed good, he has to struggle against the temptation which those desires provide. And if he is to do intentionally what is in fact good, he needs true beliefs about what is good.

Now it would, I suggest, have been wrong of a divine individual to allow himself to become incarnate in such a way as to open the possibility of his doing objective or subjective wrong. Hence it is incompatible with his perfect goodness that he should do so. For it is wrong of anyone to put themselves in a position where they are liable to wrong another—intentionally allow themselves to forget their duties, or to take drugs which would lead to their being

---

[12] For fuller discussion of this claim see my *Responsibility and Atonement*, especially ch. 2.

[13] I shall have more to say about the strength of God's reasons for becoming incarnate in Ch. 10.

strongly tempted (without having a stronger contrary desire) to do some wrong. A divine individual in becoming incarnate must ensure that in his human actions he has access to such beliefs as will allow him to be aware of his duties, and must ensure that he is not subject to a balance of desire to do believed wrong. Even though he cannot do wrong, he may however, through not allowing himself to be aware of his divine beliefs, be inclined to believe that he may succumb to temptation to do wrong and thus, in the situation of temptation, he may *feel* as we do.[14]

Now, while it is wrong to put oneself in a position where one is liable to do wrong, there is nothing wrong in putting oneself in a position where one is liable not to do the best action (or best kind of action), if there is such. Indeed, an action which had the foreseen consequence of putting oneself in that position might itself occasionally be the best thing to do. A generous man might well give away so much in order to do some supererogatory good that thereby he greatly endangered the possibility of his doing even more supererogatory good in future. Compatibly with his perfect goodness, a divine individual could choose to allow himself to act on a limited set of beliefs which included inadequate beliefs about what is most worth doing; and he could allow himself to be subject to a balance of desires to do lesser goods, to a weakness of will, so long as it did not include any proneness to wrong anyone. He would then need to discover what was most worth doing; and he would need to fight against the balance of desire to do the lesser good and it would be possible that he should yield to the temptation to do a

---

[14] Morris, *Logic of God Incarnate*, 147, urges that 'it is the *epistemic* possibility of sinning rather than a broadly logical, or metaphysical, or even physical possibility that is conceptually linked to temptation'. Our concern in this context is with doing wrong rather than with sinning in the sense of doing wrong against God. But, if we take that into account, Morris's point would seem to be that you are tempted if and only if you believe that you have open to you a choice of what is wrong to which you may yield. That seems doubtful to me; if you do not really have such a choice, then you have the mere illusion of temptation. However, as I concede in the text, someone falsely believing that he can choose what is wrong is indeed in an unfortunate situation which is like our situation of temptation in its psychological aspect. Morris's useful point is spoiled by his examples that concern agents who correctly believe that they can try to do some wrong action which it is physically impossible that they succeed in doing. But subjective wrongdoing is trying to do a believed wrong, and although objective wrongdoing is not possible for those agents, subjective wrongdoing is. Hence the felt inclination to do subjective wrong is a temptation. The 'metaphysical or physical' possibility of subjective wrongdoing remains open to agents in Morris's examples, which do not therefore illustrate his point.

lesser good. He might choose to put himself in this position in order to share our lot as fully as possible. God the Son, in his divine consciousness, in perfect freedom would continually will (as part of the good of his incarnation) that he would do whatever (other than the wrong) he chooses to do under the influence of desire and limited belief. The former (second-order) will or choice would not be influenced by desire; only its execution would be so influenced, but it is good that it should be. Desire would have influenced God, but only to the extent to which God, uninfluenced by desire, allowed it to do so.

If in his human consciousness Christ were on occasion subject to a balance of desire not to do the best action, then his overcoming this balance would be a free act for which he would be praiseworthy. Almost all the actions by which he is supposed to have made available atonement for the sins of the world—his sacrificial service, culminating in allowing himself to be crucified—were not obligatory but supererogatory.[15] No divine individual had any obligation to allow himself to be crucified, and Christ must have been subject to desires of considerable force not to go through with the Crucifixion, and highly plausibly a balance of desire not to go through with it. In that latter case he was crucified as a result of a free choice contrary to temptation. It was a supererogatory act, and one which surely he believed to be supererogatory; and hence highly praiseworthy. In doing that supreme act and other supererogatory acts during his life freely and contrary to desire, he would have used well the freedom which we ordinary humans have abused by our sins. If he had failed to perform those acts, he would have done us no wrong; but doing them he did us great benefit. Yet if such

[15] The supererogatory character of Christ's work consists in his living a holy life and allowing himself to be killed rather than deny his vocation as Messiah (see Mark 14: 61 f. for his affirmation of his Messiahship before Caiaphas, and the parallel passages in the other Gospels in which he refuses to deny his Messianic role which he has affirmed before his disciples); and in intending that supererogatory work to be the means of our salvation. On my account of the Atonement (see *Responsibility and Atonement*, ch. 10) it is the means of our salvation by being something which we can offer to God in place of the lives which we ought to have lived. In order to be supererogatory in the latter respect, the life must have been lived and laid down with the intention that it should be so available. That is, in his human consciousness Christ must have intended that his life and death be in some way the means of our salvation. It is hard to interpret Christ's words of institution at the Last Supper, 'This is my body', and 'This is my blood' (e.g. Mark 14: 22–4) in any other way than as expressing an intention that they commemorate the sacrifice of his life, which benefits those who partake of the Supper.

heroic acts were inevitable, he would have had an advantage that we sinners did not have, and his redeeming acts would have been taking on and rightly directing a human nature crucially unlike ours in the respect in which we had gone wrong. That he performed supererogatory good actions, while we ordinary humans did wrong, although both he and we were equally well positioned to do good or ill is, I repeat, crucial for theories of the Atonement.

So, yes, God the Son could subject himself to temptation, but only to do a lesser good, not to do wrong. He must protect himself from the proneness to do wrong which is original sinfulness. Original sin includes minimally this original sinfulness, this proneness to do wrong. It has, however, been thought of by many as including some responsibility for the sin of others, including our ancestors ('Adam'). Yet any 'solidarity' with them in sin can arise only as a result of their being responsible in very small part for our existence, which would not arise in the case of Christ, who, being God, does not owe his existence to them at all. So, since such solidarity has no application to an incarnate God, if God protects himself—as he must—from original sinfulness, then in becoming incarnate, he does so, as many creeds vigorously affirmed, without inheriting original sin at all.[16]

One important form of wrongdoing which the divine Word must ensure that the incarnate Christ does not do is deceive his hearers and thus the Church with respect to the content of revelation. He must not tell us that God wished the Church to celebrate the eucharist regularly or to incorporate new members by baptism, if that was not what he really wished it to do; or that the pure in heart and peacemakers are blessed, if they are not. For that would be deceiving people with respect to the way to salvation.[17]

---

[16] As I have argued elsewhere, such 'solidarity' in sin which we have with our ancestors is not guilt for their sin—see *Responsibility and Atonement*, ch. 9.

[17] I distinguish between the content of Christ's teaching and the assumptions of his culture in terms of which it may have been expressed. On how this distinction is to be made see my *Revelation*, ch. 2. I also distinguish between the content of Christ's solemn teaching on matters of religious doctrine, his revealed teaching given with authority (often, it seems, introduced by the phrase, 'Verily I say unto you') and any other bits of information which he might have sought to convey (e.g. about the dates of the kings of Judah). I cannot see that God the Word needs to ensure that the incarnate Christ does not convey any false pieces of information (that he is inclined to believe in his human consciousness) which are such that no great harm will come to anyone who believes them; any more than any of us have any obligation not to overtire ourselves lest we honestly mislead someone on trivial matters.

If it can be good that Christ allow himself to act subject to a balance of desire to do an action less than the best, *a fortiori* it can be good for Christ to allow himself to be subject to desire to do some one among equal best actions (or one of an infinite number of good acts, each less good than some other of the number)—for example, to be subject to particular desires to benefit particular people more than others (when reason does not dictate such a choice). His perfect freedom would not be impaired, so long as he continually chooses (in his divine consciousness) as a best act that he act under the influence of some good (but not necessarily best) particular desire.

So then God the Son, being divine, must remain omniscient, but he can allow his human actions to be guided only by his humanly acquired inclinations to belief. He must remain omnipotent, but there is a limit to what he can do in a human way and, when he does act in a human way, he need not be fully aware of having more power than that. Being divine, he must remain perfectly good and perfectly free, but he can in perfect freedom and because of the perfect goodness of doing so, allow himself to make a choice under the influence of desire to do a lesser good and allow himself to be subject to particular desires to benefit particular individuals. But an incarnate God could not do wrong. The Chalcedonian definition is not merely self-consistent but consistent with the New Testament picture of Christ as acting in ignorance and weakness, and subject to temptation. A divine individual could become human in a rather fuller sense than its traditional interpretation allowed.

What in effect the 'divided mind' view is claiming is that the divine and human natures are to some extent separated, and that allows the human nature of Christ to be not a nature as perfect as a human nature could be (e.g. in Heaven), but a nature more like our human nature on Earth, subject to ignorance and disordered desire, yet one connected enough with the divine nature so that Christ does no wrong. In particular the two wills are kept to some extent separate, so that when Christ wills under human conditions, he wills under the conditions, not of perfect humanity, but under conditions more like those of our humanity, i.e. conditions of ignorance of some of the remote consequences of his actions, limited awareness of power, and open to the influence of desire. The 'subjection' of the human will to the divine must then be read only as a subjection which ensured no wrongdoing, but not in the more full-blooded way that always Christ had to will as he would will if he knew all the possibilities open to him and was not subject to influence by desire.

The monothelites saw that having two natures and only one will (in the relevant sense) would ensure that the human aspect of Jesus was purely passive; whereas the dyothelites and especially Maximus the Confessor and his disciple Anastasius saw that a genuine humanity needed a certain active independence.[18] I have suggested that the divided mind can give content to that requirement.

Total Interpenetration

The monothelites had objected to Maximus—does not dyothelitism have the consequence that 'the Logos and man would be related to each other as strangers'?[19] In answer Maximus adumbrated a doctrine, which was fully developed by St John Damascene in the eighth century, which ruled out the 'divided mind' account and, I believe, lay behind the unsatisfactory way in which Chalcedon was expounded by the scholastics. This was the doctrine of περιχώρησις φυσέων, the 'interpenetration' of the two natures of Christ.[20] It is 'each nature giving in exchange to the other its own properties;[21] or more correctly, as St John corrects himself a little later, it is the permeation of the human nature by the divine—the divine nature 'imparts to the flesh its own peculiar glories, while abiding itself impassible and without participation in the affections of the flesh'.[22] What this means is that the human properties of Christ are as divinized as they can be, that is, made as like those of a divine individual as the properties of a creature can be.

Hence as a man Christ was omniscient, not necessarily omniscient, or with a divine way of knowing—but he knows as man all

---

[18] On these arguments of dyothelites and monothelites, see J. A. Dorner, *History of the Development of the Doctrine of the Person of Christ*, div. 2, vol. i (Edinburgh, 1861), 186–90.　　　　　　　　　　　　　　　　　　　　[19] Ibid. 190.

[20] περιχώρησις φυσέων, the interpenetration of the natures of Christ, is not to be confused with the περιχώρησις ὑποστάτων—which I discussed in Ch. 8—the interpenetration of the persons of the Trinity, i.e. the mutual knowledge and support of each of the persons by the others, taught by Gregory Nazianzen and other Cappadocian theologians who sought thereby to explain in what consisted the unity of the persons of the Trinity and thus defend themselves against the charge of tritheism.

[21] St John Damascene, *De fide orthodoxa*, 3. 4.　　　　[22] Ibid. 3. 7.

a human could conceivably know.[23] So, John denies that Christ really advanced in wisdom and knowledge. Like Augustine before him, John Damascene held that Christ had always before his mind things that God alone can know, such as 'the hour' at which 'Heaven and Earth shall pass away'; the apparent denial by Christ that he knew this hour was, said Augustine, to be read simply as a claim that he was not prepared to announce the hour.[24] Likewise, although Christ's human nature was 'not by nature omnipotent. But yet it was omnipotent because it truly and by nature had its origin in the God-Word.'[25]

Likewise, given total permeation, the perfect goodness of the divine nature so permeated the human nature that Christ's strongest desires were always for the perfectly good; any sensory desires for food, drink, etc., in a situation where it was not overall a best act that he should eat or drink (as in the temptation in the wilderness—see e.g. Matt. 4: 2 ff.) were automatically overruled by stronger desires, so that there was not the slightest possibility that he would yield to any inclination to do a lesser good. Thus Damascene wrote: 'The soul of the Lord . . . willed . . . those things which his divine will willed it to will. It was not in inclination but in natural power that the two wills differed from each other.'[26]

John Damascene is an author quoted very frequently by Aquinas —after the Bible, Aristotle, Augustine, and Pseudo-Dionysius, probably the author most quoted—and we find in Aquinas, as in Damascene, 'interpenetration of the natures', but not, I think, quite as total an interpenetration as in Damascene. Thus the human Christ knows everything actual (e.g. about past and future) but not all the possible actions that God could do and does not do.[27] And the human Christ was not, claimed Aquinas, omnipotent. And although there was not the slightest possibility that Christ would do wrong, Aquinas did not always sharply distinguish between doing wrong, and failing to do supererogatory good; however, he does in one place say that 'difficulty in doing good'[28] was among the disabilities Christ did not acquire. In these matters Duns Scotus followed Aquinas.[29]

---

[23] 'His human nature does not in essence possess the knowledge of the future, but the soul [i.e. the human or rational soul] through its union with God the Word himself and its identity in subsistence was enriched . . . with the knowledge of the future, as well as with the other miraculous powers', ibid. 3. 21.

[24] St Augustine, *De Trinitate*, 1. 23.

[25] St John Damascene, *De fide orthodoxa*, 3. 18.   [26] Ibid.

[27] *Summa theologiae*, 3. 10. 2.   [28] Ibid. 3. 14. 4.

[29] See e.g. on the human Christ not being omnipotent, Duns Scotus, *Commentary on the Sentences*, 3. 14.

Christological controversy flared up again in a mild way at the Reformation—between Lutherans on the one side and the 'Reformed' tradition in a more technical sense, i.e. Calvinists (together with some Catholics) on the other side.[30] What was at stake here was explicitly the doctrine of total interpenetration advocated by Lutherans who used John Damascene as an explicit source. The Lutheran *Formula of Concord* recognized three 'genera' of communication of properties, divine and human, in Christ. The first genus was simply the *communicatio idiomatum*—that the human and divine properties were predicable of the same individual, Jesus Christ who was the Son of God. This was accepted by all disputants; but the other genera involved the interpretation of the *communicatio* so as to involve total interpenetration. The second genus of communication was that by which 'the perfections that are truly divine, together with the authority and power resulting from them, the honour and supreme glory, are communicated to the human nature of Christ.'[31] Hence, Christ was omnipotent in virtue of his human nature. The third genus involved Christ's actions, which pertained to his office: 'The union of the two natures in Christ occurred so that the work of redemption, atonement, and salvation might be accomplished in, with and through both natures of Christ.'[32] So both the divine essential properties and the actions of redemption belonged to Christ in virtue of belonging both to his human nature and to his divine nature. In this controversy the Calvinists stressed Chalcedon's affirmation that the union of the natures was 'without confusion' (ἀσυγχύτως), while the Lutherans stressed Chalcedon's affirmation that the union was 'without division, without separation' (ἀδιαιρέτως, ἀχωρίστως).[33] I suggest that we support the Calvinists in this controversy. Calvin was right to comment that the Lutherans 'deprive [Christ] of his flesh'.[34] Total interpenetration rules out the divided mind view which alone does justice to the New Testament and makes for a viable theory of the Atonement. Total interpenetration is not a necessary development of Chalcedon. St John Damascene's reason for advocating the doctrine was clearly to affirm

---

[30] On this controversy, see (e.g.) J. Pelikan, *The Christian Tradition*, vol. iv. *Reformation of Church and Dogma* (University of Chicago Press, 1984), 352–9.

[31] J. W. Baier, *Compendium of Positive Theology*, cited in Pelikan, ibid. 357.

[32] Pelikan, ibid. 358.   [33] Denzinger, 302.

[34] J. Calvin, *Institutes of the Christian Religion*, 4. 17. 32. The Lutheran/Calvinist controversy about the relation of the two natures of Christ came to prominence in connection with the alternative doctrines of the eucharist to which they led; and this quotation form Calvin comes from his discussion of the eucharist.

the divinity of Christ in an unattenuated form, but I have argued
that it is not needed for that purpose. Even Aquinas resisted
total interpenetration; and, I have argued, we need significantly
less interpenetration than he allowed.

Hypostatizing the Natures

The final development of the Chalcedonian definition on which I
need to comment was a simple piece of philosophical muddle by
the scholastics.

Christ was divine and human and so he had a divine and human
nature. But human nature as Aristotle and, I suspect, almost every-
one else up to the fifth century AD understood it, is a universal. What
made a human the particular human he was, we noted in Chapter
2, according to Aristotle, was the matter of which he was made. I
saw reason in that chapter to consider this last view unsatisfactory,
and argued that a human is the human he is in virtue of the individual soul (in my sense) which is joined to matter (whether physical
matter, or soul-stuff, or perhaps no stuff at all). The resulting individual is human if the soul and body have universal characteristics
of the kind analysed in Chapter 1. In the case of normal humans
the individual soul is an individual essence which is a restriction of
a wider form, for example, animate being; in the case of Christ, I
have suggested, it is a divine nature individuated by its relational
properties. So in the Incarnation the divine soul of Christ, in
acquiring a human nature, acquires those additional properties that
are necessary for the humanity of any other individual, and also, no
doubt, acquires some properties that are peculiar to the human
which was Christ but which could in principle be possessed by
many other humans. He also acquired a particular body, but that is
not what individuated him.

Now what makes an individual the individual he is cannot be
possessed by anything else. If ordinary human beings could not
be other than human (instead, as I suggested in Chapter 1, of being
able to be instead animate beings of other kinds), each human soul
would be an individual human nature (instead of being an individual
animate nature). But such a nature would be the essential core
of the individual—what made him who he is—and could not be

possessed temporarily or accidentally by anyone else. Christ therefore could not have an individual human nature. His human nature
must be universal, in no way peculiar to Christ—it is just a set of
properties which he acquires. I have also claimed that, since humans
can become animate beings of other kinds, the same applies to
ordinary humans too.

Many of the Fathers saw that the human nature of Christ is a
universal, in no way necessarily peculiar to Christ. There was no
such thing as an ἀνυπόστατος φύσις, a nature which exists without
existing in an individual or hypostasis, claimed the sixth-century
Leontius of Byzantium; the human nature of Christ, not being
a hypostasis, exists only ἐνυπόστατος, that is, in virtue of the hypostasis in which it exists;[35] or what Leontius was, I believe, getting
at—to speak of an individual human nature is merely to speak
(misleadingly) of the universal human nature as joined to a hypostasis. Christ's human nature is impersonal (in my view just as also
ours is)—but that makes him no less of an individual human being
when that nature is united to the soul (in my sense) that is the
Second Person of the Trinity.

That clear philosophical point began to get forgotten, and theologians began to think of the Incarnation as the Second Person of
the Trinity adopting an individual human nature. This mistake
was already adumbrated by earlier talk of Christ's divine nature or
human nature being able to do or suffer this or that. But natures do
not do things (unless they are themselves individuals); individuals
do things, and their nature or natures give them the power to do
or suffer this or that. Thus the Prologue to the definition of the
Council of Chalcedon denied that the divine nature of Christ was
παθητής (passible, able to suffer);[36] what it should have said was
that Christ was not παθητής in virtue of his divine nature, only in
virtue of his human nature. By a similar mistake the 'rational soul'
of Christ began to take on a life of its own—not being a human way
of thinking that belonged to Christ, but more a soul in the sense in
which I have used the term.[37]

Aquinas too had adopted such a way of talking which was bound
to lead to trouble. For all humans other than Christ Aquinas held

---

[35] The 'nature' (φύσις) of Christ 'has its being in another' (ἐν ἑτέρῳ ἔχει τὸ εἶναι),
wrote Leontius (PG 86: 1277D), just as a shape has its being in the body of which
it is the shape. (See also Leontius, PG 86: 1944).
[36] Denzinger, 300.   [37] See Additional Note 15.

(and in this he was followed by Scotus and Ockham),[38] the human person is the same thing as his or her individual human nature; a human nature is a substance composed of a body and a rational soul. (The necessity of a body is something against which I have argued, but that is not where Aquinas goes wrong in this matter.) What, according to Aquinas, distinguishes Christ from other humans is that while Christ is a person who is a human being, he is not a human person—I suppose that what this means is that Christ is not essentially human, while the rest of us are. I have suggested that the rest of us are not essentially human either. But if the only contrast to be made is between the human and divine (and the possibility of us becoming angels or crocodiles is ignored), then Aquinas's point may be allowed. Since Christ is not a human person, what makes him human is not something essential to his being the person he is. So far so good. But now, Aquinas assumed that since it is for ordinary humans, so also for Christ, a human nature is an individual substance and it is this which is joined to Christ in the Incarnation and makes him human. The union of human soul and body constitutes us ordinary humans as the individuals we are; but in Christ that union that forms a nature is joined to God the Son; 'The composite comes to an already existing person or hypostasis.'[39] But the question then arises as to why this human nature has to be joined to Christ; could it not be joined to someone else, temporarily or permanently? Aquinas seems to claim that this nature depends on the divine individual to which it is joined for its very existence.[40] But the question remains—why should it be thus? Why cannot a composite of soul and body exist on its own?

Scotus and Ockham took this way of talking to its logical conclusion and said that these things were possible; the human nature which Christ assumed was only contingently assumed by him. Christ need not have assumed it, in which case it would be a complete human person on its own; or he could temporarily have taken the human nature of Socrates for two weeks, in which case Socrates would not exist for two weeks although his nature would. But then

---

[38] For the subsequent analysis of the difference between the Christologies of Aquinas on the one hand and those of Scotus and Ockham on the other, I am much indebted to Alfred J. Freddoso, 'Human Nature, Potency, and the Incarnation', *Faith and Philosophy*, 3 (1986), 27–53.   [39] *Summa theologiae*, 3. 2. 5. ad 1.

[40] See Freddoso, 'Human Nature', app., for an exegesis of Aquinas's views on this.

how can Socrates be the same thing as his nature if these things are possible?[41]

This whole mess has been produced by forgetting that human nature, and certainly Christ's human nature, is a universal; what individuates him is something else. Even if what individuates other humans is an individual human soul, in the sense of a restriction in the form of humanity, a divine individual cannot acquire such a soul. For such a soul would already be the individuating principle of a human. He can only take on a human soul in the sense of a human way of thinking and acting; and a soul in this sense (even with a body) is not enough to individuate a human.

My conclusion to this chapter is that the Chalcedonian definition is an internally coherent account of the Incarnation; and, spelled out in a certain way, coherent with things said in the New Testament about Christ and with doctrines of the Atonement. John Damascene's doctrine of the total interpenetration of the two natures is not however consistent with my favoured explication of Chalcedon and should be rejected, as should the hypostatization of the human nature of Christ. I turn in the final chapter to consider what grounds there are for believing the Chalcedonian account of the Incarnation to be true, or whether any rival modern account is preferable.

[41] For detailed references to Scotus and Ockham, and demonstration of the contradictions to which their account leads, see Freddoso, 'Human Nature'.

10

The Evidence of Incarnation

Why should anyone believe the Chalcedonian definition to be true? It is certainly not necessary that a perfectly good God should become incarnate. On this Christian tradition has been more or less unanimous, at least until the last two centuries.[1] It is not necessary for God's perfect goodness that he create human beings. That follows from the argument of Chapter 8. It is necessary that a divine individual be involved in causing the existence of other conscious beings with whom to share. Whatever number he brings about, it would be better to cause the existence of even more. But we saw that the need to cause existence would be adequately satisfied within the Trinity by each member causing or sustaining the existence of the others. God does not need to create a universe of humans, good though it is that he should. If he does create a world of humans, he need not create them with the possibility of sinning; he could have created them as purely rational beings. But if he does create humans liable to sin (and if there is a God, clearly he has done so), and they do sin and stand in need of reconciliation, does he need—in virtue of his perfect goodness—to become incarnate in order to make available that reconciliation?

On this there have been two main views among Christians. The first is that humans could not be reconciled to God except by God becoming incarnate to make available atonement for human sin through his perfect human life and death. Anselm held this.[2] Anselm also held that in virtue of his perfect goodness, God having created man liable to sin, was obliged to redeem him when he sinned: 'What man was about to do was not hidden from God at his creation;

---

[1] One writer who might be arguing that a perfectly good God had to make men liable to sin and to become incarnate to redeem them is Hegel, see (e.g.) his *Philosophy of History*, 3. 3. 2, 'Christianity'. As so often, Hegel tries to show that what does happen has to happen; but whether he is claiming exactly what I am attributing to him is not altogether clear.

[2] *Cur Deus Homo?* 2. 5–11, trans. S. N. Deane (Open Court Publishing Co., 1903).

and yet by freely creating man, God as it were bound himself to complete the good which he had begun.'[3] A different version of this first view is that in creating man God had not thus bound himself, and so his perfect goodness did not require him to become incarnate to redeem us. The second and more normal view is that God could reconcile humans to himself without becoming incarnate. He could forgive the penitent without the need for any act of atonement, or he could accept some imperfect act of an ordinary human or some act of an angel as the atoning act without himself needing to become incarnate. This second view is that of both Aquinas and Scotus and also most of the Reformers.[4]

I believe this second view to be correct. A wronged person, in this case God, can forgive the penitent without requiring reparation for the offence. Innumerable human examples confirm this point. However, unless the obligation is remitted by the wronged person, the guilty person is under an obligation to make reparation, and it is often good that the wronged person should allow the guilty one to take his wrongdoing seriously by making proper reparation; and if he does not have the wherewithal to make proper reparation, it would be very good if the wronged person made that accessible to him. What humans owe to God their creator is a good life, and if they have all failed in living such a life, one perfect life not already

---

[3] Athanasius has a slight variant on this view. He holds (*De Incarnatione*, 1–12) that God could forgive us without the need for atonement. But God had vowed in creating us that sin would be punished by death, and since all humans had sinned, all had to die. Yet a God incarnate as man would represent all humans, and his death would constitute the execution of that sentence, and allow humans to have again the possibility of eternal life. Death could not have the ultimate victory over an immortal God, and so by his death alone could life finally be won for all. Athanasius seems finally to hold (to express it in my terminology) that in virtue of his perfect goodness God had to ensure that his plan in creating humans that they should enjoy eternal life was ultimately successful, and so had to become incarnate. If we suppose God to have made a solemn vow of the kind described, then Athanasius' view becomes more plausible; but there seems to me no reason to suppose this, and so I prefer what I describe in the text as the 'second view'.

[4] Aquinas, *Summa theologiae*, 3. 1. 2—'It was not necessary that God should become incarnate to secure the redemption of human nature. In virtue of his omnipotence God could have redeemed human nature in many other ways.' This is integral to Scotus' position, for according to Scotus, God can make any good act have the 'merit' he chooses, and so make any good act meritorious enough to redeem the world. Calvin held that there is no 'absolute necessity' that our mediator 'be both true God and true man'. 'Rather it has stemmed from a heavenly decree'— J. Calvin, *Institutes of the Christian Religion*, trans. F. L. Battles (The Westminster Press, 1960), i. 464. For the other Reformers also see R. S. Franks, *The Work of Christ* (Thomas Nelson & Sons, 1962), 326 and 338.

owed to God would be a proper reparation which humans who
take their sin seriously can offer back to God as the life it would be
good if they had led. If humans through their proneness to sin are
very unlikely to lead a life of that sort, God might well intervene
on earth in order to do so. But God would be perfectly good if
he accepted other atoning acts instead. No wronged person can
be under an obligation to provide any means of reparation for the
guilty to offer; and though it is a good thing that a wronged person
should do this where the wrongdoing is serious and the guilty finds
it difficult to make reparation, it cannot be necessary for God's
perfect goodness that he should live a sacrificial human life culminating in allowing himself to be killed, for this purpose. He could
perfectly well accept less committed lives of less perfect saints for
such a purpose.[5] And yet of course he is our creator and a perfectly
good creator would be concerned for our redemption. Yet the concern need not take the form of an incarnation. But of course there
is a generous propriety in it doing so.

So given that there is no necessity for God to become incarnate,
do we have reason to expect that he will? One such reason, is the
reason already considered—to make available to us a means of
atonement by living a perfect human life. And that has certainly
been the primary reason which Christians have adduced for expecting an incarnation. But many other reasons have been suggested.
Aquinas[6] lists some ten such reasons, for each of which he gives a
supporting quotation from Augustine. I shall boil his ten reasons
down to five.

First, human nature is such a good thing that given that he has
created it, it is a fitting nature for God to adopt. There is in humanity
a unique mixture of the rational (humans see and pursue the good
as such), the sensory (have sensations, and are influenced by non-
rational desires), and the physical (operate through bodies situated
in a beautiful law-governed universe). It would be appropriate for
its creator to put on such a nature, as it is for a designer to wear a
coat he has designed. Thereby he evinces solidarity with his creation.
Secondly, by God adopting human nature, 'we are taught how
great is the dignity of human nature'.[7] (Aquinas and Augustine do

---

[5] I summarize here briefly the argument of my *Responsibility and Atonement*
(Clarendon Press, 1989), esp. ch. 10.   [6] *Summa theologiae*, 3. 1. 2.
[7] Aquinas cites Augustine, *De vera religione*, 16 (PL 34: 134 f.) writing that God
showed us 'how high a place human nature has among creatures'.

not seem to distinguish my first and second reasons. The first
reason concerns the goodness of God adopting human nature in
itself; the second concerns the goodness of God showing this to
us). A third reason for God becoming incarnate is that he might
show us, by identifying with us, how much he loves us.[8] Under
this heading it is appropriate to mention Kierkegaard's parable
of the King and the Maiden. The King seeks to win the love of the
humble maiden, but if he appeared to her as a king he might elicit
her love for the wrong reason. So he comes as a servant—but
not in disguise, for that would be deception, but really becomes a
servant.[9] A fourth reason for God becoming incarnate is to show
man an example of how to live a human life. Mere propositional
revelation may not give the flavour of what a life of love amounts
to; and propositional revelation will not inspire in the way that an
actual example will.[10] A fifth reason is to reveal propositions. Now
of course God can provide propositional revelation in other ways,
and no doubt he has often done so. He could dictate propositions
to a prophet who was not divine and then provide some authenticating miracle.[11] But clearly if there is any other evidence that a
certain prophet is God incarnate, then that evidence increases the
force of any other authenticating evidence that his teaching is
God's.[12]

A further consideration not adduced by Aquinas makes the first
three reasons considerably stronger than they would be otherwise.
God made humans subject to pain and suffering of various kinds
caused both by other humans and by natural processes. God, being
perfectly good, would only have permitted this subjection if it
served some greater goods. Theodicy seeks to explain what are the

---

[8] Aquinas cites Augustine, *De Trinitate* 13. 10—'nothing is so needful for us to
build up our hope than for us to be shown how much God love us'.
[9] *Philosophical Fragments*, trans. D. F. Swanson (Princeton University Press,
1962), ch. 2.
[10] Aquinas quotes a sermon of Augustine (Sermon no. 371. 2 (PL 39: 1660), *De
nativitate Dei*)—'It was in order that God might be shown to man and seen by man,
and that there might be someone for man to follow, that God became man'.
[11] For the need for miracle to authenticate propositional revelation, see my *Revelation* (Clarendon Press, 1992), esp. ch. 6.
[12] 'Greater assurance is guaranteed when the belief rests on God himself speaking'
—Aquinas, *Summa theologiae*, 3. 1. 2. Aquinas quotes Augustine, *De Civitate Dei*,
11. 2—'In order that man might advance more confidently towards the truth,
the truth itself, the Son of God assuming humanity . . . established and founded the
faith.'

relevant greater goods[13]—for example, the great good of humans
having significant free choice that involves the possibility of their
doing considerable harm to each other. We humans sometimes
rightly subject our own children to suffering for the sake of some
greater good (to themselves or others)—for instance, make them
eat a plain diet or take some special exercise for the sake of their
health, or make them attend a 'difficult' neighbourhood school for
the sake of good community relations. Under these circumstances
we judge it a good thing to evince and show solidarity with our
children by putting ourselves in somewhat the same situation—
share their diet or their exercise, or become involved in the parent/
teacher organization of the neighbourhood school. A perfectly good
God would judge it a good thing to share the pain and suffering to
which he subjects us for the sake of greater goods—by becoming
incarnate.

Although there was dispute between Dominicans (including
Thomas Aquinas) and Franciscans (notably Duns Scotus) about
whether there would have been an incarnation, if there had been
no need for atonement, those such as Aquinas, who said that there
would not, affirmed that there were other reasons for an incarnation,
even if God would not have acted on those in the absence of need
for atonement. I can hardly see that either party has any very
strong a priori argument (or even a posteriori argument from
Scripture) to allow them to say what God would have done under
certain unrealized circumstances. My only point is that God had
available to him various good reasons for becoming incarnate. Some
of these reasons are, it might seem, reasons for an incarnation on
more than one occasion. And the scholastics in general wished to
allow the logical possibility of that,[14] but they claimed that incarnation had in fact only happened once. However, as regards the
major reason for incarnation, atonement, it seems to me that there
is good reason for supposing that there would only be one incarnation. A perfect human life lived so sacrificially that it led to death
by crucifixion is an adequate offering for human sin. It trivializes
the notion of atonement to suppose that it would suffice for ten
billion but not for twenty billion sinners. What atones is the quality

---

[13] For my theodicy, see *The Existence of God* (Clarendon Press, 1979), 152–60,
and chs. 10 and 11. I intend to give a much fuller theodicy in the fourth volume of
the present tetralogy, on *Providence*.

[14] See Aquinas, *Summa theologiae*, 3. 3. 7.

of one life, not the number of lives. Suffering is as such a bad thing and God would not subject himself to it when it served no good purpose. One atonement suffices. And the other reasons might well seem adequately satisfied by one incarnation. There seems far less reason to expect a second incarnation than a first.

But, granted some reasons for expecting an incarnation, what would show that it had occurred by a certain human, Jesus Christ, being God Incarnate? Two kinds of reason. First, that Christ had lived the sort of life which fulfilled the reasons for incarnation— namely, a life which was a life of perfect goodness, offered as an atonement, a life showing love for humanity, and teaching them on authority important truths otherwise unknowable. For if God was to adopt a human nature for these reasons, he must ensure that there is enough interpenetration of the divine and human natures for him in his incarnate life to understand the goodness of him living this sort of life (that, in a wide sense, it was his 'vocation' to do so). We need to look at the record of Christ's life to see whether it came up to these requirements. Of course treating the Gospels and other New Testament writings as simple historical documents provides some evidence that Christ's life was of the requisite sort, but being ordinary historical evidence it is weak. Even if the evidence suggests that much of the public life of Jesus was perfectly good, how do we know that he did not have secret malicious thoughts?

The public evidence needs topping up. We need revelation for two reasons; first, to confirm that both the public life and the private life of Jesus Christ was a life of perfect goodness, offered as an atonement. I have argued elsewhere that, given that there is some historical evidence that the Resurrection of Christ occurred in something like its recorded form (historical evidence which need not be too strong in view of good a priori reason for expecting such a miracle), that would constitute God's seal of approval on Christ's teaching.[15] Christ's commissioning of the twelve apostles constituted them (and the society founded on them) as witnesses to that teaching, and the account of the Church founded on them as to what Christ taught and did is to be believed, since authenticated by God. Revelation confirms the public evidence that Christ lived the sort of life that God Incarnate would be expected to have set himself to live.

---

[15] See my *Revelation*, esp. pt. 3.

Secondly we need revelation to confirm more directly that Jesus Christ was God Incarnate. He might have taught this explicitly; and in that case evidence of the New Testament treated as a mere historical document, together with the Church's confirmation thereof, would be such evidence. Alternatively, Christ might not have taught this explicitly—both because people might have misunderstood him if he had (by coming to suppose that like the Greek gods who were said occasionally to acquire human bodies, he did not have a real human nature), and because he wanted people to work out his status for themselves (and a lot of Jesus's teaching suggests that his method in general was to get people to work things out for themselves),[16] and perhaps because in his human nature he was not fully aware of his divine status. But it might have been implicit in his teaching and actions that he was God Incarnate, 'implicit' in the sense that his having the belief that he was God Incarnate might be the best interpretation of the things that he did say and do. For example, given the conventions of understanding at the time, his forgiving sins, his commissioning the apostles to baptize in the name equally of the Son (i.e. himself) as of the Father, etc., might be best so understood. And central among the evidence that much of the sayings and actions of Jesus are best so interpreted would be the fact that soon after his Resurrection his disciples did so interpret them. That takes us to the issue of how many of the individual New Testament writers believed Jesus to be God. There can be little doubt that 'St John', the author of the Fourth Gospel did; how many other writers did is a matter of dispute, if we are assessing the New Testament documents by historical criteria without bringing in their status as revelation.[17] Once the Church is recognized as having some authority to interpret those documents in the right way, then their testimony to the divine status of Jesus is clear, for that is how the Church interpreted them—namely, as saying or implying that Jesus was divine. But in order to recognize the Church as having that authority, we do need some historical evidence

---

[16] See his use of parables—e.g. Mark 4: 33 f.—as the main means of popular instruction, and his getting disciples to recognize his Messianic status by showing them how he acted, rather than telling them directly—Mark 8: 29, Matthew 11: 2–6.

[17] Cf. the more conservative account of the New Testament documents so interpreted, by C. F. D. Moule, *The Origin of Christology* (Cambridge University Press, 1977), with the more radical account in John Macquarrie, *Jesus Christ in Modern Thought* (SCM Press, 1990), chs. 1–6.

(assessed by criteria that do not presuppose that authority) that the Church was commissioned by Christ, whose status as revealer was authenticated by God in the Resurrection, and such historical evidence must not contradict too clearly or violently what the Church said that Jesus taught or did—if it did, that would cast grave doubt on the Church's reliability.[18]

So much for what would be evidence of Christ being God Incarnate. The reader must judge, in the light of the work of biblical scholars, whether we have enough of it—given the framework that I have provided of the sort and limited amount of such historical evidence as we need.

The Alternatives to Chalcedon

I have so far only operated with the traditional orthodox account of the Incarnation. How does it compare with rival accounts of how God was related to Christ?

The two alternatives rejected by the Council of Chalcedon were monophysitism and Nestorianism. A monophysite[19] holds that not merely is there one hypostasis ($\dot{\upsilon}\pi\dot{o}\sigma\tau\alpha\sigma\iota\varsigma$, which I translate 'individual') but one $\phi\dot{\upsilon}\sigma\iota\varsigma$ (nature); a Nestorian holds that not merely are there two natures, but two individuals. Now these doctrines are only opposed to Chalcedon if their exponents meant by the crucial terms the same as the Fathers of Chalcedon meant, and history suggests that some of them meant the same and some of them did not. Some monophysites, and among those their leading pre-Chalcedonian champion Cyril of Alexandria, in affirming one 'nature', were affirming little more than one individual. And some Nestorians, including perhaps Nestorius himself, in affirming two hypostases, were affirming little more than two natures. I shall not consider the historical issues of which theologians before or after Chalcedon were really in disagreement with it, but simply set out

---

[18] On all these matters, see my *Revelation*, pt. 3.

[19] On monophysitism and its successor doctrine monothelitism, see J. N. D. Kelly, *Early Christian Doctrine*, 5th edn. (A. & C. Black, 1977), 330–4; J. Tixeront, *History of Dogmas*, iii, 2nd edn. (B. Herder Book Co., 1926), chs. 3–6; and J. Pelikan, *The Christian Tradition*, ii. *The Spirit of Eastern Christendom* (University of Chicago Press, 1974), 49–61.

sharp, clear forms of monophysitism and Nestorianism in which they contrast with the Chalcedonian definition, and point out their disadvantages. My criticisms of them in those forms will apply in a more sophisticated way to more sophisticated forms; and the criticisms may well have no application at all to many, including churches, which are labelled 'Nestorian' or 'monophysite' but whose views are really those of Chalcedon.

Monophysitism, holding that the Incarnate Christ had only one nature, normally understood that to be the divine nature, although some understood it as a compromise semi-divine, semi-human nature. I shall consider it in the stark form of a doctrine that the incarnate Christ had only a divine nature, in the Chalcedonian sense of nature. He had a human body; and the connection with that leads to the human sensory desires—pain, thirst, etc. So this is not Docetism, the view that Christ's body was mere 'appearance' and Christ did not really suffer. But it is what the century before Chalcedon knew as Apollinarianism, the view that the Incarnation consisted in the Word of God acquiring a human body but not a 'rational soul'—which I have interpreted in the previous chapter as a human way of thinking and acting. The Christ of Chalcedon, as I have developed it, was not subject merely to the sensory human desires—pain, thirst, etc.—but to the more complex human desires for fame and fortune, and under circumstances where they were not automatically outweighed by stronger desires for better goods; he had to choose on which desires to act when he did not have full access to knowledge relevant to the choices. All this was what would have made the Incarnation the taking on of an additional nature. A monophysite incarnation would be a very limited incarnation.

The a priori reasons for expecting a monophysite incarnation are far less strong than the a priori reasons for expecting a Chalcedonian-type incarnation. Christ would not have made atonement for our sins by living well in circumstances where we live badly—for he would not have needed to do his works of supererogation by struggling with human-type desires under conditions of limited access to knowledge. And the first four of the further five reasons for expecting an incarnation are all reason for expecting a Chalcedonian-type incarnation far more than for expecting a monophysite incarnation. For monophysitism does not allow God to live a full human life. And any appeal to revelation to support monophysitism will clearly have far less force than any appeal to revelation to support the Chalcedonian definition. An ecumenical council of bishops of the Church rejected monophysitism; the vast majority of Christians in a thriving Church have followed in the Chalcedonian tradition, and confirmed that tradition by similar formal decisions (e.g. in the similar rejection of monothelitism). I suspect that the main appeal of monophysitism was to avoid the other extreme view—Nestorianism—in a coherent way. In showing the Chalcedonian definition to be coherent, I hope that I have removed any appeal monophysitism might have.

Nestorianism[20] holds that there are two hypostases—a divine individual and a human individual linked in the one Christ. The link is a causal link; the human Jesus is caused to be fully open to the inspiration of the divine Son who, in turn, feels his sufferings. But again the reasons for an incarnation favour much more strongly an incarnation of the Chalcedonian kind than a Nestorian incarnation —though they favour the latter more than they favour a monophysite incarnation. On the Nestorian account there has been a fully human life offered in atonement, and shown as example. But God has not shown his love for humanity by himself coming to earth, nor has he adopted a human nature because of its goodness, nor has he thereby shown us its goodness, nor has he provided extra authentication for propositional revelation. And Nestorianism has its own problems. According to it, the human Jesus was a separate individual from God. If further—as I have represented Nestorianism as claiming—God the Son controlled the human Jesus in such a way that he led a perfect life, then the latter would have been a puppet. There would only be worth in the human life in so far as it was led freely—but for some freedom there cannot be total causal control by God the Son. Suppose the control merely partial—God the Son ensures that the human Jesus does no wrong, but does not make him do supererogatory acts. Jesus nevertheless does them and hence makes an atonement and provides an example. But the human Jesus is a creature and so, like all of us, he has a lot of obligations to his creator; quite a lot of his life is owed to God—and so the causal control of the human Jesus by the divine Son would need to remain considerable. This does not arise if Christ is himself divine—*qua* God, he has no obligations to God as his creator.

---

[20] On Nestorianism see Kelly, *Early Christian Doctrine*, 310–17; Tixeront, *History of Dogmas*, iii. ch. 2; and Pelikan, *Christian Tradition*, 39–49.

(Unlike ordinary humans, the second person of the Trinity is not created by a voluntary act of will.) Hence the range of his obligations is much less. And so any mechanism to ensure that he does no objective wrong would be much less constraining. If the Nestorian Jesus is to be prevented from doing wrong, there has to be very considerable control of his actions. The question then arises whether it would be good for God to control so much of someone else's actions in a puppet-like way; especially if this is in order to allow him to make atonement for our sins. The alternative of supposing that God allows the human Jesus to do wrong, but in fact, Jesus does not do wrong, breaks the causal link—and leads to a different form of Christology which I will discuss below. And Nestorianism shares with monophysitism the major problem that any attempt to appeal to revelation in its support is going to be far less powerful than the appeal to revelation of the Chalcedonian tradition. Nestorian Christianity virtually died out after a few centuries. If Christ founded a church which would survive to carry on his work and to teach the central doctrines of revelation, the Nestorian account of Christ cannot be among those central doctrines.

Modern Humanistic Christologies

After the monothelite controversy, Christological disputes lost their prominence. The framework of the Chalcedonian definition was accepted by the vast majority of Christians with little questioning, until the spirit of the Enlightenment led to the emergence in the nineteenth century of apparently less supernatural accounts of the Incarnation. Some of these, it seems to me, were straightforwardly Nestorian in their Christology—though those who put them forward explicitly denied being Nestorian.

One clear example, to my mind, of Nestorianism in modern guise is the account of Christology given by Schleiermacher. Christ could not, Schleiermacher claimed, be literally both human and divine, for 'everything human is essentially a negation of omniscient omnipotence'.[21] But 'The Redeemer . . . is like all men in virtue of the identity of human nature, but distinguished from them all

[21] F. Schleiermacher, *The Christian Faith* (T. & T. Clark, 1928), 412.

by the constant potency of his God-consciousness, which was a veritable existence of God in him.'[22] This 'God-consciousness', awareness of God, had to develop in Christ 'gradually in human fashion'.[23] But it was God who was active and made it develop; the divine is the active, the human the passive.[24] It is not a freely chosen matter. So we have the Nestorian picture of God causing the man Jesus Christ to be aware of him and conformed to him and so a causal link between two separate individuals.

Schleiermacher goes on further and consistently to claim that 'as certainly as Christ was a man, there must reside in human nature the possibility of taking up the divine into itself, just as did happen in Christ'.[25] We can all 'become divine'. The 'taking up' is simply the bringing into causal union of two separate individuals. It cannot be read literally as a man becoming divine for, as Chalcedon and all the scholastics rightly—I have argued—assumed, God can become man, but man cannot become God, because being divine is an essential nature—a divine individual would not exist unless it were divine, and so any divine individual cannot be the same individual as any individual not previously divine. Of course a lot of Christian theologians, early Fathers of the Church and more especially later theologians of the Eastern Orthodox tradition, talked of θεοποίησις, the 'deification' of man, as something at which the process of sanctification initiated by Christ aimed. But they did not mean literally 'man becoming God'. By 'deification' the early Fathers simply meant in some vague way coming to share the divine life, not becoming divine.[26] More precisely, wrote Maximus the Confessor whose championing of this notion led to its prevalence in the Eastern Orthodox tradition, 'deification' meant becoming 'all that God is, except for an identity in οὐσία (essence, nature) one becomes when one is deified by grace'.[27] And the 'except' of course makes all the difference. Deification is being made like God in many ways, including no doubt perfect goodness and maybe such properties as omniscience—but those properties would belong to a human contingently, not essentially. The sense in which a human can 'become God' is

[22] Ibid. 385.   [23] Ibid. 381.   [24] See ibid. 408.   [25] Ibid. 64.
[26] 'It is of first importance to bear in mind that "deification", for Origen, Athanasius, and their successors, did not mean a sharing in the divine "substance", but enjoying the divine *relation* of Son to Father, sharing the divine life', Rowan Williams, *The Wound of Knowledge*, 2nd edn. (Darton, Longman, & Todd, 1990), 51.
[27] Maximus, *Book of Ambiguities*, 41 (PG 91: 1308).

a long way away from the sense in which Christ was God—on the Chalcedonian account. Schleiermacher's account of Christ is not an account of God becoming *incarnate* at all. Just because it is a straightforward Nestorian theory, there remains against Schleiermacher's system the original objection to Nestorianism.

John Macquarrie, in his book about modern Christology, calls Schleiermacher's system 'humanistic Christology', and writes that 'many of the basic ideas have been reexpressed and given new applications, and we have met what I am calling the 'humanistic' Christology in different forms in such near contemporaries with ourselves as Pittenger, Pannenberg, Rahner and others'.[28] While I do not wish to attribute Nestorianism to any one of the individuals mentioned, it seems to me that Macquarrie is correct in his implied judgement that very many modern theologians share in essence Schleiermacher's Nestorianism. There is, however, in some of them one possible difference from Nestorianism as I have found it in Schleiermacher. In the original Nestorianism as I represented it, and in Schleiermacher, God acts on the man Jesus either totally or at any rate to the extent of ensuring that he does not sin. Other modern theologians who are basically in this tradition seem to allow to Jesus a certain freedom of will in respect of whether or not to yield to sin. 'Seem' is, however, the word because these writers are not always very clear about the kind of freedom to resist temptation which they ascribe to the human Jesus—whether it is 'free will' in my sense of a freedom to act one way or another independently of prior causes, or whether it is freedom of some weaker kind. Thus, to take a very recent example, John Macquarrie himself very cautiously suggests that Jesus's situation might have been as follows:

Sin may be briefly described as alienation from God. Anyone born into human society is bound to know this alienation—that is what we call 'original sin'. Surely Jesus must have known this distance from God as he grew up in ancient Palestine. His 'sinlessness', in spite of the negative formation of the word, consisted in his highly affirmative overcoming of the distance, his deepening union with the Father through the deeds and decisions of his life, in which he overcame sin. I would not hesitate to call this a progressive incarnation in the life of Jesus.[29]

To describe 'sin' as 'alienation from God' seems to me a very vague account; 'sin' is wronging God, and the worthwhile content

---

[28] J. Macquarrie, *Jesus Christ in Modern Thought*, 373.   [29] Ibid. 398.

of the notion of 'original sin' is original sinfulness, a proneness to wrong God.[30] However, the main point which I wished to bring out by the quotation is Macquarrie's attribution to Jesus of his 'highly affirmative overcoming' of the alienation, which suggests Jesus's doing so by free choice, which if Macquarrie's account of freedom is the same as mine, indicates that the man Jesus in freely rejecting sin, made himself God. That then contrasts with Schleiermacher where the union of God with man in Jesus is due entirely to God's act; for Macquarrie the man Jesus seems to be largely responsible for it. In each case of course the union is a union of two separate hypostases, causally linked—not, as with Chalcedon, a union that is simply the fact of the same individual being both divine and human.

Is a modified Nestorianism of the type that (possibly mistakenly) I have attributed to Macquarrie any improvement on the original Nestorianism? What can be said in favour of this version of 'humanistic Christology'? Since, on this view, God does not act in a supernatural way in Christ more than in any other human—Christ has as much free will to act contrary to the will of God as any of us does—none of the a priori reasons as to why God should have so acted in Christ have any application. Likewise the theory can make little appeal to revelation—whatever the New Testament writers may or may not have thought about the issue, clearly this view was virtually unheard in the Church between the third and eighteenth centuries. So its advocates cannot claim that it is revealed doctrine. And, given all that, what grounds are there for believing that Christ was or even became perfectly 'open to the divine' (in the stated sense)? His public acts, in so far as they are on record in the New Testament, do indeed show considerable 'openness to the divine'. But that is quite inadequate evidence for the nature of his private thoughts—who knows how many bitter and lustful thoughts he indulged, even if after a few minutes he suppressed them, before going to his Passion? Since it was up to Christ how he acted and he was not caused to act as he did and he was just like us in his initial formation, God no more acted in him than he does in the rest of us and so there cannot be a priori evidence for what happened in Christ; nor can there be evidence from revelation that Christ was totally open to God. This second version of humanistic Christology

---

[30] On this see my *Responsibility and Atonement*, ch. 9.

is simply unevidenced. There is no good reason to believe it, even less reason than to believe the original Nestorianism.

Why have people been tempted to advocate some form of humanistic Christology? For two reasons, I suspect. First because they have believed that the Chalcedonian picture of Christ was an inconsistent one. A divine being could not really be fully human. I have argued otherwise in Chapter 9. And secondly because of a deep hostility to the supernatural—God does not, these writers deeply believe, intervene in history. But either there is an omnipotent God or there is not. If there is, he can intervene in history and I have suggested reason to suppose that he will. If there is not, there is not a God in anything like the traditional sense.

The Kenotic Theory

One new Christology quite different from the humanistic kind, that arose in the nineteenth century, is worth a special mention. This is the kenotic theory.[31] As with monophysitism and Nestorianism, so with the kenotic theory, in order to subject it to clear criticism, I need to set it out in a sharp, explicit form. Some theologians who have been called exponents of a kenotic Christology do not clearly seem to hold a kenotic theory at all,[32] and others do

---

[31] So called after the description of the Incarnation in St Paul's *Epistle to the Philippians* in which St Paul writes that 'Christ Jesus, being in the form of God, counted it not a prize to be on equality with God, but emptied himself (ἐκένωσε, ekenose), taking the form of a servant, being made in the likeness of men' (Phil. 2: 6–7, RV).

[32] Thus Macquarrie, *Jesus Christ in Modern Thought*, 249 f., cites Charles Gore as the 'most prominent' British theologian to develop a kenotic Christology. But a study of his *Dissertations on Subjects Connected with the Incarnation* (John Murray, 1895), does not reveal him as clearly kenotic on my classification. It is true that he writes of the need for theology to affirm 'a real abandonment on the part of the eternal Son, in becoming incarnate, of divine prerogatives inconsistent with a proper human experience' (p. 204). But Gore goes on to emphasize that the 'abandonment' applies only to the activity of the Word of God within the sphere of his human operation (p. 206), and claims that this is perfectly compatible with the Word continuing to operate in his government of the universe with 'the fullness of divine power'. So Gore seems to me to be fully Chalcedonian, in that really—despite his unfortunate use of the word 'abandon'—he claims that the Word remains divine. Chalcedon holds that the Word takes on an extra and limited way of operating; and that may well be Gore's claim, though at this point I find him confused. However, he certainly claims that his views are fully consistent with the Chalcedonian definition.

not hold it in such a sharp form as I shall set out. My criticisms of the kenotic theory can have application to the writings of the latter group only in a qualified form. However, in the sharp form in which I shall criticize it, it was expounded classically by G. Thomasius[33] and subsequently advocated by a number of other theologians and a few modern philosophers of religion.[34] The basic idea of kenotic Christology is that God is not essentially as I described him in Chapter 7. In particular, omnipotence and omniscience are not of the essence of God; a divine individual is normally omnipotent and omniscient, but he can at any rate temporarily abandon these properties while remaining divine. The Incarnation involved the Word of God, the second person of the Trinity abandoning some of the properties traditionally supposed to be essential to him and adopting human properties instead. Such a theory brings out the generosity of God in abandoning such properties as omnipotence, and the resulting doctrine might seem to be less paradoxical than initially, but I have urged, mistakenly, the Chalcedonian definition might seem to be. If being omnipotent seems inconsistent with being human, the seeming inconsistency is removed.

Thomasius, as a Lutheran, thought of himself as taking Luther's advocacy of the doctrine of the total interpenetration of the two natures to its only viable conclusion, and in thinking that, he may be correct. As I argued earlier, total interpenetration is internally consistent. The problem is that it is not consistent with other things, and in particular with a viable doctrine of the Atonement, such as would be very important for a Lutheran. Thomasius quotes Luther's remark that 'if I believe that only the human nature suffered for me, then to me Christ is a poor saviour'.[35] To secure an interpenetration which would leave the human Christ ignorant, weak, and fighting temptation, and also totally penetrated by the divine nature, he consistently denied that omniscience, omnipotence, and necessary

---

[33] G. Thomasius, *Christ's Person and Work* (1853–61). The central part, pt. 2, 'The Person of the Mediator', is translated in C. Welch (ed.), *God and Incarnation in Mid-Nineteenth Century German Theology* (Oxford University Press, 1965), from which I take my quotations.

[34] Modern philosophers of religion who have explored the kenotic theory sympathetically include Stephen T. Davis, *Logic and the Nature of God* (Macmillan, 1983), ch. 8, and Ronald J. Feenstra, 'Reconsidering Kenotic Christology', in R. J. Feenstra and C. Plantinga (eds.), *Trinity, Incarnation, and Atonement* (University of Notre Dame Press, 1989). See also Thomas V. Morris, *The Logic of God Incarnate* (Cornell University Press, 1986), ch. 4.   [35] *Christ's Person and Work*, 36.

perfect goodness are essential to deity. So what remains essential to
deity? Thomasius' answer is 'absolute power, truth, holiness, and
love'. These are the 'immanent divine attributes', which are 'inseparable from the essence of God'[36] and which revelation reveals. And
how is 'absolute power' to be distinguished from omnipotence? It
is as 'the freedom of self-determination, as the mighty will completely his own'. 'Absolute truth' is 'the knowledge of the incarnate
one concerning his own essence and the will of the Father'. These
are not very precise accounts, but it is clear that these 'immanent
attributes' are more restricted than what he calls the 'relative
attributes' of omnipotence and omniscience. Christ 'did not actively
rule the world at the same time as he walked on earth as man. He
was no omnipotent man.' Nor did he then know the future.[37] However, the relative attributes belonged again to the glorified Christ
after the Ascension.

The difficulty with such a theory is that all the arguments to the
existence of God are arguments to a simple source of all, such as
described in Chapter 7, to whom omnipotence and omniscience
belong essentially; and any being who was divine would have to
have the same essential properties as such a creator—otherwise he
would be less than the creator source of all, and there would be no
incarnation of God. To try to meet this point, one can represent a
kenotic theory as claiming that, to be divine, at some time a being
needs to have the traditional properties listed in Chapter 6, including
that of being creator and sustainer of any universe there may be,
unless he chooses to abandon them for a prearranged interval. But
in that case could God the Father temporarily abandon the traditional properties at the same time as God the Son and God the
Spirit? If so, then there can (metaphysically) be a universe without
there being a God in control at that time. If that be admitted, what
argument could there be from the universe for supposing that there
is a God at all since his control would not be needed to explain its
existence, and what reason would there be for believing that God
would ever be in control again? And if we suppose that there is
some mechanism to ensure that one divine being is always in control,[38] our hypothesis is beginning to become very complicated and
for that reason less likely to be true. The hypothesis of the existence

---

[36] Ibid. 67 f.   [37] Ibid. 70 f.

[38] For a suggestion along these lines, see Feenstra, 'Reconsidering', 141 f.

of a being who has the divine properties essentially (and of any other such being whose existence is entailed thereby) is much simpler than the hypothesis of the existence of a kenotic God. And of course the criterion of revelation lends much more support to the Chalcedonian definition than to the kenotic theory.

The intentions of kenotic theory are admirable—it is trying to capture the simple idea behind all vaguely orthodox theories of the Incarnation that in some way God humbled himself and lived a human life. Where it differs from Chalcedon is in supposing that that was and could only be achieved by God the Son ceasing in some way to have the divine properties; the humility involved a giving up. Chalcedon, by contrast, affirms that the humility involves a taking on. The king humbles himself by becoming a servant as well as being a king. I am arguing, in defence of Chalcedon, that God cannot cease to be God but that that is compatible with his living a truly human life.

The Virgin Birth

In conclusion I ought to comment briefly on two doctrines associated with the Christian doctrine of the Incarnation, doctrines which concern the beginning and end of the earthly life of Jesus Christ. I begin with the Virgin Birth. Christian creeds affirm that Christ was born 'of the Virgin Mary', that is, they accept as literal the accounts in St Matthew's Gospel (Matt. 1: 18) and St Luke's Gospel (Luke 1: 34 f.) that Christ was born of a virgin, that is, conceived without sexual intercourse with a male human. Now these stories could be understood as expressing in a parable some doctrine of Christ having a supernatural nature, for example, the traditional doctrine of incarnation or something less exalted; and the stories of the shepherds hearing the angel choir and Joseph being warned in a dream do suggest to the modern mind suspicious of the supernatural (and right to be suspicious initially, to a moderate degree) that the infancy narratives do not belong to the genre of eyewitness-report history. Nevertheless they do not seem to me to belong to the genre of expressing theological truth through prose-poems. My own view, and that, of course, is not that of an expert, is that they do—despite appearances—purport to be eyewitness-report history; and while our suspicions of the unusual and miraculous should lead us to doubt many of their details, the coincidences between two very different narratives on the point of the Virgin Birth (a phenomenon not suggested by the then current Messianic expectations—unlike the other main point of coincidence between them, the birth being at Bethlehem), is significant evidence in its favour.

Now a virgin birth or anything else unusual is not necessary for God to become man. No natural processes dictate which soul is joined to which body, and so—as I wrote in Chapter 9—God could ensure that the soul joined to a certain human body was his own, without disturbing any natural processes. However, a God who becomes incarnate must, I argued in Chapter 9, protect himself from original sinfulness, i.e. from a proneness to wrongdoing to which he might yield. Our proneness to wrongdoing arises from our moral beliefs being in conflict with genetically caused desires, e.g. for food, drink, sleep, and sex when the subject has no right to them. These desires arise in humans from physiological sources which are genetically inherited.[39] There are different ways in which a human soul could be protected from the possibility of yielding to such desires. One is by a certain 'stiffening' at the mental level; the soul could already be strong enough so as to resist such desires automatically, without effort, at its first moment of human operation. Alternatively the desires themselves could be made to operate properly; that is, to influence the soul only when it would not be wrong (even if not the best act) for the soul to yield to them. This might be effected by tampering with the genes which determine their conditions of operation—and of course those modern humans who wish to improve humanity by genetic engineering have a vision of such a programme. A virgin birth, or a virgin birth from a virgin with a particular set of genes, could be such a mechanism. So a virgin birth is a possible mechanism whereby God could ensure that his incarnation was of a proper kind. This is one way in which it would have a role in effecting the Incarnation.

The other role for it would be that of performative act—God showing to humans that the resulting child was someone more than human. A virgin birth is a violation of natural laws and so, if there is a God, the act of him who controls the laws of nature,

---

[39] On this see my *Responsibility and Atonement*, ch. 9, esp. 142–4.

setting them temporarily aside. In older societies messages of importance are often conveyed and expected to be conveyed by symbolic acts.[40] God setting aside the laws of nature to produce a child in a supernatural way is an obvious way of showing the supernatural character of that child. But of course this supernatural act—if it occurred—was a very private act, compared, say, with the Resurrection, evidence only to Mary and those to whom she told it and who believed her. Still, it would have been a very obvious way to convey the message if the message was to be conveyed.

So there is some reason to suppose that an incarnate God might have a virgin birth, and some reason in the coincidence of testimony of two Gospels, as also in the subsequent witness of the Church to it in its creeds, to suppose that it occurred. But clearly the Church has not thought the Virgin Birth to have had the importance possessed by the Incarnation, to which—if it occurred—it was a means and witness. Though I am inclined to believe that the Virgin Birth did occur, I regard it as unfortunate that mention of the virginity of Mary occurs in creeds; it is not a central enough doctrine to justify that. One suspects that a motive for emphasising the virginity of Mary was a feeling that there was something 'impure' about the normal sexual method of generation, a feeling which I believe to be unjustified and ill-supported by the Jewish tradition of thought on these matters out of which Christian moral thinking arose.

Ascension

After Christ's resurrection from the dead, the various New Testament books tell us, he appeared to his disciples on a small number of occasions, and then his earthly ministry ended. St Luke's Gospel (and its companion work the Acts of the Apostles) tell of an 'ascension', forty days (says Acts) after the Resurrection, at which Jesus Christ was carried up into 'heaven', that is, the sky, and covered (says Acts) by a cloud.

I shall not say anything in this volume about the Resurrection. That it occurred in bodily form is central to Christianity, as God the Father's symbolic miraculous act whereby he accepted the

[40] On this see my *Revelation*, 26 f.

atoning sacrifice of Christ and gave his seal of approval to the teaching of Christ (both continued in the Church), and showed symbolically to humans the possibility of redeemed life after death. I have written of this elsewhere.[41] But it would be appropriate to say something here about the Ascension, as traditionally marking the end of the earthly life of Jesus in the way that the Virgin Birth (or more accurately virginal conception) marked its beginning.

The creeds all say that 'Christ ascended into heaven' or 'the heavens'; but this can, not unnaturally, be read simply as saying that Christ gave up his earthly life to live solely the divine life. For the confession of most creeds that Christ 'descended from the heavens' (ἐκ τῶν οὐρἀνων) to become incarnate is clearly to be read simply in the sense that he became human and lived an earthly life. That Christ was seen on earth only for a short period after his Resurrection is clear, and so the Ascension in this minimal sense can hardly be a problematic doctrine for those who affirm an incarnation.

But generally the Church has believed two further things about the Ascension, though one of them has not appeared in creeds and the other has only appeared in some lesser creeds. The first is that the account in St Luke's Gospel and Acts reports a true historical incident. The οὐρανός there is then to be read as 'the sky', and not in the metaphorical sense of the life of the Trinity in which Christ is said to have descended ἐκ τῶν οὐρἀνων. If God the Father did indeed raise his incarnate Son from the dead by a miraculous act, I do not see anything surprising in that he should symbolize the end of his earthly life by another symbolic act, of his being taken away into the sky, symbolizing the life of God, and being covered by a cloud, which for a Jew symbolized the presence of God; it was by the accompanying cloud that God was known to the Israelites in the desert.[42] But this understanding of the Ascension is no explicit part of creeds.

Some lesser creeds and church pronouncements[43] have stated that the union of God the Son with human nature (soul and body) was, after the conception of Christ, permanent; that Christ took away with him at the end of his earthly life his human nature and body.

---

[41] See (e.g.) *Responsibility and Atonement*, 160, 171, and *Revelation*, 110–13.

[42] e.g. Exodus 19: 9.

[43] The Lateran Council of AD 649, e.g., implies this in stating that at the Last Judgement Christ will come to judge 'the living and the dead' in the flesh and rational soul which were assumed by him', Denzinger, 502.

If we are to rise again with our bodies, as creeds have normally claimed explicitly, there must in another space be a place for us, which if he so chose Christ could inhabit with his human body. If he did so, God thereby would have been continuing to give content to three of the reasons for the Incarnation that I discussed earlier in the chapter—to express and show to us the goodness of human nature and to show his love for us. Maybe then there is that interpenetration of the divine and human natures of Christ which, I argued, there was not on earth. But again I cannot see the permanent union as a central Christian doctrine.

Conclusion

Leaving these last two lesser doctrines, what I have argued in this second part of the book is this. This simplest account of what the existence of God amounts to is that described in Chapter 7. Given arguments of some reasonable degree of probability for the existence of God, it is to that God that they lead, more probably than to any other. It follows from that that there is very considerable reason to suppose that there are three divine individuals 'in one substance', and quite considerable reason to suppose that one such might become incarnate. A religion that claims to have a revelation of Trinity and Incarnation is therefore very likely to be a religion with a true revelation, which is to be believed in respect of what else it tells us about the Incarnation—where and when it happened—and other central matters.

It is a mistake to divide Christian doctrines into those that can be known by natural reason (i.e. arguing from general features of the publicly observable world) and those that can only be known by revelation (i.e. those known because contained in Bible or Church creeds, which may be shown by independent argument to be reliable sources of information). Plausibly, both reason and revelation have a role in respect to most items of doctrine. But for some items the weight of evidence comes more from natural reason and for other items more from revelation. The existence of God is more a matter of natural reason—though the statement of a prophet whose testimony is confirmed by miracle that he was sent by God may have some small role to play. Conversely, that God became incarnate in

Christ is knowable mainly through revelation, though a priori arguments that God has reason for acting in that sort of way have their part to play. It is an integrated web of argument from the whole of experience which leads to the Christian doctrine of God; and that doctrine is justified to the extent to which that web is a seamless garment.

Many recent theologians have tried to construct a moderately traditional doctrine of God, but have balked at a traditional doctrine of the Incarnation. That doctrine—that God walked on earth—they claim, is 'unbelievable by modern man'. But there really is no special problem with that doctrine, if you accept a Christian doctrine of God. If you accept that the whole physical world owes its existence from moment to moment to the sustaining action of a personal God, there is no special problem about that God relating himself in a special way to one bit of that world, that is, making it his body and dividing his mind in such a way as to be related to that body in the way in which we are related to our bodies. What the radical theologians are really objecting to is the traditional doctrine of God which allows for the possibility of a traditional incarnation. It is really that which, speaking on behalf of 'modern man', they claim to be 'unbelievable' by him. I have argued elsewhere[44] that arguments which use the inductive criteria which 'modern man' uses in science and history point beyond science and history to a creator personal God.

[44] *Existence of God, passim.*

Additional Notes

1. Hartry Field has argued persuasively, and to my mind convincingly, for a fictionalist view of mathematics. '2 + 2 = 4' is, he claims, true only in the sense in which sentences of fiction are true, namely, they fit with the rest of the literary work. However, it is useful to suppose fictional sentences of mathematics to be true, because they facilitate inference. Field defines a mathematical theory M as 'conservative', 'if and only if for any assertion A about the physical world and any body N of such assertions, A doesn't follow from N + M unless it follows from N alone' (H. Field, *Realism, Mathematics and Modality* (Basil Blackwell, 1989), 58). It is the sentences of such a theory M that we, fictionally, suppose true; and thereby inference from N to A is facilitated, because adding sentences of M to N provides us with easy and clear steps. In supposing the sentences of M to be true, we suppose their names (e.g. '2' and '4') to refer to objects, and so we suppose such objects as 2 and 4 to exist. Mathematics is not, Field claims, theoretically indispensable for stating the physical laws that govern the physical world; merely useful for their succinct exposition. See ibid. *passim*, and *Science Without Numbers* (Princeton University Press, 1980). Field does, however, assume a strong view of the necessity of the laws of logic, while denying that that involves any existential commitment. I shall come to discuss the status of the laws of logic in Chapter 5.

2. One theory about the nature of fundamental 'particles' may be supported by evidence of observation against a rival one in the following way. A theory which says that material objects have thisness allows the possibility of distinct states between which we cannot ever tell the difference, i.e., that are indistinguishable. In that case, given certain further initially plausible assumptions, we might expect to find certain kinds of indistinguishable states (namely, those which correspond to more than one distinct state) more often than others (namely, those which correspond to just one distinct state). By contrast, a theory which says that material objects lack thisness might, given further initially plausible assumptions, lead us to expect various indistinguishable states with equal frequency (since indistinguishable states are non-distinct states).

As I read it, modern physics does suggest that this kind of inductive evidence for the presence or absence of thisness may be in principle available. It tells us that there are two sorts of fundamental particle out of which the large-scale inanimate material objects are made—fermions (such as electrons and protons) and bosons (the energy-exchange particles, such as photons and gluons). Any two such particles which have the same hard properties are, it claims, indistinguishable.

To distinguish large-scale inanimate objects we need to take into account their past-directed soft properties of spatio-temporal continuity. Consider two billiard balls at a time t_1: b_1, at place p_1, and b_2 at p_2. Then at a later time there are, among others, two possible distinct states: the two having remained in the same places (b_1 at p_1, and b_2 at p_2) and the two having exchanged places (b_1 at p_2, and b_2 at p_1) and by observation of spatio-temporal continuity we can recognize which has occurred. Contrast this case with the case of fundamental particles belonging to a system such as a gas. Here there are no corresponding distinct states at a later time between which we can tell a difference. We cannot keep track of the particles to see if they change position because in general 'particles do not move in well-defined trajectories, so the question of spatio-temporal continuity of trajectory does not arise' (S. French and M. Redhead, 'Quantum Physics and the Identity of Indiscernibles', *British Journal for the Philosophy of Science*, 39 (1988), 233–46, 244). Fundamental particles may move discontinuously on the quantum scale—e.g. an electron orbiting a nucleus may 'jump' from one orbit to another without passing through intervening space. For particles there is just the earlier state of a particle at p_1 and a particle at p_2, and the later similar state of a particle at p_1 and a particle at p_2. Distinguishable states are clearly distinct. But what of the indistinguishable states? Are there really distinct states—the particles remaining in the same position and the particles having exchanged position—between which we are unable to tell the difference? Or are the indistinguishable states in fact the same state? Our answer will depend on how we read Quantum Theory.

On what is called the 'first quantized' version of Quantum Theory, particles are given labels; and the difference between them not being a matter of any monadic or relational property, whether hard or soft, they are in effect supposed to have thisness. However, statistics governing particles (the Bose–Einstein statistics for bosons, and the Fermi–Dirac statistics for fermions) work on the assumption that distinguishable states are equiprobable states and from that assumption we can derive correct results for the behaviour of large observable assemblages of particles. (On this see M. Born, *Atomic Physics*, 8th edn. (Blackie & Son, Ltd., 1969), 223–30.) That assumption is intrinsically plausible if all distinct states are distinguishable states (and so amounts to the assumption that distinct states are equiprobable) and so all indistinguishable states are identical, but otherwise requires some explanation. That explanation would be provided by a hypothesis that there are physical principles which prevent the occurrence of all but one of each of the distinct but indistinguishable states. As French and

Redhead put it in developing this account, 'states with the wrong symmetry get eliminated because they are not *accessible* to the joint quantum system, not because there are no such states' ('Quantum Physics', 237). However, on the 'second quantized' version of Quantum Theory, 'particles' are merely excitations of a quantum field, and there is no difference between the particles continuing to occupy the same position and their positions being reversed; indistinguishable states are identical. But since the question of spatio-temporal continuity does not arise for fundamental particles, that leaves us with [E] as the strongest principle affirmable for them. The applicability of quantum statistics is explained without the introduction of a further physical hypothesis. So whether one attributes thisness to particles depends on which version of Quantum Theory one treats most realistically, as giving a more accurate picture of physical reality. My quick gut reaction is to regard the 'second quantized' version as giving the more realistic physical picture. It is simpler without the additional hypothesis about accessibility, and the 'first quantized' version gives an extraordinary complex picture of every electron in the universe somehow being 'entangled' with each other electron. 'Every electron . . . partakes of the state of every other electron in the universe, according to the antisymmetrization requirement', ibid. 244. A simpler hypothesis which accounts equally well for the data is as such more likely to be true than a complex one.

The issue of just how to read the two versions of Quantum Theory is a difficult one and I have moved quickly over some difficult ground, but my main concern is to show the relevance of physical theory to the issue of thisness, rather than to settle exactly what modern physics in its current state suggests. But if I have read Quantum Theory correctly, then it favours the view that fundamental particles do not have thisness.

3. Aquinas also held the view that human souls are forms which are also substances, 'subsistent forms'—see *Summa theologiae*, 1a. 75. 2, though he claimed that the disembodied soul is not fully a human being. A major reason why Aquinas held the view that human souls are subsistent forms was to allow for the possibility of their existing on their own without bodies (as Aquinas held that they did temporarily after death—in Purgatory or Heaven or Hell—before final reunion with their bodies), while suggesting that embodiment is the natural state for a soul. For if a human soul is a form it is something like a shape fitted for a particular body. And clearly particular human souls with their particular desires and beliefs are suited to operate through particular bodies. Aquinas, however, unlike Scotus, held that the identity of a soul is constituted by the body to which it naturally belongs and with which it is suited to be reunited; that is, a soul is the soul it is in virtue of having a particular relational property—e.g. 'fitted to be united to body B'. (See *Summa Contra Gentiles*, 2. 81.) Scotus objected that inclinations to occupy one body rather than another do not

exist on their own (*inclinatio non est entitas absoluta*). There cannot be 'bare dispositions', to use a modern term; such inclinations presuppose a distinction between souls founded in some other way (*Ordinatio*, II. d3. p1. q7. nn. 230–1). I do not find that argument too convincing, because it is not clear to me why there cannot be bare dispositions. But my earlier arguments suggest that such a relation to a particular body would not individuate a soul, since another soul could have had just that relation. If souls are forms which can exist on their own, those forms have thisness and so are individual essences.

As Aquinas abandoned the hylemorphic theory for disembodied human souls, he also abandoned it for angels, whom he regarded as pure forms—see *Summa theologiae*, 1a. 50. They were each individuated by essential properties, additional to the essential properties of angels as such.

    4. Hume himself, in *A Treatise Concerning Human Nature*, 1. 3. 14, gave two different accounts of causation, one of them analysing α 'causing' β in a subjective way as a mere propensity of the mind to pass from the thought of α to that of β (where α is precedent and contiguous to β). But the empiricist tradition has largely followed his alternative regularity account which (with the omission of the requirement, stated only in the *Treatise*, that cause and effect be contiguous) I stated in the text. In *An Inquiry Concerning Human Understanding*, sect. 7, pt. 2, Hume equates his regularity account of α 'causing' β with 'if the first object had not been, the second had never existed', i.e. a counterfactual relation (see text) between α and β. I point out in the text that there can be regular succession without such a counterfactual relation. Hume ought not to equate the two.

    It might well seem, however, that there are better prospects for analysing causation in terms of counterfactuals than in terms of regular succession; and in recent years David Lewis has sought to develop a counterfactual analysis of causation—see his 'Causation' in his *Philosophical Papers*, ii. (Oxford University Press, 1986), 159–213. In summary, his account is as follows. C causes E if there is a chain of events from C to E, each event in the chain being causally dependent on its predecessor. E is causally dependent on A is read as: if A had not occurred, E would not have occurred, symbolized as '$\sim A \;\Box\!\!\rightarrow\; \sim E$'. The basic trouble with this analysis is that it might on some occasion be the case that the world be otherwise the same up to the relevant time, A not occur, and then quite unconnectedly E not occur '$\sim A \;\Box\!\!\rightarrow\; \sim E$' might be 'barely true', not grounded in A which has the causal power to produce E being absent and so not exercising that power. If such unconnected succession would be what would happen if A were not to happen, then A would not have caused E. True, we could not observe the difference between the two possible scenarios if A were not to happen, but in a world where A happens we cannot observe either of the scenarios. What is at stake is what a claim about causation does commit us to by way of the unobservable, and the answer is that it commits us to more than mere counterfactuals. That it is caused by A explains why E occurs. Counterfactuals merely describe what would happen in different circumstances. They do not explain why what happens does happen, and what would happen would happen. That it is caused by A does explain the occurrence of B; and its powers and liabilities do explain why A causes.

5. Two recent books have advocated the thesis that talk of laws of nature is reducible to talk of causation by particular substances (the basic metaphysical fact) rather than vice versa, a thesis that goes against the whole stream of the empiricist tradition. The first is R. Harré and E. H. Madden, *Causal Powers* (Basil Blackwell, 1975). We are, they argue, directly aware of causal power, both when we act intentionally and on other occasions. The second is Nancy Cartwright, *Nature's Capacities and Their Measurement* (Clarendon Press, 1989). All attempts to reduce causal talk to talk about regularities in the succession of events along Humean lines fails, she claims. She argues explicitly, as I have done, that both parts of the Humean programme—the programme of reducing singular causality to laws of nature, and laws of nature to regularities of successions—are mistaken. John Foster in his *A. J. Ayer* (Routledge & Kegan Paul, 1985), 254–63, makes a more limited point. He points out that any laws of nature that relate events involving only general properties (i.e. 'all events of kind A physically necessitate events of kind B') could leave it indeterminate which event caused which. Thus if there were a law that 'heating metal-K causes a flash 2 metres distant', and there were two lumps of metal-K 3 metres apart, duly heated, followed by two flashes, both within 2 metres of each lump, it would be indeterminate which heating caused which flash. If talk of causation were reducible to talk about laws of nature, there could be no truth about which heating caused which flash. Yet, claims Foster, intuitively there would be such a truth, even if we could not know it. He goes on to urge, more powerfully, that if all truths about brain events causing mental events were general truths—e.g. 'all brain events of kind B physically necessitate mental events of kind M', they could not determine in which (in my terminology) soul M occurred. The laws would have to have the form 'all brain events of kind B in body *b* physically necessitate mental events of kind M in soul *s*'. That would be a quite different kind of law from the kind always envisaged by scientists and philosophers of science; and, to my mind, moves us on towards affirming the primacy of causation by substances.

An argument of exactly the same kind as Foster's metal-heating argument is also among the arguments given by Michael Tooley for rejecting the view that singular causation is reducible to causation by law. (See his *Causation* (Oxford University Press, 1987), ch. 6; and 'The Nature of Causation: A Singularist Account', in D. Copp (ed.), *Canadian Philosophers*

(*Canadian Journal of Philosophy* Supplement, University of Calgary Press, 1990). For Tooley, however, causation is by events, not substances. Tooley's other arguments for this thesis depend on accepting a causal theory of time, i.e. a theory that temporal order is reducible to causal order. Tooley does not give arguments for a causal theory of time; I do give arguments for such a theory in Ch. 4 of this book. In *Causation*, Tooley claimed that laws are necessary but not sufficient for causation—i.e. that a substance can (logically) cause an event only in virtue of some property such that any other substance having that property would cause (with physical necessity or with such-and-such a degree of physical probability) an event of that type. In his later article he has abandoned that view, holding that one event can cause another without instantiating a law. But he still leaves himself with an unnecessarily swollen ontology by holding that there are laws of nature as well as causation; some laws are causal, some non-causal, and causal laws are just those in which the physical necessitation is causal. But it seems to me that all talk of non-causal laws is reducible to talk of causal laws (and initial conditions). If it is physically necessary that events of type A are correlated with events of type B, then either the former phys-ically necessitate, i.e. cause, the latter, or conversely, or the only events which cause events of type A are also events that cause events of type B. But if all laws are causal laws, then talk about laws can be reduced to talk about causation. If it is a làw that events of type A cause events of type B, then since an event of type A will consist in the instantiation of some property P in a substance of type S, (by my argument in the text) what the law amounts to is that all substances of type S have also the property of the power to cause an event of type B and the liability to exercise that power when the property P is instantiated in them. It is the universal coinstan-tiation of properties (e.g. the relevant causal power in substances of type S and the liability to exercise it when property P is instantiated) which is the ultimate (non-causal and non-law-dependent) logically contingent fact and which Tooley represents as a 'contingent relation between universals'. Tooley claims (in 'The Nature of Causation', 293) that 'The concept of causation is parasitic upon the concept of a law of nature.' I have claimed in the text that we derive the concept of causation from ourselves causally acting and being causally acted upon, and then come to recognize succes-sions of events in the world as exemplifying causality.

6. Although philosophers have normally ruled out the logical possibility of backward causation, they have usually allowed the possibility of simultan-eous causation and often affirmed its actual occurrence. Kant claimed that 'the great majority of efficient natural causes are simultaneous with their effects' (*Critique of Pure Reason*, trans. N. Kemp Smith (Macmillan, 1933), B 248). He illustrates this with the example of the ball lying on the cushion. The action of the ball in forming a hollow is, he claims, simultaneous with

the formation of the hollow. But Kant gives no argument in favour of the claim that these are simultaneous, let alone in favour of his wide general claim; and he seems to have casually supposed that where he was unable to observe a time interval between the ball beginning to exert its gravitational force (concentrated at the ball's centre of gravity) and the first depression of the cushion, there was in fact no interval. But Kant's casual supposition was mistaken; special relativity can now tell us the length of that very small interval. In the Middle Ages it was generally supposed that light had an infinite velocity, and Newton and his successors supposed the force of gravity to act with infinite velocity; and infinite velocity involves the simultaneity of cause and effect. The Special Theory of Relativity has the consequence that all causal action is propagated with finite velocity. But, if my arguments in the text are correct, it did not need special relativity with its empirical foundation to show this; it follows from logical considerations alone. It did of course need empirical considerations to show that the velocity of light is the fastest signal. Hume, by contrast, had an argument to show the logical impossibility of simultaneous causation (*Treatise*, 1. 3. 2). He argues that cause and immediate effect must be as close as possible. (If an earlier event causes a later event separated from it by an interval of time, it can only do so via a chain of close events which connect the two.) And how close is close? If cause and effect could be simultaneous, argues Hume, they would be; and then all effects would be simultaneous with their causes and that would lead to 'the utter annihilation of time'. So cause and effect cannot be simultaneous, and the requirement of closeness will have to be satisfied by mere contiguity in time. But Hume gives no argument as to why if nature allows one effect to be simultaneous with its cause, it has to allow all so to be. My claim in the text is that the *Treatise* contains the resources for a much stronger argument.

7. In this chapter I showed how the notions of 'proposition' and 'statement' may be introduced as the content of public sentences; but I argued that the propositions and statements so introduced were fictional constructs, and that logical necessity belonged ultimately to and logical relations held ultimately between public sentences. Logic was constituted by the linguistic behaviour of language users in the context in which they used their sentences. I thus gave a nominalist account of these matters. Since the notions of 'proposition' and 'statement' are notions of claims about how the world is, and since we can express such claims not merely in public sentences but in private thoughts, the notions of 'proposition' and 'statement' may be introduced instead as the meaning content of such thoughts. But I shall argue that that way of introducing them also does not require a Platonist account of the resulting notions—for such talk is ultimately talk about how people think privately in various contexts of thought.

Our thoughts, we want to say, have the content the thinker supposes them to have even if he cannot put them into words. That seems right if by the 'content' of the thought we mean the content that does not depend on which public objects or properties in the outside world his referring devices latch on to, that is, on the referential context of his thought. What he knows infallibly is what he would express in words of a public language if he knew a suitable public language well enough, and which is independent of the referential context of his thought, about the nature of which he may well be mistaken. Since—in the usage that I have commended—linguistic conventions alone suffice to determine which proposition is expressed by a public sentence, the content to which the thinker has infallible access is a proposition. When I have the thought that my desk is brown, the thought that I have is the one that, if I knew the English language well enough, I would put into words by 'My desk is brown.' Knowledge of language does not add to my thought but merely allows me to express it. And that content of my thought about which I cannot be mistaken is that which would be expressed by any sentence of any language synonymous with 'My desk is brown'—in any context (the propositional content of a thought is what some philosophers have called its 'narrow content'; on these issues, see more fully my *The Evolution of the Soul* (Clarendon Press, 1986), ch. 4, 'Thoughts'). But there is another sense of 'content' in which the content of my thought is other than a proposition. My thought concerns an individual object—'my desk'; and if in some sense I do not know what my desk is, in that sense I do not know what the content of my thought is. I may not have a desk or it may be other than the one I think it is. The content in this other sense is the individuals about which I am thinking and the properties that I am attributing to them, and in so far as I am ignorant about which individuals those are, then my thought has a content of which I am ignorant. This aspect of content of which a thinker may be ignorant is that which is determined by the referential context of his thought. So we can introduce the notion of a statement as the content of a thought—in the sense of that which is common to any sentence by which the thinker could express his thought if he knew a suitable public language well enough and any other sentence which predicated the same properties of the same individuals at the same times and places.

Thoughts contain other thoughts; and a thinker can only be the final authority on the content of his thought if he is the final authority on which other thoughts are contained in it. So the proposition that a thinker thinks will have the minimal entailments that he recognizes it as having, and the entailments that are connected to it by a chain that he will recognize. A thought-proposition is logically necessary if its negation entails what the thinker will recognize as some proposition and also the negation of that proposition. No one can have a contradiction as the explicit content of his thought, in the sense that no one can suppose true both some supposition and its negation. For supposing the negation of some supposition to be true is just supposing the original supposition not to be true. However, human thoughts can certainly contain implicit contradictions, in that on reflection the thinker will acknowledge that his original thought involves a commitment both to some other thought and to its negation. We may say that a thought-proposition is *ultimately* coherent if it does not implicitly involve a contradiction.

But if the notion of proposition is introduced in this way as the content of a thought which some thinker has, there is again no need to think of propositions as timeless entities or the relations between them as timeless relations. They exist and are related only in so far as there are thinkers who have thoughts, and they form the content of those thoughts, and are related to each other only in the ways that the thinkers acknowledge. To talk publicly of these propositions we need a public human language, but putting those propositions into public words may suggest that they have a more precise content with more remote consequences than they do in fact have.

If the notion of statement is introduced as the content (in the second sense) of private thought, then which statement is the content of some thought depends on how the propositional content of the thought latches on to the world (both which individuals his thoughts pick out, and perfectly ordinary facts about them). Although the thinker cannot be in error about which proposition constitutes the content of his thought, he can, as we saw, be in error about how that proposition latches on to the world, that is, about which statement is the content of his thought (and indeed he may suppose that it expresses a statement, when it does not; maybe the referring elements of his thought do not pick out anything in the external world). But again we can say all we need to say without hypostatizing the notion of statement. Whether a thought contains a certain statement just is a matter of how its propositional content latches on to the world, and it expressing a necessary statement just is a matter of some thought that contains the negation of that statement having as its content a proposition that entails a self-contradiction. And whether this holds or not is a matter as well as of the contingent consideration of how the propositional content latches on to the world, of which propositions the thinker would—if fully informed about the referential context—recognize as latching on to the world in the same way, and which entailments he would recognize them as having.

And so, the notion of statement, like that of proposition, remains a fictional construct. If propositions and statements are introduced as the content of thoughts, then talk of logical relations between them and of their logical necessity just is talk about which thoughts people will recognize as involved in which other thoughts and how their thoughts latch on to the world. The truths of logic concern now not *nomina*, public words, but thoughts (and the contexts in which the thoughts are had); and so we may use the medieval term 'conceptualism' to describe this account of their nature, as logical conceptualism. Either way, there are no timeless entities logically related, just the ways and contexts in which rational beings use words and operate with their thoughts. Platonism is false.

8. In 'Eternity', *Journal of Philosophy*, 78 (1981), 429–56, Stump and Kretzmann tried to spell a notion of 'ET-simultaneity', analogous to but different from our ordinary notion of simultaneity in which God's causal actions and awareness in an 'eternity' not temporally related to our time would be ET-simultaneous with their mundane effects and objects of awareness, so that in a sense he causes them and is aware of them 'as they happen' without literally being prior to, simultaneous with, or later than them. Their definition (p. 439) is as follows:

(ET) For every x and for every y, x and y are ET-simultaneous iff

1. either x is eternal and y is temporal, or vice versa; and

2. for some observer, A, in the unique eternal reference frame, x and y are both present—i.e. either x is eternally present, and y is observed as temporally present, or vice versa; and

3. for some observer, B, in one of the infinitely many temporal reference frames, x and y are both present—i.e. either x is observed as eternally present and y is temporally present, or vice versa.

The first clause of this definition simply lays down by fiat that every eternal event is 'ET-simultaneous' with every temporal event, and vice versa. One hopes for more content from the other two clauses. What (2) and (3) amount to depends on what it is for an eternal observer to 'observe' a mundane event as 'temporally present', and a temporal observer to 'observe' an eternal event as 'eternally present'. Stump and Kretzmann tell us that such observations are not observations of simultaneity, but of 'co-occurrence' of the state observed with the observation. No further illumination however is provided of what this amounts to, and hence I am unclear what (2) and (3) add to (1). Stump and Kretzmann indicate that the observers referred to need not be actual observers; potential ones will do. For there must be actual temporal events, as well as eternal events, that are not observed by any temporal observer. But the question remains as to what it would be for such observers to 'observe' events of other frames as 'present' when they are not 'present' in the literal sense of being simultaneous with their being observed. In default of such illumination being provided, I cannot see what (2) and (3) add to (1), which lays down by fiat that every eternal event is 'ET-simultaneous' with every temporal event. Such definitions of the supposed relation that eternal and temporal events have to each other would be harmless if some other word had been chosen to denote it—e.g. 'ET-disjunction'. But to call the notion 'ET-simultaneity' suggests that what has been defined has some analogy to normal simultaneity, and no reason has been given for supposing that it does. Hence no reason has been given for supposing that if God has an existence outside time, he can have any relation to the events of time that would be in any way analogous to 'causing' or 'observing' them. The objection to the coherence of the 'timeless' doctrine remains, and in my view remains conclusive.

9. What I have written about the divine necessity and the impossibility on theistic grounds of ontological arguments for his existence is very much, I believe, in accord with things Aquinas wrote in *Summa theologiae*. He claimed (1a. 2. 1) that there could not be a valid ontological argument to the existence of God from premises known by humans to be true. For to give such an argument we would have in some sense to grasp the divine essence and show that it involved existence. Any mere description of God as, say, 'that than which nothing greater can be thought' (1a. 2. 1 ad 2) would beg the question whether that description described anything. And so any description of the divine essence as the essence of that than which nothing greater can be thought, would also beg the question as to whether there was such an essence. For on Aquinas's understanding of essence (alias form or nature), one cannot define essences into existence; there are only essences of those things which exist actually or potentially (i.e. such that there is some mechanism whereby they can be actualized, and so according to Aquinas's view that any potential must sometime or other be actualized, have been or will be brought into existence—1a. 3. 4). Since God is not the sort of thing which can exist potentially—if he exists at all, he exists always—there can only be a divine essence if there is a God. Hence 'God is the same thing as his own nature or essence' (1a. 3. 3). But in the course of a normal earthly life we do not 'see the divine essence' (1a. 12. 11), which seems to be what he means by 'we do not know what it is to be God' (1a. 2. 1), and so we can only argue to the existence of God from the effects of his actions. But what we argue to is the existence of an essentially simple, limitless, perfect, good, eternal, etc. being. If we did 'see' the divine essence, as, Aquinas claims, we may hope to in the beatific vision, we could argue to God's existence from that, but since that is the same thing as God, we would not be arguing to the existence of God from some other fact. Nowhere does Aquinas suggest that there is some other fact, e.g. a truth of logic, which makes it the case that there is a God. On the contrary, the description by which we initially come to refer to God is as 'the first cause', i.e. as that which does not have a cause of its existence. 'It is not possible that anything should cause itself' (1a. 2. 3). And even if

ruling out God having a cause does not explicitly rule out there being a sufficient reason (e.g. of some logical kind) why there is God, it is very much in the same spirit to deny that there is. God is too ultimate for anything else (however necessary that thing) to provide a sufficient reason why there is a God.

10. Those who claim that there are timeless necessarily true statements or propositions are faced with the question of how God is related to them. If there is a timeless truth expressed by '2 + 2 = 4' which is true in every possible world, it is not something created by God's free act of will and so seems to be something which is equally ultimate with God. The normal defence of the Platonist theist is to claim that God, who is a logically necessary being, necessarily brings about (as an act of essence, to use my terminology) any necessary truths and other abstract objects which have to exist. This view, adumbrated by many Platonists, by Leibniz, and by Plantinga has been developed recently by Morris and Menzel, and called by them 'theistic activism'. The eternal propositions and relations between them are thoughts which God necessarily thinks. (See G. W. Leibniz, *Monadology*, sect. 46; A. Plantinga, *Does God Have a Nature?* (Marquette University Press, 1980), 26–61; and T. V. Morris and C. Menzel, 'Absolute Creation', *American Philosophical Quarterly*, 23 (1986), 353–62.) The notion of the eternal forms as ideas in the mind of God is, of course, an ancient part of the currency of Christian Platonism, but a clear notion of logical necessity in terms of which these modern writers develop it was not. But even given the Platonist account of logical necessity and that God's existence is among the logical necessities, it remains hard to see how the truth expressed by '2 + 2 = 4' could depend on the existence of God. For surely if—*per impossibile*—there were no God, 2 + 2 would still equal 4. And the point made in the text suggests that if there were a sound ontological argument for the existence of God of the traditional kind, the necessity of God's existence would derive from some necessary truth more ultimate than that of God's existence, rather than God's existence being the ultimate necessary truth as theistic activism affirms.

11. The medieval theologians wanted to claim, in accord with Christian orthodoxy, both that there is only one God and that there are 'three divine persons'. Various of the arguments which they gave for the former seem to me to be such that if they worked they would also refute the latter. However, they seem to me not to work. Richard of St Victor has the simple argument that there could be no more than one (essentially) omnipotent being, because then one could deprive the other of omnipotence—*De Trinitate*, 1. 25. He does not recognize the point that such an act would be bad, and that for quite other reasons omnipotence must be construed in such a way as to rule out the possibility of God doing a bad act. Duns Scotus has a more subtle argument against the possibility of more than one (essentially)

omnipotent being of the kind which I used in connection with the example of Abraham above—'if two omnipotent beings exist, each will make the other impotent, not indeed by destroying the other, but because one by his positive will could keep non-existent what the other wills should exist'. Interestingly he goes on to suggest that his opponent might suggest 'sophistically', 'that they voluntarily agree on a common way of acting through some sort of pact', but claims that the result of the pact would be to leave neither of them omnipotent. But he does not see the point that to break a pact would be a wrong act; and that God's omnipotence must be construed in such a way as to rule out the possibility of his doing wrong. See Scotus, *Ordinatio*, 1. d2. q3; trans. A. Wolter, *Duns Scotus: Philosophical Writings* (Hackett Publishing Co., 1987), 90.

12. There is a possible compromise position between the view that divine individuals have thisness with the consequence that there can only be one of them, and the view that they do not have thisness with the consequence that there can be more than one of them—the view that either alternative is a logical possibility; that divine individuals can have or lack thisness. In that case the first divine individual could have thisness, but it would remain the case that subsequent divine individuals could not have thisness—for there would be no reason to bring about this second divine individual rather than that one. Yet subsequent divine individuals could have as essential individuating properties not merely general relational properties (e.g. 'being caused by a divine individual') but particular relational properties (e.g. 'being caused by this divine individual'). The thisness of the first divine individual would then be what constituted the individuality of subsequent divine individuals, and of the collective. This compromise view does then have the same consequences for the Trinity as those of the second view above, to be developed subsequently in this chapter. In some ways it is an attractive view. But against it are to be ranged first the objections at the end of Ch. 7 to divine individuals having thisness; and secondly the very strong objection that surely all individuals of the same kind must be individuated in the same sort of way. Two individuals could not both be divine if the sort of thing that constituted their individuality was totally different for each of them.

13. It is compatible with my philosophical argument that there must be an asymmetry of dependence between divine individuals, that it be either an asymmetry of causal dependence only for an initial (beginningless) period of time or an eternal one. In the first system the first divine individual actively causes the second and (with him) the third during an initial period. Subsequently each is only the permissive cause (i.e. permits the existence of) the others. In the second system the first divine individual actively causes the second, and (with him) the third throughout all time. But for each period of time that has a beginning the first continues to exist only

because the second and the third permit this, and the second continues to exist only because the third permits this. Which system will operate depends on which system there is most reason for divine individuals to bring about. In favour of the first, more limited, system of dependence is the argument that under it the first and second individuals would be, as it were, less stingy in handing over influence. In favour of the second fuller system of dependence is the argument that since dependence is good, the more of it the better; and the first and second divine individuals would see that the best act would be one which maximized dependence. I hesitate to pronounce on which system reason favours most. That part of the Christian tradition that understands God being eternal as his being outside time will, of course, demand that all causal dependences that exist once exist always. But that part of the Christian tradition that understands God being eternal as his being everlasting would seem equally at home with either kind of asymmetry.

14. While Apollinarianism, explicitly claiming that Christ had no human soul and that the Incarnation consisted simply in the Word, the second person of the Trinity, acquiring a body was explicitly rejected as a heresy as soon as it appeared towards the end of the fourth century, the Fathers before then were clearly somewhat torn as to whether they should say that Christ had a human soul. Maurice Wiles's conclusion from a study of the history of this issue is that: 'From the very start, the mind of the Fathers was clear that when thinking soteriologically they must affirm the fact of Christ's possession of a human soul. On the other hand, when thinking of the unity of Christ's person they were . . . almost equally clear that the idea must be repudiated' ('The Nature of the Early Debate about Christ's Human Soul', *Journal of Ecclesiastical History*, 16 (1965), 139–51). When 'thinking soteriologically', they wished to affirm that Christ had a human way of thinking and acting. When thinking of 'the unity of Christ's person', they wished to affirm that there was only one individual. But the Fathers were insufficiently sensitive to the different possible understandings of ψυχή (soul) arising from the Greek philosophical systems which they used. For Plato, as for me, the soul is an entity separate from the body. For Aristotle it is a way of thinking and acting. Chalcedon wished to deny that the Word of God was joined to a separate human individual (this is Nestorianism—see Ch. 10), and so cannot be read as affirming that the Word acquired a Platonic human soul, merely that he acquired an Aristotelian human soul.

15. We can see that this is at stake in the Christological disputes in the West of the first half of the twelfth century, described by Peter Lombard in *Sentences*, 3. d6. The issue addressed by different theologians was 'In what sense did the Word, the Second person of the Trinity take on something (*aliquid*) when he became man?' The Lombard expounds three

current answers to this question. The first, having some affinities with that of Hugh of St Victor, held that a certain human substance, separate in essence from God though not existing prior to the Incarnation, was made God. The second, a version of Gilbert Porreta's account, was regarded by the Lombard as close to the third theory which he himself espoused. This was that the Word put on a human soul and body like a garment (*velut indumento*), i.e. as accidental (i.e. non-essential) attributes. The Lombard, to my mind correctly, rejects the first view, on the grounds that God cannot become a substance which is not divine. His own view was condemned by Pope Alexander III in AD 1170 as 'nihilianism', the view that Christ was not a human substance at all (see Denzinger, 749 and 750). It is generally agreed that this is a misrepresentation of the Lombard's view, which is in effect the view that I have been expounding myself as the only tenable exposition of Chalcedon. Aquinas was clearly influenced by Pope Alexander's condemnation. He quotes the part of the letter of the Pope, extracted as Denzinger, 750, as authoritative in an article (*Summa theologiae*, 3a. 2. 6) leading him to adopt the tenet that 'human nature did not come to Christ in the manner of an accident', a tenet going well beyond what Alexander wrote and surely one at odds with Chalcedon. While acknowledging the appropriateness of the 'garment' metaphor in some respects, Aquinas denies its appropriateness in the respect that whether one wears a garment and which garment one wears is accidental to the person. Aquinas's own positive view (see my description in the text) seems to be a compromise between the first and third views. The individual human nature of Christ was a separate thing; it was assumed by the Word, but it did not become the Word. This view seems to me untenable for the reasons which I give in the text.

Index